YOUR Horse's Health
LAMENESS

OLIVER C.DAVIS MRCVS

D&C
David and Charles

Mom and Dad

Dedication
To my mother and father,
for everything

A DAVID & CHARLES BOOK
Copyright © David & Charles Limited 2007

David & Charles is an F+W Publications Inc. company
4700 East Galbraith Road
Cincinnati, OH 45236

First published in the UK in 2007

Cover image and running head images copyright © Horsepix 2007

Photograph on page 133, lower by Matthew Roberts Copyright © David & Charles Limited 2006

Text and all other photographs copyright © Oliver Davis 2007

Illustrations on pages 33, 44 and 90 by Maggie Raynor copyright © David & Charles Limited 2007. Illustrations on pages 24–25 and 99 copyright © George Bingham 2007. Illustration on page by Visual Image 9 copyright © David & Charles Limited 1997

Oliver Davis has asserted his right to be identified as author of this work in accordance with the Copyright, Designs and Patents Act, 1988.

A catalogue record for this book is available from the British Library.

ISBN-13: 978-0-7153-2643-5 hardback
ISBN-10: 0-7153-2643-0 hardback

ISBN-13: 978-0-7153-2893-4 paperback
ISBN-10: 0-7153-2893-X paperback

Printed in China by SNP Leefung
for David & Charles
Brunel House   Newton Abbot   Devon

Commissioning Editor Jane Trollope
Assistant Editor Emily Rae
Designer Jodie Lystor
Production Controller Beverley Richardson
Project Editor Anne Plume

Visit our website at www.davidandcharles.co.uk

David & Charles books are available from all good bookshops; alternatively you can contact our Orderline on 0870 9908222 or write to us at FREEPOST EX2 110, D&C Direct, Newton Abbot, TQ12 4ZZ (no stamp required UK only); US customers call 800-289-0963 and Canadian customers call 800-840-5220.

Contents

Foreword

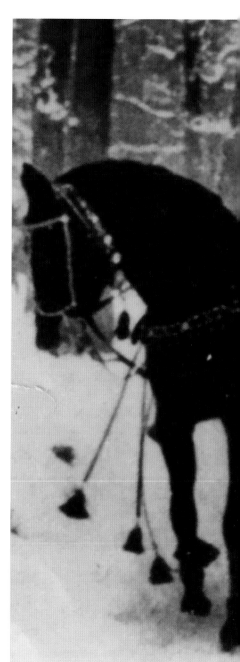

Man's history is inextricably bound up with that of the horse. The widespread domestication and admiration of this animal is an attest to the influence it has had. As a tool for travel, commerce and agriculture, it shaped the countryside beneath its hooves. As an instrument of war, it proved an invaluable weapon.

This close bond between man and horse was of benefit to the *equidae* in a broad sense, but does not preclude the immense suffering and hardship that it has endured. Millions of horses have fallen as casualties of war. Through this quiet servitude, man has come to admire and speak about the horse almost as if it were one of his own. In his gripping history *1812* about Napoleon's ill fated venture to Moscow, Adam Zamoyski recounts the exploits of Melet, a dragoon of the French Guard who throughout the thousand kilometre retreat risked his life on an almost daily basis for the sake of his horse's companionship. Enduring bitter cold, famine and danger, Melet foraged for food for his horse, Cadet, first before attending to his own needs. Against all odds, both he and Cadet returned safely back home to France.

Man's reliance on the horse is not even that distant. One hundred and thirty years later, my grandfather was to serve as a veterinary officer on the same western front. Even more recently, with the end of the Cold War and the fall the Berlin Wall, I can remember travelling through remote parts of Poland and Romania and seeing horses still cultivating farm land.

Both the economic and emotional dependence have fostered in man a desire to understand and attempt to heal lameness in the horse. The ancient Romans already had a well documented interest in farriery and horse medicine. With the mass production of the motor car and later the tractor in the immediate post war years, many had claimed that the demise of the horse was unstoppable. But subsequent generations, though no longer dependant on the horse as an economic tool, have been unable to sever the strong emotional bond that exists between man and horse. No longer only a pursuit of the wealthy, equitation is one of the most popular sporting activities in the world to date. As a direct consequence, understanding equine movement has once again become an important skill, albeit a difficult one for each and every horse owner.

Unfortunately, modern life has dulled our practical skills – we now rely on technology to answer medical issues. Just as the calculator and the computer have caused a deterioration in mathematical and spelling skills, so too have radiography machines, ultrasound scanners and MRI equipment caused us to rely on these too heavily for answers. Practical medical skills, most importantly the use of the hands to assist in diagnosis, are now being completely supplanted rather than complemented by a vast array of machinery.

Along with this technology comes new knowledge and even more vocabulary. Although complex, these can and should be explainable to the horse owner. The aim of this book therefore, is not to replace the skilfully researched veterinary tomes on the subject, most notably, *Adam's Book on Lameness*. It is hoped however, that it will impart a coherent and common sense approach to owners and students alike to help understand and deal with one of the most common and yet elusive problems in animal husbandry – the lame horse.

4

5

Introduction

How to Use this Book

We live in busy times, and it is a rare luxury to be able to take time out to sit down and read a book from cover to cover. This book is meant to accommodate the hurried reader, and as such, main points are highlighted on each page. Lameness is divided into forelimb and hindlimb problems, starting with the foot and moving progressively up the leg, just as you would approach a lame horse.

For those readers keen to learn more about the subject, including the recognition of lameness in the horse, I have attempted to intermingle the inevitable chapters of anatomy and medical terminology with real-life anecdotes and stories, to lessen the blow of overly academic material. This is not a lecture book, but a practical guide intended to impart an approach to understanding and solving lameness problems. Instead of trying to guess what is wrong with a horse, it is meant to train your eye, to guide your hand so that you learn to investigate problems in a systematic fashion. Figuring out why a horse isn't moving properly is not easy, but it is a surmountable problem if the approach is methodical.

I use a multi-layered technique when approaching a lameness. Instead of trotting the horse up and down once and feeling obligated to know the answer, slow down in your approach. Listen carefully to the history. Then take a good look at the horse from all angles. See any potential problems? Once you've made up your mind, carefully run your hands over the whole horse.

Do you feel any signs of stiffness or discomfort? Does what you feel correspond to what you have seen before? If it does, then there is a good possibility that you might at least have an idea as to which leg or legs are affected, and the problem is acute or chronic.

Now watch the horse walking in a straight line, over and over again: does this correspond to your findings? Is the animal walking shorter on the limb that was most definitely sore? These are the mental acrobatics that should go on in your mind. Now you can watch the horse work faster, flex the limbs: but by that time, you should already have quite a good idea of exactly what is going on in the horse's movement.

The first job is completed; now the task of actually pinpointing it begins.

My grandfather with his favourite horse Stasja

To recap, each and every lameness should be approached in the same way:
1. Listen to the full history.
2. Look at the horse from all angles.
3. Palpate the entire body of the horse.
4. Watch the horse walk in a straight line for a longer period of time.
5. Watch the horse trot in a straight line.
6. Watch the horse walk in circles.
7. Perform flexion tests.
8. Watch the horse lunged.
9. Watch the horse ridden.

If these basic concepts are understood and implemented, I am certain that both owner and student will find the task of lameness assessment less mysterious, and far more fun. If so, I will have fulfilled my aim.

Good luck!

Learn the Jargon

Diagnosing lameness in horses is a complicated business; trying to impart some understanding of the subject matter upon the casual reader who has an interest, but no scientific foundation upon which to back it, is a daunting one. In writing this book I have purposefully kept in mind that the best teachers are able to take the most complicated subject and present it in a simple fashion. However, the matter contained herein needs to be actively engaged, and certain things must be, dare I say it, understood and memorized. Notwithstanding the modern trend of 'dumbing down' matters, I have purposefully set the bar high. If you truly desire to understand what is going on with your horse, a bit of work is in order.

When the sun finally set upon the Roman empire, along with heroes, aqueducts, wine, and lots of legends, the Romans bequeathed to us their language: Latin. This forms the basis for many of our modern European languages, including English, but in its purest form it has become the cornerstone for medical jargon, since the Latinization of the medical (and veterinary) world was supposed to allow these professions to communicate with each other, regardless of nationality. Even now, many European countries require a certain amount of Latin proficiency in order to be accepted as a medical student.

Unfortunately, keeping in line with the Anglo-Saxon phobia of languages, both in Britain and America, the Latin terms have either been 'anglicized' or forgotten completely. For instance, a pododermatitis purulenta diffusa is now termed by all English-speaking vets the length and breadth of this country as 'pus in the foot'.

This leads us to another interesting point: all these words mean something! The literal translation for the Latin version for pus in the foot is a 'diffuse, purulent inflammation of the skin in the foot'. So even if you were a Japanese doctor, provided you spoke Latin, you could still make matters out.

So when you see a long series of words, don't panic, but try to find where these words have been joined at the hip, and interpret their meaning. And if you don't understand the meaning of one word, look it up! Take the word 'laminitis' for instance: in the horsey world it is nearly ubiquitous, particularly around yards with a monopoly in little fat ponies. But have you ever taken into account what 'laminitis' really means? It means an inflammation of the laminae, which is the area that binds the hoof to the coffin bone. If one can understand this, then understanding the ensuing pedal bone rotation of the coffin joint becomes a doddle.

Every structure within the body therefore has a Latin name which has been hammered out passionately by the anatomists who, true to character, every now and then decide to change the name of some obscure blood vessel or nerve to confuse even those of us 'in the know'! But the most important thing to remember for now are the directional words, which although seem to be confusing at first, allow extremely accurate directions to be given via either the written or the spoken word. For instance, instead of saying 'upward', vets say 'dorsal'; instead of saying 'downward' in relation to the body, vets say 'ventral'; towards the middle is medial, and towards the outside is lateral. Please take some time to look at the different directional terminology, and do not hesitate to keep referring to this page, or to consult the glossary, until you have grasped the individual meanings of each.

Though similar, horses are not the same and can vary both anatomically and in temperament

Like man, the horse is a warm-blooded mammal. Support and protection come via an internal skeleton surrounded by muscles and tendons. During the course of evolution, the appendages have adapted to optimize their use. Unlike man, all four of the horse's legs have slowly developed for one main purpose: speed of movement to help it flee from its predators. Its legs have become more upright, slowly evolving it into an ungulate. Simultaneously, unnecessary toes have been shed or reduced to support the main weight carrier: the third metacarpal/metatarsal bone, or cannon bone. If it is understood that the horse is essentially walking on what is the equivalent of your third finger and third toenails, then the anatomy of the horse becomes much clearer.

A joint is a structure necessary to join two or more bones together, and both the structure and function of a joint will differ, depending on its use. For instance, the joints in the skull need only to fuse the various bones together to help protect the skull. In the limb where movement is needed, however, bones are joined by synovial joints. A typical synovial joint is pictured at right. The ends of the bones are covered with articular cartilage to give them a smooth surface and to reduce friction. The shape of the ends is determined by the movement needed. For instance, the hip is a ball-and-socket joint which allows nearly 360 degrees of movement in all directions, while the fetlock is a hinge joint, which limits movement in one plane. Together with short, tough collateral ligaments, the fibrous joint capsule encloses the joint and helps keep the joint together. Depending on how they are arranged in relation to the joint, these ligaments are termed collateral, cruciate, accessory, and so on. Ligaments are very strong but inelastic, and are therefore prone to injury if exposed to undue strain. Because of the poor blood supply afforded them, healing is prolonged and the result inferior in strength.

The joint is filled with a viscous fluid which acts not only as a lubricant, but as nourishment for the articular cartilage. Any changes in the fluid will not only have a direct effect upon the physical properties of the joint, but can directly affect the joint cartilage. This becomes

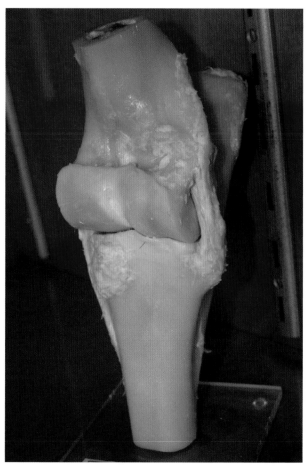

Powerful ligaments hold a joint in place

Many unprofessional explanations offered resemble the anatomy of a bird more than that of a horse

important in understanding the aetiology of arthritis, or degenerative joint disease (DJD), as it is commonly referred to in the horse.

Below is an overview of the horse's skeleton in which both common and scientific terms are given.

Bones (ossa) are complicated structures. Not only do they provide structure to the body, but the marrow serves to produce the red and white cells in the blood. Surrounding the bone is a thin film called the periostrum which carries the nutrient blood supply into the interior of the bone. When damaged, the periostrum can serve as a catalyst for splint formation.

Attached to the various bones are muscles which fill out and support the skeletal frame. They also provide the basis for movement. They are attached to the bone by tough ligaments at two points, the origin and the insertion, usually in opposing pairs. Depending on the position of the muscle in relationship to the joint, it is either an extensor or a flexor.

Finally, the limbs are controlled by sensory and motor nerves. Even though there are minor individual anomalies, the location of all these follows the same basic pattern. This is important to know when attempting to anaesthetize a nerve in order to figure out where a horse is going lame.

9

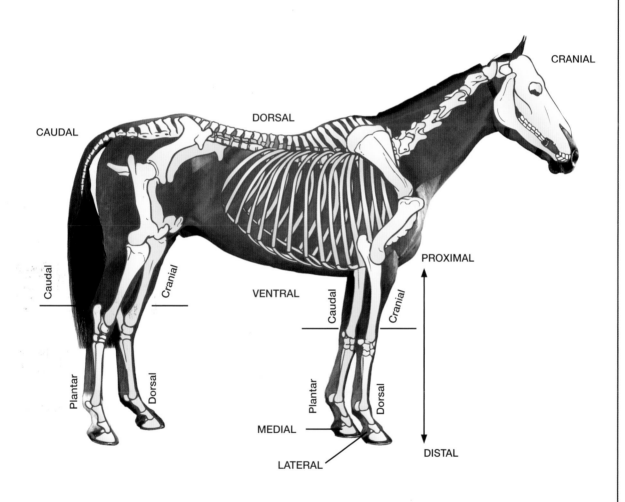

SECTION 1 LAMENESS EVALUATION FOR THE HORSE OWNER

Take a Good Look

What do we mean when we talk about the conformation of a horse? In simple terms, we know that a horse generally has four legs and a head and a tail, but it is how these things are put together that will (theoretically) determine a horse's athleticism. That is how the concept of 'showing' a horse developed. Those animals deemed to have the most perfect build were chosen over the rest because they were the most likely to be able to continue a productive working life. Unfortunately this is a fact that is all too often forgotten today, and often more weight is given to looks and presentation than to actual conformation.

Of course, the conformation of a horse must be evaluated in relationship to its classification (draft horse, light horse or pony) and type (pleasure horse, hunter, stock horse, sport horse, racehorse). As each of these animals is used for a different purpose, their conformation will also vary somewhat. However, the judgement of conformation is similar in all.

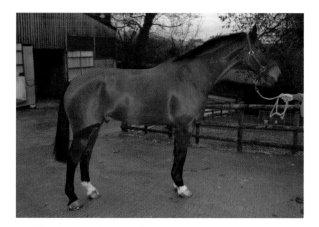

Evaluating the horse

Begin your evaluation of a horse in the same way and systematically continue your examination in the same fashion each and every time.

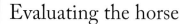

In this manner, you will not forget to look at something which may be of importance. With the horse at rest, stand to the near (its left) side and back up five steps or so. Look at the animal carefully, always searching for clues. Is it standing comfortably and square, or does it shift its weight around continuously? If it is restless, is that just part of its personality or is it really uncomfortable? Perhaps it is insecure or missing its friend? Look at its demeanour: are the ears forward? While it is true that horses can't talk, understanding their body langauge can tell you a lot.

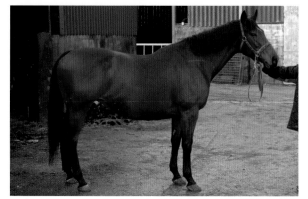

Viewing from the side
Move your eyes from the horse's head down the upper line of the neck (crest) and along the back to the rump. The head should be set at an angle of roughly 60 degrees to the ground, and at a right angle to the neck. Is the back straight or dipped? Is it evenly muscled? Is there evidence

Every breed has an ideal conformation that will best suit the task for which it was bred

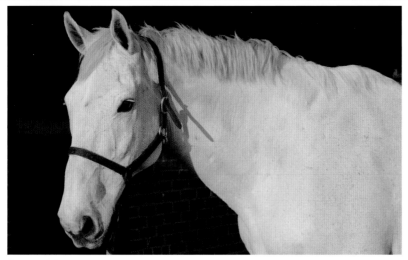

The neck is an important factor in determining a horse's speed and jumping ability

in the form of scarring of a poor saddle fit? Is the croup well muscled, or does it lack muscle mass?

A lack of muscle always indicates a lack of use. So is this perhaps due to insufficient fitness, or does it point to a more chronic problem?

Now let your eyes return to the head and neck. The length of the neck generally will determine the animal's speed and jumping ability. Therefore, a longer neck is essential for a hunter or sport horse, while a draught horse should exhibit a shorter, thicker, and more powerful neck. Is the neck well muscled? How is it set on to the torso? Take a few seconds to watch the horse move its head. Is the neck reasonably flexible? Does it happily bend in an arc, or does the entire neck muscle look stiff and rather immovable?

Inspect the shoulder and try to determine the angle at which it is set. As a general rule, the more oblique the angle of the shoulder, the greater the stride a horse will be able to make. A straight shoulder is undesirable in nearly every type of horse. Is it well muscled? In general, the longer the shoulder blade, the more muscle mass is able to attach to it, thereby increasing a horse's power and speed.

From the shoulder, inspect the lower forelimb. Is the limb straight and unblemished? Is there any sign of joint swelling? Particular attention should be placed on the flexor tendons along the back of the leg. Are they clean,

without swelling, and remain unbowed – that is, show no signs of previous injury? The pasterns should be sloped similarly to the angle of the shoulder to help alleviate concussion to the lower limb, but the fetlock must remain upright and should not collapse down, thereby placing strain on the tendons and ligaments of the leg.

Finally, the foot demands careful scrutiny. Has the horse been trimmed and shod properly? Are the toes sufficiently short to take the pressure off the lower joints? Have the heels been given enough support to bear the weight of the horse and rider? Compare the side profile of the two front feet. Is one more upright than the other? Perhaps the horse has collapsed heels, a common feature in Thoroughbreds. If a line were drawn from the shoulder (the *tuber spinae* of the scapula) would it bisect the limb to the fetlock, and then land at the heel of the foot? It should do in all horses.

Scrutinize the lower limb of the near hind in a similar fashion, paying close attention to the hock and stifle. The stifle joint should never be swollen, as this almost always points to a significant pathology. The angle of the hock is also important: ideally, when standing square, the point of the hock should be exactly in line with the line of the buttock.

An obviously bowed tendon. Note the bar firing lines

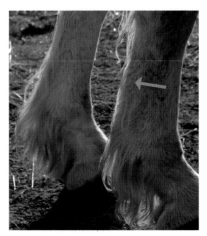

However bowed tendons are not always immediately obvious

A swollen hock joint should be recognized instantly. A 'chip' fracture is not an uncommon finding, particularly in horses over 15hh

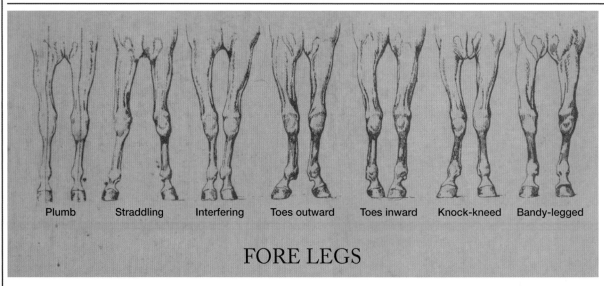

| Plumb | Straddling | Interfering | Toes outward | Toes inward | Knock-kneed | Bandy-legged |

FORE LEGS

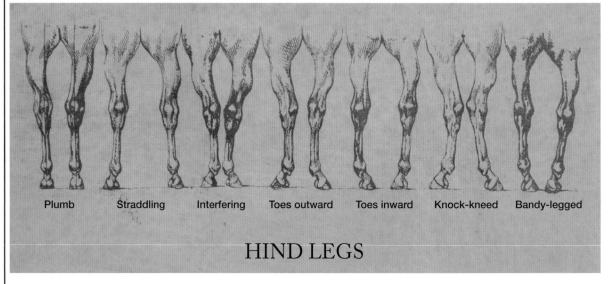

| Plumb | Straddling | Interfering | Toes outward | Toes inward | Knock-kneed | Bandy-legged |

HIND LEGS

The importance of good conformation has long been recognized, as revealed by these 19th century diagrams, which show a wide variety of poor leg structures, compared to the two ideals on the left-hand side

Viewing from the front

Now move in a clockwise fashion to view the horse from the front. From this position it is now possible to assess symmetry in the neck, shoulders and forelimbs. Is the neck held naturally straight, or does the horse have a tendency to keep it crooked to one side?

Are the shoulders symmetrically muscled? What kind of chest does the horse have: is it narrow or broad? Are both chest muscles the same size?

Now compare one forelimb to the other: are the legs straight – that is, if a line is dropped from the point of the shoulder, does it bisect the limb completely? Often, the leg diverges from the knee or fetlock downwards. A turned-in toe in conformation is fairly frequent (pigeon-toed).

'What does this mean for the horse? Is it really important?' I am often asked. I usually answer it this way: stand with your legs shoulder-width apart and flex your knees. Now point your toes inwards and flex your knees: notice the difference? There is a lot more pressure on your ankles, and in horses, it is the same. That doesn't mean that they can't be sound. What it does mean is that the pressure distribution within the foot isn't equal, and this can lead to problems in the future.

At this stage, note any sign of splint formation on the cannon bones. Remember that splints can arise not only from trauma, but also from chronic imbalance. For example, a horse with a narrow conformation in front will be more prone to knock the inside of the legs, thereby causing a splint. At the same time, if it is pigeon-toed with long untrimmed hooves, the increased stress and concussion along the inside of the cannon bone can also cause a splint in that area.

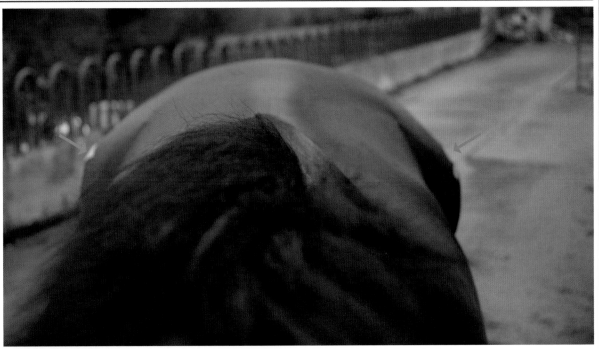

Small pieces of tape placed on the hip bones can be used to assess symmetry in the pelvis

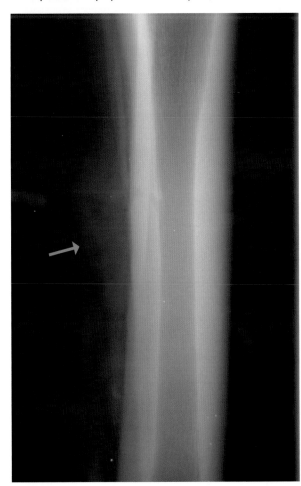

This x-ray reveals a large splint on the inside of this horse's cannon bone

Continue your walk round the horse and evaluate the off (right) side of the horse, constantly comparing it to what you have already observed.

Viewing from behind

Finally, view the horse from behind. With your eyes fixed on the croup, observe the top and side profile of the gluteal muscles to each other. You can often pick up muscle wastage in this area. Compare the hip bones to each other too, as these can be good indicators for pelvic rotation. Now let your eyes travel down the leg to the gaskins: these should be well muscled and symmetrical. Pay careful attention to the hocks, as from this angle, it is easy to see signs of bone and/or bog spavin. Is the point of the hock clean or swollen (capped)? Are the legs straight, or is the horse cow-hocked? Continue down the lower limb, making careful note of any signs of splints or tendon damage. Finally, check the fetlocks for windgalls, and note the conformation of the heels.

It is particularly useful to stand in a raised position some distance behind a horse, because you can then view the shoulders, back, hips and buttocks as well as the curvature of the spine. As in humans, some horses suffer from scoliosis. Dropped hips are also easily noticed from this vantage point. Exercise caution when performing this examination, as many horses will naturally feel uneasy and vulnerable with you towering over them. Ask the handler to give the horse plenty of time to observe you from a distance, then have it led past you, with plenty of space between, before it is made to stand squarely several yards ahead. In this way, there can be no danger to anyone!

Use Your Hands!

It is well recognized that during the course of evolution, man's reliance on his eyes has caused him to neglect the use of his other senses. Particularly in the field of medicine with its emphasis on the use of high-tech equipment, the 'hands-on' techniques are easily dismissed. This is a trend which must be stopped, for one simple reason: eyes alone are unreliable testimony! Nevertheless, if we conduct a thorough visual evaluation of a horse's conformation and make a mental note of any flaws we see, we can then check these against what our hands tell us.

Before beginning, let's take a brief look into our patient's psyche. In simple terms, we are predators and the horse is a prey animal, so it is important that we do not approach quietly, or from behind, or make sudden movements, because that is exactly what a predator would do! Instead, walk up naturally to the horse, preferably arriving at the near shoulder. Exude confidence, because any insecurities you have will immediately be transferred to him.

I like to speak to horses in a normal, soothing tone of voice. Do not make full eye contact, and do not square your shoulders, as these moves can be interpreted by the horse as being aggressive. And when you arrive at the horse's shoulder, allow him some time to adjust to your presence; usually just a few sniffs of your hand or clothing will be enough to make him feel more relaxed.

Examining the horse

I like to begin my examination on the near side, and I start with the neck and work backwards: that way, the horse has time to get accustomed to me, and is relaxed by the time I reach that potentially dangerous back end.

Palpating the neck

- Place your hands on either side of the neck, and work up slowly to the poll of the horse, the area just behind the ears. This part can be quite sore in horses with chronic lameness problems, because they will 'lock' the head in an attempt to reduce the pain they are feeling. It is also here that inexperienced horsemen can cause soreness through the use of artificial aids such as draw reins and side reins, forcing a horse to 'collect'.

- If a horse reacts nervously to your touch, you should always try to distinguish whether it is because it is feeling true pain, or is merely apprehensive about your palpations so close to the ears and head. If the horse is defensive, move your hands away from the position, soothe the animal, and then come back to the same place. This time however, only palpate superficially in order to get the horse used to it before you begin to apply more pressure.

- From the poll, move your hands slowly down both sides of the neck along the vertebrae, noting any increased muscle tension, fibrous areas, or abnormal bony protrusions. Then, using your left hand, gently palpate the musculature at either side of the base of the neck: the muscles in a nimble, athletic horse will feel loose, and will scarcely notice your manipulations, but in horses with chronic underlying problems – with navicular disease or even chronic laminitis, for instance – the muscles here will feel taut and fibrous, and the animal will attempt to evade your attentions. In my opinion, problems in the horse's neck arise from a natural tendency to use the neck to displace weight off the affected area. Although not always, a chronic lower limb problem in a forelimb often leads to a stiff neck on the same side, because the horse will stretch its neck away from the affected limb in order to place less weight upon it.

Remember: the more horses you examine, the more discerning you will become. After all, it is only once you know what normal is like, that you will be able to recognize abnormal pathology.

Palpating the chest and foreleg

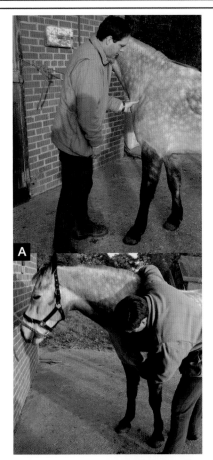

- From the base of the neck, palpate the shoulder before sliding your hand forwards to feel the pectoral muscles. Sometimes an obvious asymmetry in the musculature can be found (A), often arising from an old kick injury, for instance.

- Now palpate the elbow joint and muscles of the forearm, with both hands clasped firmly around the leg. Moving downwards, check the joints of the knee for abnormal filling, and the cannon for any signs of splint formation.

- Next, palpate the suspensory ligament, the deep digital flexor tendon, and the superficial flexor tendons individually for signs of swelling or discomfort, and in more acute cases, heat. If this palpation elicits a painful response, be sure to compare the reaction with that of the opposing leg as horses can be naturally quite sensitive in this area.

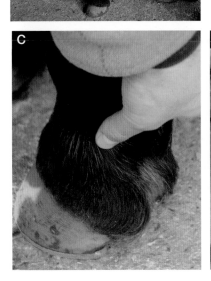

- Now palpate the fetlock joint. The joint can be felt in three places: on the front of the leg, on the side of the leg, and just above the sesamoid bones. Feel these bones for symmetry (B).

- Check the digital pulse: facing backwards, grasp the back side of the pastern between thumb and forefinger (C), and follow the palmer digital nerve, vein and artery into the back of the heel; once again, check for a pulse. Any acute lameness arising from the foot will increase the magnitude of the pulse in that foot.

- Pick up the foot. Looking down the back of the pastern, check to see whether the heels are of a symmetrical shape (D). Also check to see whether the foot has been balanced properly by the farrier. Is the shoe wearing equally or is it showing abnormal wear on one side? Using both hands, palpate the cartilage in the heel and the coronary band around the top of the hoof.

- Gently flex the lower limb to get an idea as to its flexibility (E). Now flex the knee and palpate deep into each joint to check once again for any joint filling which you may have missed initially.

- Supporting the back of the knee, now move in front of the horse and slowly stretch the entire front leg. This will allow you to judge the horse's flexibility in the shoulder and underarm areas.

- That was just the first leg! Now repeat the same procedure for the other forelimb.

15

Examining the back

We now have the back to examine, and this should always be undertaken thoroughly: after all, someone is going to sit there!

■ First note the withers: do you see any white hairs, telltale sign of an ill-fitting saddle? Place the flat of your hand in the area where the saddle would normally rest: are the muscles healthy and symmetrical, or is one side wasted away, perhaps indicating a primary back problem, a secondary lameness problem, or yet again a poor saddle fit, or perhaps even an unbalanced rider? Continue to run the flat of your hands down the left side of the horse's back until you reach the croup: did that feel comfortable and natural to the horse?

■ Now come back to the withers area and using your thumb, carefully palpate down the top of the spine. Can you feel any bony protrusions, or perhaps a lack of space between two vertebrae? Note that, given the natural curvature of the spine, the intervertebral space just behind the saddle area will be smaller. However, an excessively straight or dipped back (roach- and sway-back) has a greater propensity for forming calcifications in the intervertebral space, which means two things: first, the horse will lose flexibility through the gradual fusing of the vertebrae. Secondly, and more importantly, the continual inflammation will be painful, so the horse will in turn hold himself stiffly in this area in an attempt to guard against the pain.

■ Finally, pull a pen or coin out of your pocket and run it either side of the spine along the muscle from the saddle area to the gluteal muscles: a flexible horse's back will naturally dip away from under you. Running it quickly along the bottom of the horse's chest should cause a similar move away from your hand. Any reluctance to move should be noted.

■ Feel the ribcage to ensure there are no broken ribs or other abnormalities.

■ Walk round the horse and repeat the examination on the off side.

Use your thumb to palpate the top of the vertebrae and the intervertebral spaces between them (for a detailed explanation of the horse's anatomy, see p.96)

16

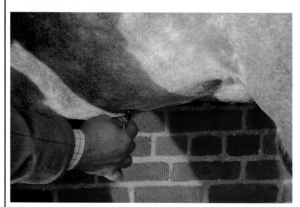

A pen or coin run lightly down each side of a horse's back and its belly is useful in assessing its reflexes

Carefully papate the hamstring for signs of tension or pain

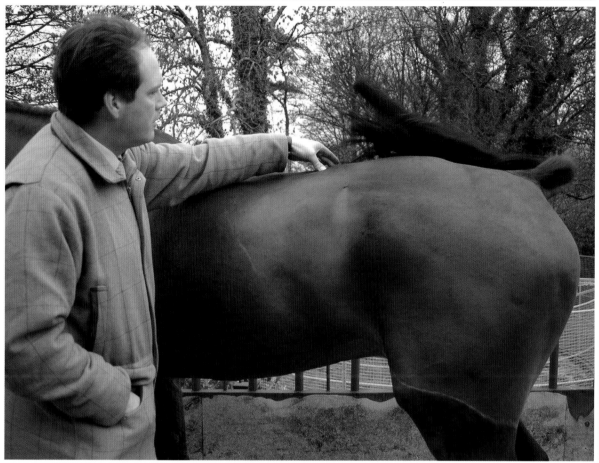

It is clear from this horse's response (tail flicking and back arching upwards) that it is not comfortable in its lower back. Now I just need to figure out why!

Examination of the hindquarters

Examining the horse's back end may put you at risk; if the animal seems edgy, forget it. Otherwise proceed as follows:

■ Standing on the near side of the horse, palpate the area around the sacro-iliac joint: essentially this area joins the hindlimbs to the spine. Check for symmetry here, then carefully palpate the horse's gluteal muscles with your fingertips. Are they soft to the touch? Does the muscle move easily under your fingers with an almost dough-like consistency, or does it feel like a tough piece of cardboard? (While examining the horse here, stand as close as you can to its hindlimb, because if it kicks, you will hopefully only be pushed away, rather than being right on the receiving end of the leg in full extension!)

■ Next, run your right hand down the groove of the buttocks and palpate the hamstring muscles; these, too, should feel loose and relaxed. Tightness in this area is often caused by something else, a hock problem for example.

■ Now grab the tail with your right hand, and with your left hand and arm placed firmly on the tuber coxae, try to pull the tail towards you. What you are actually checking for is the amount of sideways flexion of the lower back. This area is often stiff for a number of reasons, and horses will react worriedly and try to step away from you, rather than allowing you to flex them in this area.

■ With your left hand, carefully feel the stifle and inner thigh areas for swelling. Once again, check the gaskin for symmetry, then feel all the joints of the hock, including the point of the hock and the Achilles heel tendon just above. Take your time, because there is a lot to feel!

By pulling the tail towards you while pushing on the hip, you can assess the tightness in the lower back

Not a position to find yourself in behind a nervous horse! Note the asymmetric pelvis shown by my hands

18

Examining the lower hindlimb

- The lower limb examination is carried out as for the forelimb. When examining the (near) hind foot, it is safest to pick it up with the left hand, facing away from the horse; then carefully stretch it backwards and step underneath it so that the front portion of the cannon is resting on your left knee (see picture opposite). Like this you will be at less risk of being kicked!

- Repeat your hindlimb examination on the off side, and compare mental notes.

- Finally, and only if the horse is absolutely safe, stand directly behind him. With the animal standing square on a flat, hard surface, palpate both hip bones with a hand on each side in order to judge whether the hindquarters are in line or not. A short tug on the horse's tail will again show how much movement there is in the animal's hip and lower back areas behind the saddle.

Checklist

- Always perform your examination in the same manner. This will help prevent you from forgetting to look at something.

- Carefully view the horse from a distance and from all angles. Decide on where its weak points lie.

- Do these observations match your previous conclusions? If so, you may be on to something. If not, keep looking.

- After you have finished with your observations, carefully and systematically palpate the entire horse. What can you feel? Where are the joint swellings, the tight muscles? Again, do these stack up with your previous findings?

Always judge how a horse is standing is it comfortable or resting a limb? In the photo above the typical laminitic stance adopted by this Shetland pony is actually due to a ruptured shoulder

Held in this manner the hindlimb no longer poses a danger

Remember to check the balance on the hind legs as well. This pony needs some serious remedial farrery

The Horse in Movement

The horse's gaits

A

As yet we have not seen the horse move, but we have gained valuable information from our visual observations, and have formulated a general impression of the horse and its possible weaknesses. This, together with the results of our hands-on palpation, should already have helped us decide whether or not the horse is suffering from a chronic problem, or whether everything is pretty much all right. This does not mean that the horse will necessarily be sound, in which case we should consider whether the lameness has cropped up suddenly. These are the issues that should flow through your mind as you first ask to see the horse move.

However, before we can judge the horse's movement, we must first take a look at its normal gaits.

For simplicity, we shall consider a horse's natural gait movements to be walk, trot, canter and gallop. Information has been added for guidance with 'gaited' horses (see pp.22–25).

The walk

Although the walk is the slowest gait, it is more complicated due to the variables of speed and limb extension. It is a four-beat gait in which all the legs move independently to one another, though importantly, there will always be two or three feet on the ground at any given time. These are called support phases.

A horse will generally begin to walk by leading with a forelimb. If the near fore leads, the sequence will be near fore, off hind, off fore, near hind. If the near hindlimb leads the sequence will be near hind, near fore, off hind, off fore.

The order of support is therefore right pair right diagonal left pair left diagonal. (Picture sequence A.)

With an increase in speed, the stride length increases from a short collected walk to an extended one. In the short walk, the hindlimbs do not reach as far as the forelimbs; in the ordinary walk, the hindlimbs more or less cover the previous forelimb print; and in an extended walk they pass them.

A healthy horse will always land either with a flat foot, or nearly imperceptibly heel first.

B

The trot

The trot is the simplest of the gaits. It is a two-beat diagonal gait in which a forelimb and the opposite hindlimb move in the same manner; thus we have a left diagonal and right diagonal. Because the fore- and hindlimbs have the same amount of work to do, this gait is the least fatiguing to the horse, and it can go long stretches in a trot. (Picture sequence B.)

As in walk, the trot can vary from a collected, to a regular, to a fast trot. Harness trotters at high speeds can show a flying trot which is so extended that the gait changes from a two- to a four-beat rhythm, because there is an asynchrony of the impact of the diagonal, with the hindlimbs touching the ground first.

Amble or pace

This is generally not a natural pace in the horse (it is in camels and cattle): it is a two-beat gait in which the two right legs and the two left legs move forwards and backwards together. In the ordinary amble there is little or no period of suspension. In the flying pace, used mainly in harness racing in North America and Australia, this suspension period increases; the maximum speed of the flying pace can exceed that of the flying trot. As in the flying trot, the hindlimb hits the ground before the forelimb on the same side, thus changing the gait from two to four beats. As there is no possibility of interference of limbs, as in the flying trot, it is easier for horses to increase their stride length. This may explain why pacers are generally faster than trotters.

C

The canter

In contrast to the other paces, the canter and gallop gaits exhibit asymmetric movement of the hind- and forelimbs. The canter is a three-beat gait in which one forelimb is unsupported by the diagonal hindlimb, therefore becoming the leading forelimb. If the near fore leads, it is a canter to the left; if the off fore leads, it is a canter to the right. That is because at both a canter and a gallop, the horse should lead to the side that it is being turned, otherwise it will be likely to cross its legs and fall. The beat is irregular because the interval between the coming down of the near fore and off hind is longest. (Picture sequence C.) It is clear that the leading forelimb is doing far more work than the other, and so if the pace is continued, the horse will often change the lead forelimb.

The gallop

The gallop is essentially the same gait as the canter, differing only in the extended reach of the forelimb, a marker of increased speed. During this time, the diagonal support limb that in a canter lands at about the same time as the hind one, begins to come after it in the gallop, thus changing the gait from three to four beats. The lead leg must also provide an extended amount of support over the other three legs, making it more prone to injury in the extension phase. There is also an increase in the interval of suspension.

The gaited horse

Due to their comfortable ride, gaited horses have always enjoyed popularity in some parts of the world, particularly North and South America where their lineage can be traced back to the Spanish Conquistadors' occupation of those lands. Given the long distances one had to travel in the Americas, it is understandable that horses able to travel in this fashion were highly prized. Centuries of selective breeding have resulted in a wide variety of breeds being born with the natural capacity to gait in this manner. Regional preferences and the genetic variety of the horses used led to a multiplicity of distinctive styles and terminology being adopted for the same basic gait; some 80 breeds of horses in the world are considered to be 'gaited'. In fact, the ability of 'gaitedness' has been detected in many primitive breeds, giving rise to the theory that it is a much older evolutionary characteristic than was once believed.

Unfortunately, the name 'gaited horse' is not a good one, since all horses have gaits, meaning the paces of walk, trot, canter and gallop. A 'gaited horse', however, is one that has another gait, usually instead of, or in addition to the trot.

Notice the outward rotation of the shoulder on this Peruvian Paso horse. This is called *Termino* and is a desired trait in these horses as it reduces the head nod in the paso llano (running walk or flat walk). Do not confuse this with 'dishing' or 'paddling', a condition which occurs in horses with crooked legs.

To review briefly, the walk is a gait with four beats in which at any given moment there are always two or three hooves on the ground. This continual support eliminates a suspension phase. Although a horse may slow down or quicken its walk either by collecting or extending, this considerable support remains and it is this that makes the walk comfortable to a rider.

The trot is a two-beat gait with diagonal support and with a moment of suspension in which all the hooves leave the ground for a brief instance before changing diagonal position and landing again. It is precisely this landing that has a jarring effect upon a rider.

The canter's three-beat gait also has a moment of suspension, but the rapid succession of the hooves landing makes the gait smoother to ride. When speed is increased to a gallop, another four-beat gait, the effect is also a smoother ride.

Clearly then, 'gaited horse' is not an accurate term, and recently introduced descriptions such as easy-gaited, saddle-gaited or four-beat gait are easier to understand.

The foot pattern of the gaited horse

The basic foot pattern of the gaited horse is always the same: off hind, off fore, near hind, near fore. It is the change in balance, speed and timing of the raising and setting down of the hooves that leads to different variations of the gaited movement. For instance, a gait may be more 'pacey' or lateral, when the legs on the same side work more together; more diagonal; or, alternatively, when all the horse's legs work independently of each other, more 'square'. This in turn has a dramatic effect on the endurance, comfort, speed and agility of the ride.

It is unquestionably true that a four-beat gait is more comfortable to ride because the moment of suspension is eliminated and the number of hooves on the ground at any given moment is maximised. However, the widely held view that a four-beat gait is less tiresome for a horse is questionable. Gaited horses require a considerable amount of muscular tension in order to move correctly. In addition, the spring effect of the lower limb suspensory apparatus as used in a light trot is lost. Therefore, a tiring gaited horse will always fall back into trot or amble first before walk becomes necessary. If one considers the differences between jogging and power walking in human athletics, the comparison between a trot and an easy-gait becomes clearer.

BREED	PLACE OF ORIGIN	BROKEN PACE	SADDLE RACK
■ Mangalarga Marchador	Brazil		Marcha
■ Campolina	Brazil	Marcha Picada	Marcha Patida
■ Paso Fino	Columbia, Dominican Republic	Ambladura	Paso corto, Paso fino, Paso largo,
■ Paso Iberoamericano	Costa Rica, Panama	Paso	Paso ideal
■ Breton/Roussin	France	Amble rompu	Amble plan
■ Icelandic Pony	Iceland	Flugskref tölt	Hreina tölt
■ Paso Peruano	Peru	Sobre andando	Paso llano
■ Afrikan Saalperd, Boerperd	South Africa	Strykstapp/Strijkloop	Trippel
■ American Saddlebred		Slow gait	Saddle rack
■ Spotted Saddle Horse		Stepping pace	Saddle rack
■ Kentucky Mountain Horse	USA	Single foot	Saddle rack
■ Missouri Fox Trotter		Singlefoot	Fox trot
■ Tennessee Walker		Flat walk, running walk	Running walk

A wide variety of gait variations carries an even greater amount of vocabulary to describe it. Listed above is a selection from the 80 odd different breeds of gaited horses

To complicate matters further, these paces are not static, but fluid within an individual, depending on the horse's speed and disposition at the time. It is up to the rider to maintain a steady and consistent gait, depending on the horse's individual potential and genetic make-up.

Of course, this potential to gait is no guarantee of ability, and just as some horses never reach their potential in other disciplines, some 'gaited' horses simply aren't as good as others. In order to help an individual horse reach its potential to be gaited, the rider and trainer is of paramount importance.

The clearest and most rhythmic of the 'gaited' movements is the tölt. An analysis is included in the photo sequence and sketch below.

A PASO IN A GAITED WALK

The footfall of the paso in a gaited walk beginning with the near hindlimb is as follows: near hind, near hind and fore, near hind leaves the ground, off fore, off hind leaves the ground, near hind.

When examining a gaited horse for lameness, it is essential to familiarize yourself with the individual attributes of the breed. What is desirable in one breed may not be in another! A thorough clinical history is also helpful. Keep in mind that poor condition, ill health, improperly fitted tack, boredom, incorrect shoeing and most importantly inept riding, can all lead to a lack of 'gaitedness' in a horse. With these thoughts in mind, begin your examination in exactly the same manner as you would for a 'non-gaited' horse. Concentrate on the walk first, as it will be slower and more familiar to you. But remember, as you watch your patient move – the very same tell-tale signs for lameness apply in the gaited horse, too!

Hoof Balance and Shoeing

Hoof balance in farriery is a term that means simply the harmonious relationship between the horse's limb, the hoof and the horseshoe. Every horse has a different conformation, some better, some worse. It is this conformation that will cause the hoof capsule to distort

due to the uneven pressures being exerted upon it. If unchecked, this will eventually lead to lameness. Proper farriery involves trimming this imbalance and shoeing the foot so that it most closely fits the needs of the limb.

A common error in farrery is to leave the toes too long. Over time this will cause the heel to collapse

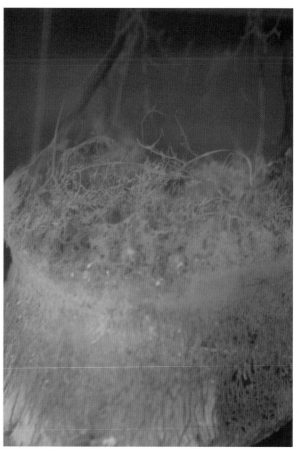

The foot is a living material that is supplied by a vast network of blood vessels

Hoof balance

Hoof balance should be assessed in a methodical way. First, stand the horse squarely on a clean, hard, flat surface and view each hoof from the front and side before picking them up. Note their general size and shape in relationship to the breed of horse. Is there any distortion of the hoof capsule? Are the hooves overgrown or misshapen?

Rings on the hoof wall can indicate several things. If they are parallel, they may signify no more than a change in diet, perhaps moving into a new field of lush grass, for example. Rings that are not parallel indicate either that significant irregular forces are being exerted upon the hoof wall, or that the nourishment or blood flow in certain areas is diminished; this happens in laminitis, for instance. Look at the foot and limb from the front (anterior view): is the limb straight, or is the hoof pointing? A line bisecting the centre of the cannon bone should cut the hoof into two equal halves. The hoof angles should be equal, and the wall on either side should not flare out or be particularly steep.

With your head pressed to the horse's shoulder, pick up the leg holding it as high up the cannon as possible,

and allow it to hang loosely. This is the best way to assess mediolateral balance in the forelimbs. A 'T'-square will allow you to be more objective in your assessment of solar surface angles, hoof wall angles and heel bulb distortion. Another view is to pick the limb up and bring it forwards, allowing it to flex naturally, and peer down the dorsal aspect of the limb.

The hindlimb of the horse is best viewed either from the front or from directly behind the way it naturally points when the animal is standing relaxed. The T-square can still be used.

When viewing the solar surface of the hoof, give careful attention to the frog as it will always remain centrally aligned while the other parts of the hoof

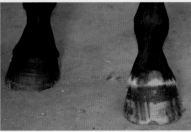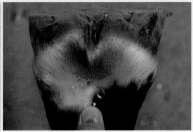

This case clearly illustrates the importance of correct balance. This horse had been seen as a second opinion following a recommendation for an expensive MRI scan. Examination of the foot clearly revealed that the foot had a broken back conformation. The lateral wall was higher, resulting in a coronary band running unparallel to the ground.

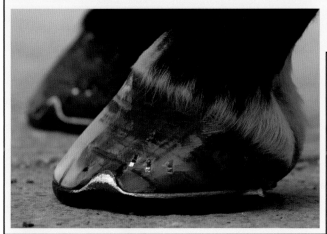

Following trimming and shoeing, these flaws were nearly completely corrected. The horse returned to soundness

Note the obviously broken forward conformation on this foal's near fore. The time to correct this problem is now, not later

distort around it. Also check for the condition of the sole (flat or overly thin), the heel bulb shape and size, and the condition of the white line.

■ The hoof/pastern axis

From the side (lateral) view, it is possible to view the hoof/pastern axis (HPA). When making this assessment, it is important to remember that the proximal third of the dorsal hoof wall will always remain in line with the pedal bone unless the animal has suffered from a rotation during an acute laminitis. In this case, radiographs are necessary to assess the HPA.

If the HPA is broken back, the laminae are placed under strain due to the leverage and extended breakover point of the toe. This may cause a widening of the white line, and signs of haemorrhage are often apparent. This conformation has also been linked to degenerative

joint disease of the coffin joint, and also to navicular syndrome because of the abnormal tension placed on the deep flexor tendon. In general, greater strain is placed upon the entire suspensory apparatus, consisting of the superficial and deep flexor tendons, the suspensory ligament and the check ligament. Finally, corns are also a common feature of this particular type of conformation.

It is essential to assess the hoof/pastern axis for each limb. This can be done by viewing the feet from the side – it should be possible to draw a straight line from the toe of the foot along the dorsal wall of the pastern to the fetlock. In other words, the dorsal wall of the hoof should be at the same angle as the dorsal angle of the pastern, unless the animal has suffered from a rotation during an acute bout of laminitis. In this case, radiographs are necessary to assess the HPA.

A particularly common finding in Thoroughbreds with long toes and under-run heels is a broken back HPA. In these cases the laminae are placed under strain due to the leverage and extended breakover point of the toe.

An upright foot is one in which the HPA is still in alignment, but it is usually narrower and higher than the opposite hoof. The heels are usually contracted. Also termed a 'boxy' foot, in warmbloods this conformation can be associated with navicular syndrome.

Finally, assess individual balance in motion while standing in front of, and to the side of the horse as it walks up and down past you.

Trimming and shoeing

Trimming remains the most important method of rebalancing a horse's foot. There are three main guidelines to remember when trimming feet:

1. The sole should be trimmed so that it is exactly perpendicular to the axis of the cannon.
2. The dorsal wall should be rasped back so that it is aligned with the proximal third of the wall. This is not always possible when trimming laminitic horses.
3. The heels must be trimmed back to the widest part of the frog.

After trimming, it is possible to realign the balance still further through the choice of shoe applied.

The importance of breakover

Achieving an easy breakover is essential in reducing strain on the lower limb joints and suspensory apparatus. A conventional shoe places the shoe directly under the toe. A rolled toe shoe will move the breakover point back 5–10mm. A rocker shoe can bring it back even further, with a square-toed shoe displacing the breakover point up to 40mm behind the toe.

Types of shoe

The type of shoe used will play a crucial role in determining whether a horse stays sound or not. The weight, rigidity, shape and size are all things to consider.

Material

Aluminium: This metal is very light and is therefore often used for racehorses on race days. However, not only is it not a particularly hard-wearing material, but because its melting point is so high, under normal circumstances it is not possible to hot shoe the horse. What you see is what you get!

Steel: Most shoes are made of steel. Although this is a heavy material, it is also hard-wearing and easy to forge.

Cast iron: Cast-iron shoes are not particularly recommendable because they are both heavy and impossible to forge. They are, however, relatively inexpensive.

Plastic: Like aluminium, plastic is light. In addition it has the advantage that it can be glued to the foot rather than nailed on, although this is a procedure which, in certain conditions, is prohibitively expensive. It is also expensive, and usually not really hard-wearing.

Bar shoe

Heart-bar shoe

Wide-web shoe with toe clip

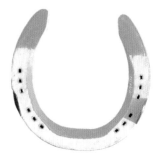

Racing plates

Four-point shoe

Quarter-clip wide shoe

Shape

The shape of the shoe determines the entire action of the foot, and sometimes even the leg. First, the width of the material should be considered. The standard width for a Thoroughbred is 19mm (¾in); if more support is needed, 'wide web shoes' are a popular option, being approximately 22mm (⅞in) wide.

There are many variations for shoes, but besides 'traditional' or 'open' shoes, the other major category comprises *closed-bar shoes*. These not only provide far more heel support, but by minimizing hoof movement, are used when repairing major horn defects. Possibly the most used bar shoe is an egg bar shoe. This has plenty of width for the heel of the foot, although because of this, it can be prone to coming off the foot. This problem can be avoided by using a *straight-bar shoe*, which is tucked in further underneath the foot.

The major disadvantage of these bar shoes is that because they shut down movement of the heels and therefore the blood-pumping mechanism within the foot, they can cause a contraction of the heels. Therefore although they may immediately improve the gait of a horse suffering from palmer foot pain, over the long term they may actually exacerbate the problem.

For horses suffering with palmar foot pain, I like to use a *short-tongued heart bar shoe*. Essentially a heart bar with half of the bar cut off to alleviate a pressure necrosis on the pedal bone, this bar can be set up into the frog, forcing pressure through the centre of the foot. This will not only give the heels more support, but as there is slightly more pressure up the centre of the foot, it will actually force the heels to move outwards every time the hoof hits the ground. This will activate the blood circulation in the foot. The disadvantage of these shoes is that it is difficult to get the amount of pressure right: too much will make the horse lame, and not enough essentially renders the shoe no more than a simple bar shoe. In addition, as the foot grows, the pressure reduces on the

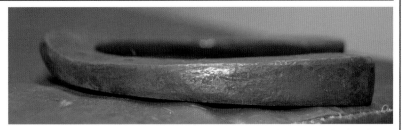

A graduated shoe can be very effective in the treament of bone spavin, locking stifles or even navicular disease. It is important, however, that exercise on soft ground is avoided

frog, thereby necessitating frequent readjustments.

A regular *heart-bar shoe* is mainly employed in horses suffering from laminitis as it supports the pedal bone, helping to prevent it from dropping further. It is essential that the bar of the shoe does not cause a pressure necrosis on the pedal bone. This can be checked with the use of radiographs.

Shoes that have recently risen in popularity again are *four-point shoes*. These do not have any clips and are not rounded in the toe area as traditional shoes, but are much squarer. The squared toe is rockered underneath, thereby creating a much shorter breakover for the horse. These shoes were redesigned after examining the natural wear within wild mustangs, and certainly in some horses they can make a huge difference. On the other hand, the argument put forth by some of their most ardent supporters that only these shoes should be employed on all feet, no matter what shape or size, is nonsensical.

Another orthopaedic shoe commonly employed is the *graduated shoe*. This is particularly useful with horses suffering from spavin. It can also be used for taking the pressure off the tendons and heel area in horses suffering from acute tendonitis, or which have injuries in these areas. Graduated heel pads are not as effective and have a tendency to produce more abrasion between the foot and the pad than a shoe would.

Finally, the *hospital plate,* right, deserves mention. This shoe is very helpful when trying to keep an injured foot clean. It consists of a closed bar

shoe that is hammered to the foot, and a piece of sheet metal is then bolted on to the shoe with four screws. In order to alleviate the pressure on the bolts, an alternative is to slot the back of the sheet metal into the back heel of the shoe and rocker the toe; that way, only one screw is used and this is suspended off the ground.

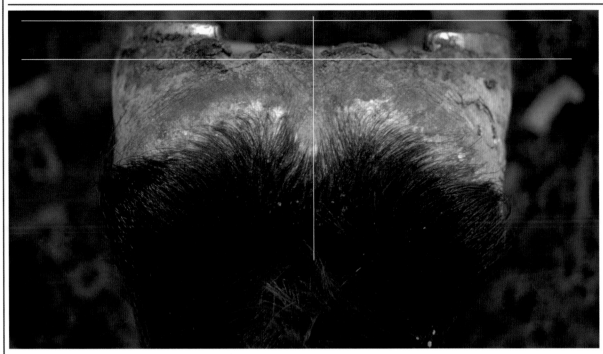

This foot is imbalanced – the lateral wall is too high

30

A vast number of leather or synthetic pads is available. These should be employed for a limited time only, however, as they trap moisture beneath the feet, not only breeding bacteria, but gradually softening the perpetually wet sole. When shoeing for mediolateral balance it is important to dress back any flares so that the wall is straight from the coronet to the sole. The sole is pared back so that the

shape is symmetrical around the frog. If trimming alone will not rebalance the hoof, the shoe can be given an extension on the medial or lateral side of the foot; this can range from just a few millimetres to more than 10cm (see photos below).

If mediolateral balance of the sole has not been possible, through a large wall defect, for example, this can be rebuilt with the use of modern acrylic and polymer hoof repair fillings.

Shoes will naturally wear most in those areas that get the most use during landing and breakover. However, always consider the age of the horse, the amount and type of work it is in, the material the shoe is made of, and the length of time since shoeing. Always remember, too, that hind shoes are often worn off square at the toe because the hock flexes in an opposite direction to the knee, with the foot moving in a lower flight arc.

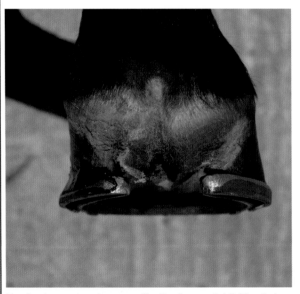 

Hoof polymers can be very effective in re-establishing balance. In these photos, the steeper lateral wall has been given increased support through a lateral extension. The weakened wall has been strengthened with a hoof filler

In the last ten years, synthetics have revolutionized the possibilities for hoof correction and shoeing, and undoubtedly there are more contributions to come. Two products in particular are worthy of mention: though expensive, Imprint Shoes, produced by Andrew Poynton, are an invaluable aid to providing support for acutely laminitic feet. Delivered with a heart bar already attached,

Imprint shoes can be attached to the hoof without nailing, which means that horses impossible to shoe before due to the pain involved, can now be immediately provided with the support necessary to help prevent further rotation of the pedal bone. Because the shoes are both light and non-invasive, they are also practical to use when correcting joint imbalances in foals.

Another product that has made life much easier is Vettec (below), which comes in several forms and colours. Applied as a paste, it hardens within minutes, and the end product is so hard that it can be rasped like a normal hoof. The rigid Vettec is good for filling in hoof defects and building up the hoof wall, while the softer product is often used for shock-absorption purposes when applied to the sole of the foot. Unlike a hoof pad, Vettec binds directly to the foot, effectively preventing moisture from getting trapped and thereby keeping the foot perpetually soft and damp. It does have one great disadvantage, however: it is very slippery, particularly when wet, so road studs should always be used in conjunction with it.

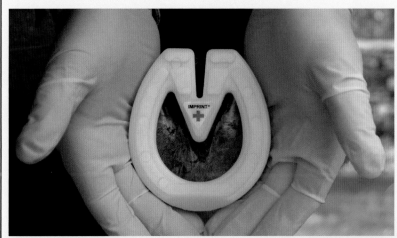

A Quick Tack Check

Entire volumes have been written about the various types of equipment that can be utilized when riding or training horses, and many of these are undoubtedly useful. However, what is questionable is the tendency to place too much emphasis on the kit and too little on the work itself. If you have fifty different bits hanging up in your tack room, I'm sure they might prove useful one day, but in most cases a simple, properly fitted snaffle will suffice; you would be far better off spending the money you save on lessons to become a better rider.

The same thing applies to saddles: so a horse's back changes slightly according to its age, the time of year, and the work that the horse is in – but unless you are a professional event rider, there is no need for you to go out and purchase three saddles for the same horse! A single saddle, properly fitted and assessed by a competent authority, will suffice.

And you could help yourself and your horse by monitoring its weight a bit: a simple measuring tape will eliminate the guesswork.

The equine mouth, bits and bitting

A wolf tooth grows exactly where the bit sits and for this reason usually needs to be extracted

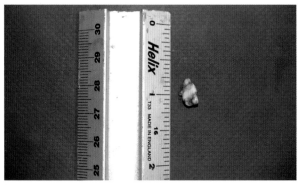

Due to their shallow roots, wolf teeth often move under a close contact

The bit can be compared to the steering wheel of your car, in that it allows you better control of the horse's head and therefore its body. Some horses don't need to be bitted, and others you wouldn't dream of trying to get on without a bit in their mouth: but remember, no matter what, a bit is the steering wheel and not the brakes on a horse, and it certainly won't stop the animal if it really wants to go.

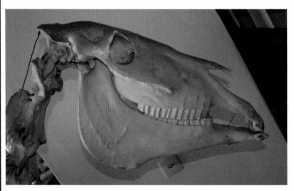

The teeth of a horse are quite large and they are constantly erupting through the jaw

Before you put a bit into your horse's mouth, you should ensure that the teeth are not causing it a problem. A quick look at its mouth anatomy is therefore in order.

The horse's dentition

Like our teeth, the horse's dentition is tailored to its chewing (mastication) needs. The front teeth, or incisors, bite or grasp the forage, while the premolars and molars grind it down in preparation for swallowing. There are also specialized teeth which, through the course of evolution, have lost their necessity, namely the large canines and the smaller wolf teeth; generally the latter do not erupt in over half of the horse population, particularly mares.

Unlike our teeth, those in a horse do not have a hard enamel coating over them for protection; to compensate for the continuous wear they are subjected to, they continually erupt into the mouth. That is why the back molars in horses are so long: they must be, for during the course of the animal's life, they are slowly pushing up into the oral cavity.

A horse naturally chews its forage from side to side, but unfortunately the wear and tear on its teeth is not even, which means that points slowly develop on its teeth,

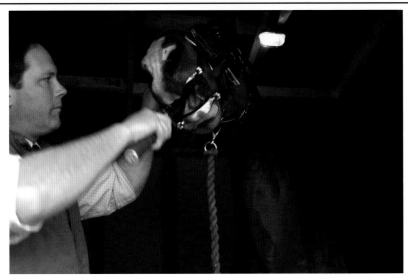

A mouth speculum is essential to do any type of dental work on a horse

as these continue to erupt. Typically these points are found on the lingual side on the lower teeth and the buccal side of the upper teeth. While true bridle lameness is extremely uncommon, these enamel points alone – never mind some of the other terrible dental pathologies that vets and horse dentists see on a daily basis – can make a huge difference to the riding pleasure of a horse. Typical histories include abnormal head movements, unwillingness to take a contact, and moving the head to one side.

Dental examination

A full mouth speculum, or 'gag', is invaluable for inspecting and rasping a horse's teeth, but generally only professionals have this specialized equipment. However, using a basic knowledge of the anatomy inside a horse's mouth, it is possible to assess whether or not a horse's teeth are in need of dental care, and most importantly, if they are the cause of riding difficulties. With the horse standing in front of you, place both hands on either side of the animal's muzzle. With the tips of

your fingers, carefully feel the upper molars and premolars through the skin of the mouth. Locate their distal edge, and feel side to side for signs of enamel pointing. Applying a bit of pressure to the area will elicit a painful response if an enamel point is present. If it does, you can be sure there are some more hooks on those lower inside edges. It is time, therefore, to get those teeth rasped so that cuts and ulcerations can be avoided, and the tongue prevented from being caught between the bit and the teeth.

This is another effective method: stand to one side of the horse, and place one hand on the bridge of the nose and the other directly underneath on the lower jaw. Push your two hands towards each other to ensure that the teeth inside the mouth are touching. While applying this pressure, try to move the jaw from side to side in an effort to mimic sideways mastication. If the jaws do not move evenly from side to side and have a tendency to lock instead, you have further indication that a dental treatment is needed.

There is one final and quick examination that I like to do, though this one is not to be recommended to anyone who doesn't deal with horses' mouths on a daily basis: get this wrong and you have a very sore finger! I slip both thumbs in the side of the horse's mouth, and push them on to the gum and second premolar where the bit usually sits; this will allow me to feel for soreness in that area, as well as determine the presence of wolf teeth and whether these are actually causing a problem.

Watching a horse eat is another good habit to get into, as it can often uncover subtle problems, and not only in the mouth! I have seen several horses that would only eat from a haynet from one side, and from this simple observation, neck pathologies were discovered, and even one case of DJD of the temporo-mandibular joint, the joint from which the lower jaw is hinged.

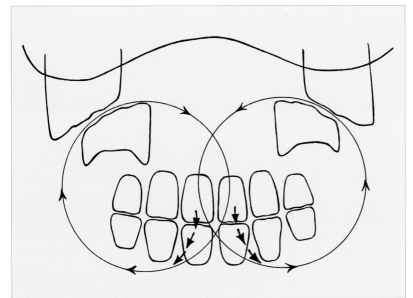

This diagram shows the circular motion horses use to chew food. Enamel hooks will hinder this movement, forcing the horse to move its jaw up and down

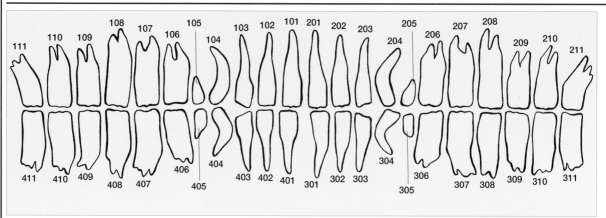

Identifying the teeth

A simple way to describe horse's teeth is through the triadan system, which divides the horse's head into quadrants. The horse's right upper teeth comprise the first quadrant, and all the teeth are labelled with a '1' in front of them. The horse's upper left teeth form the second quadrant so are labelled with a '2' in front of them; the lower left teeth are the third quadrant and carry a '3'; and finally the lower right teeth form the fourth quadrant and carry a '4'. Teeth are counted from the inside incisor (#1) backwards until the last molar, tooth #11. Thus the upper back left-hand molar on a horse is 211, and the first incisor on the lower right-hand side, 401.

It is clear from the diagram that the bit fits between the gap of the canines (104 and 204) and second premolars (106 and 206). As the first premolars, the wolf teeth are very small and have shallow roots; they usually interfere with the action of the bit, and need to be removed in a relatively minor extraction procedure. In many cases it is also advisable to rasp the edge of 106 and 206 to make it difficult for the horse to 'get the bit between his teeth', thereby negating your control over it. This is called a 'bit seat'.

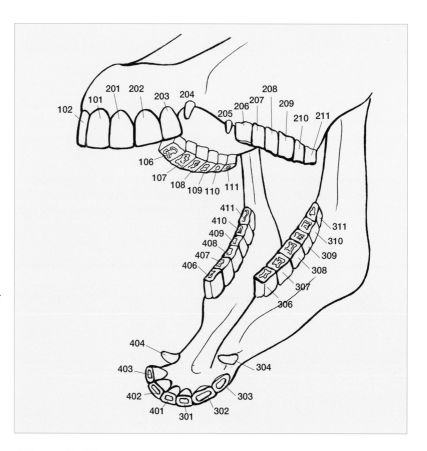

Bits and bitting

An obvious but overlooked fact is that the internal anatomy of the mouth will help determine what bit a horse feels more comfortable with. Lifting the lips covering the diasthema, have a look at the horse's tongue. Does it fit narrowly within the contours of the mouth, or does it bulge out to the side? As it has been shown that the tongue is used by horses to push the bit around, the fleshier the tongue, the more it will push against the bit, keeping it from making contact with the bars. The configuration of the hard palate is also of interest, as a low one will usually necessitate a thinner bit.

A conventional standard for assessing the width of a horse's windpipe, and therefore its ability to get air down into the lungs, was set as the width of a man's fist. This idea can be extended further to assess the width of the lower jaw. If you have a horse with a fleshy tongue but a narrow jaw, for example, it would in fact not be comfortable in a 'mild' *thick* mouthpiece.

Fitting a bit

Width: A snaffle bit should be long enough to protrude approximately ½in (13mm) from either side of the mouth. Pelhams, Weymouths and other straight bits may be fitted *slightly* narrower.

Height: A jointed bit should create only one slight wrinkle at the corner of both sides of the mouth. Straight-bar bits should never cause more than a slight wrinkle. The only exception to this is in the occasional short-mouthed horse that needs to be bitted slightly tighter in order to keep the bit from banging on to the incisors.

When assessing for bit difficulties, it is important to look at the lips of the horse, particularly the corners. Injuries here are often indicative of a bit being too thin, or having been adjusted too high.

Rubber straight-bar loose-ring snaffle

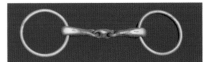
Double-jointed loose-ring snaffle

Loose-ring Cambridge snaffle

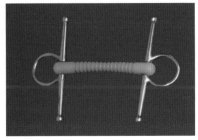
Rubber straight-bar with cheek pieces

Vulcanite pelham

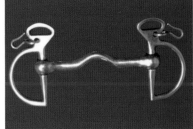
Kimblewick

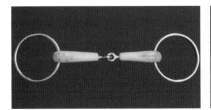
Rubber jointed loose-ring snaffle

Double-jointed loose-ring snaffle

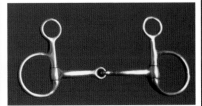
Hanging cheek (half cheek) snaffle

Eggbutt snaffle

Eggbutt bridoon

Eggbutt French-link snaffle (Dr Bristol)

Saddles

The saddle had already found widespread use as far back as the fourth century. It is used to help the rider to adopt and maintain the correct seat for the purpose intended. It is no wonder then, that there is a wide variety of different style saddles on the market today. The most commonly found saddles in the western world are the English saddle and the Western saddle.

It should be remembered that these two forms of riding grew out of very different, distinct needs. The English saddle was born out of the requirement to send cavalry troops into the pitch of battle. The horses had to be quick, responsive to every signal given by the rider. The rider was to be balanced, athletic and mobile. The Western and Spanish saddle traditions grew out of a very different necessity – the need to travel long distances – days or even weeks in relative comfort. The saddle cut became deeper, essentially holding the rider in the saddle without the need for strenuous leg work. Perhaps this is how the different styles of horsemanship were also born. Instead of worrying about controlling the animal, the rider learned to rely on it. In order to do so, he had to be more receptive to the emotions of his travelling companion. After all, if the horse dumped him and bolted, leaving him stranded in the inhospitable elements, miles away from anywhere, it could have grave consequences.

Various styles of English saddle. Clockwise from top left: racing, jumping, dressage, general purpose

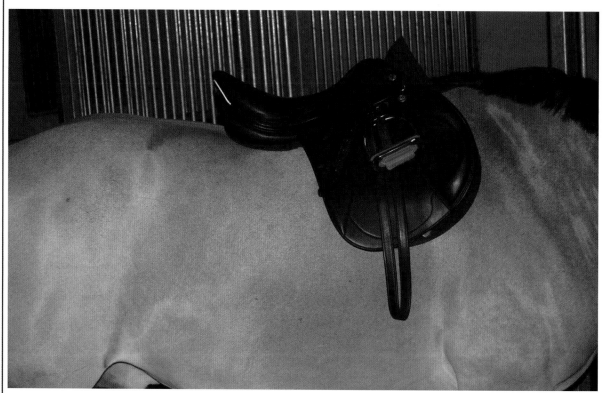

This saddle is too large for this horse's relatively short back, tipping the rider's weight on to the weaker lower back. Note the swellings just behind the saddle

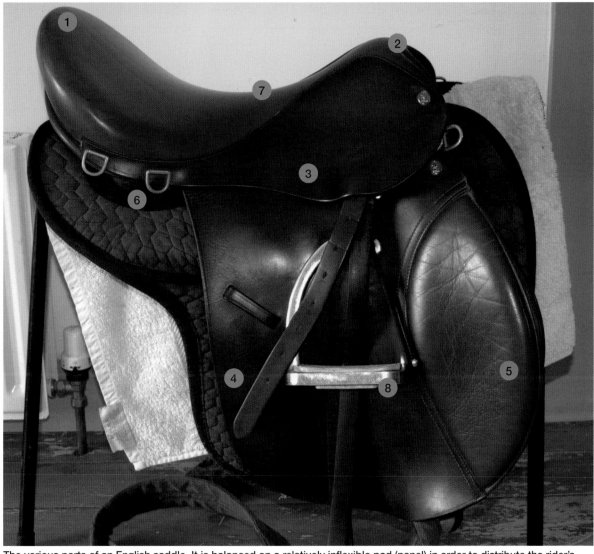

The various parts of an English saddle. It is balanced on a relatively inflexible pad (panel) in order to distribute the rider's weight more effectively

1	cantle
2	pommel
3	skirt
4	flap
5	knee roll
6	panel
7	waist
8	stirrup

English saddle

Viewing an English saddle from the top and the side, the eye falls naturally upon the raised part of the seat, the pommel, then down into the seat before rising again to the back edge, the cantle. The large side panels are simply called flaps, and are stitched into place under the overhanging leather from the seat, namely the skirts. Under the flap are the girth straps and girth safe which lie on top of the now exposed panel. The forward edge of the panel is rolled into a knee roll, the back edge becomes a thigh roll. It is the underside of the panels that make contact with the horse's back, forming a gullet between them so as not to press on to the spine.

A quality, well fitted saddle is essential. To fit a saddle properly, place the saddle on the horse, partially up the withers and slide it back just behind them. After girthing, check the saddle from the side to ensure that it is lying in balance. With the rider sitting, ensure that the gap between the withers and the front arch of the pommel is at least 5cm (2in). This will ensure that there is no contact between the two. Standing from behind in a raised position, look down the gullet to ensure that there is plenty of space for the spine. The weight-bearing surface of the saddle should be as broad as possible to distribute the weight evenly. The back of the cantle should not be more than 4cm (1½in) from the surface of the horse's spine. The front of the panel underneath the knee roll should be checked to ensure that there is a symmetrical and snug fit to the musculature of the back. It is essential that the rider's weight should not fall back into the weaker, lower back. To avoid this, it may be necessary to sacrifice rider comfort in favour of a slightly smaller seat.

As long as you have a well fitting saddle, a wide assortment of gel pads, riser pads and so on are not necessary, and in some instances are counter productive as they hinder the contact between horse and rider!

Depending on their cut and the positioning and prominence of the knee and thigh rolls, English saddles can be classified as jumping, dressage or general purpose saddles. Specialized saddles would include show saddles and saddles that are used for playing polo or for riding endurance.

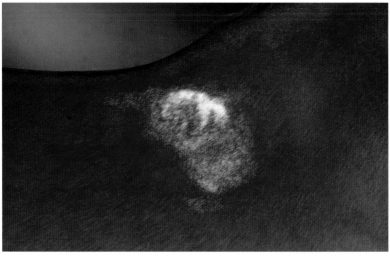

White hair is a tell-tale sign of an ill-fitting saddle

Western saddle

Western saddles were designed for comfort for long hours of riding. They have a wide, comfortable seat and wide, long stirrup leathers and stirrups which allow the leg to stretch out and forward. These features ensure more comfort, and also more security in the saddle.

Although the saddles are much heavier than English saddles, they distribute the weight of the rider more evenly. Because they lack a tree and are much flatter than English saddles, they will fit most horses. They were specifically designed this way so that cowboys could change their own saddle on to almost any other horse. Instead of a cantle, there is a swell with a horn attached to it. This horn was originally intended for cowboys to tie a roped cow onto after lassooing the animal. The saddle is worn with a thick saddle pad underneath. They have two cinches – one that is tied where a normal girth is, and one that is tied further behind in order to prevent the saddle from tipping forwards when roping cattle.

Working saddles are usually plain leather, whereas show saddles can be intricately decorated. Western saddles can be categorized as roping, cutting, reining, or barrel-racing saddles.

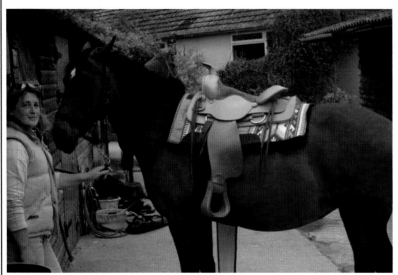

A traditional Western saddle

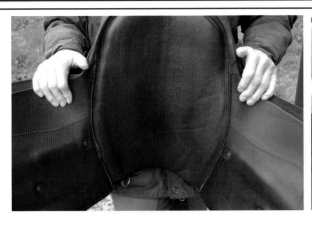

↑↓ Three alternative forms of English saddle: a treeless saddle, an adjustable tree and saddle pad and an air-filled saddle. Although these ideas are to be recommended, in most cases a traditional properley fitted saddle is to be preferred

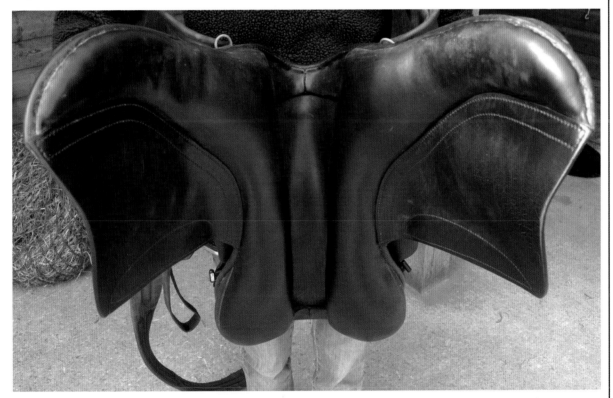

← Side-saddle is a very traditional and specialized form of riding

The Influence of the Owner/Rider

It is little wonder that in the current climate of affixing blame rather than assuming personal responsibility, the influence of the owner is all but forgotten within the amateur riding community. However, *the owner plays the single largest factor in maintaining soundness in his/her horse*. Fitness, nutrition and hoof, dental and veterinary care – all of these factors are the sole responsibility of the owner. There is no quick remedy, no single jab, no bit of fancy equipment that is going to overcome poor horsemastership.

There are two key issues that warrant closer attention: the individual horse and the individual rider.

A lot of work, effort, time and money went into the training of this horse and rider partnership to get them to this point

The individual horse

When considering treatment or rehabilitation, or even just during training or routine care, it is prudent to recognize the character of the horse you are dealing with. Some horses are afraid of being alone. When injured therefore, it may be wise to place them in a 'sick' paddock next to their friends, rather than leaving them alone to worry in their box while the others go out. Other horses get easily impatient or bored, so if they kick the stable door a lot, don't wait for their habit to catch up with them: pad the door with a soft mattress, and try to keep them out for as long as possible. The same thing goes for horses that weave: get them outside where they can entertain themselves in a healthier manner!

On the other hand, if you own a little fat pony that is prone to laminitis, it is quite obvious that the worst thing for its health is for it to be outside on good pasture all day long. Get a sick paddock for it, and if that is not possible for whatever reason, *change yards*. The same thing goes for a horse that is prone to mud fever: keep him out of muddy fields and filthy stables. Be proactive: don't wait until the obvious happens, but *change*

yards, even if it means leaving a yard with all your friends. You can enjoy chatting with them in the pub in the evening, when you have a sound horse and they don't!

I remember being called out to see a lovely Irish hunter suffering from raging laminitis. As my eyes wandered over the distended belly to the radiographs of its feet, I asked the owner what she was feeding the animal. After listening to her textbook answer, two and two weren't quite making four: 'What are you *really* feeding her?' I asked. There was a pause, a slight shuffling of feet, and with a blush she said: 'Well, she has six jam doughnuts every Sunday – she really likes those. And a pint of Guinness a day, and….' Needless to say, I made it perfectly clear that both she and I knew that I didn't have a hope of curing her horse until those little feeding sessions ceased.

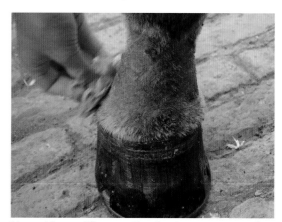

Many skin conditions are the direct consequence of unhygienic surroundings

I have clients that let their animals graze next to a sewage processing plant because it's inexpensive – but all that money comes right back out of their pockets during the autumn when the heavy rains force the plant to flood the fields with the toxic overflow causing mud fever in their horses.

Finally, there is no doubt that, like people, horses have individual pain thresholds. In general, it is said that pony mares are the toughest, whilst Thoroughbred geldings can be a bit sensitive. However, each animal is certainly different in how much or how little they are willing to put up with. It is well known in veterinary circles that Thoroughbreds in particular can lose the will to live when they are in severe pain. If you find yourself in this unfortunate situation, it is important to do what you can to enhance the animal's attitude.

Rider balance is essential in maintaining soundness

The horse is not the only one that needs to be fit

Years ago I was introduced to a lovely paint mare who through a retained placenta, had contracted a desperate case of laminitis. I can remember looking at her lying in the deep shavings of her hospital stable, wondering if she would have the fight to keep on. But we had one thing going for us: Skippy loved bananas. I asked the nurse to bring her a small piece of banana three times a day in an attempt to lift her spirits. Sure enough, no sooner did the nurse enter the barn, when Skippy's friendly 'Wicker, wicker' could be heard in gleeful anticipation of that little bit of banana. I know what the school book would say, yet I am certain that those little morsels of her favourite food helped Skippy overcome those agonizing weeks and live happily in the pasture for another seven years.

Consider these stories the next time you go riding and your horse goes lame under you. As you slide off your saddle, you should already be thinking, 'Am I dealing with a thin-soled, flat-footed Thoroughbred, or a tough 12-year-old hunter that has never seen a day's lameness in its life?' If it's the latter, you would certainly be right to be more concerned about its lameness.

The individual owner/rider

My first introduction to the influence of the rider happened while I was a young assistant. I was called out to perform a lameness investigation on a young lady's horse; but as she trotted the lame animal up and down, an uncomfortable feeling came over me. 'Doesn't the boss usually come and treat your horse?' I asked. There was a slight hesitation before she blurted out, 'Why yes, he does. He came only yesterday. And when he got out, he looked at me and my horse and said, "Martha, you're too damn fat to be riding that horse." And then he left.

…I know he's right, but I still want my horse fixed.' So we nerve blocked and x-rayed and treated her horse's coffin joint inflammation – but we all knew that the *real* treatment was either for my lovely new client to lose some weight, or to buy herself a new horse.

Fitness

Being overweight isn't the only factor to consider. The reality is that for many riders, 'equestrian sports' should really be rephrased 'equestrian leisure'. Many people ride just for fun nowadays, and why not? I'm all for it, but for one minor detail: particularly in the English style of riding, you have to have some form of fitness, some strength in the leg, in order to ride properly. I use the term 'properly' loosely here. I don't mind if you don't ride well, but you should try to ride loose and balanced. And this is where another small problem occurs: many riders have never performed any form of athletics in their life, and so have no concept of how difficult it is to achieve and maintain fitness. Try running three or four miles a day for a few weeks: only then do you begin to understand how difficult it is. And you begin to understand the importance of stretching, warming up and cooling down.

You begin to understand another thing, too: some days you feel light, as if you could run twice as far in the same time, and on other days it seems hard work.

Proper diet is essential in maintaining health and fitness

Preparation is the key here, and the amount of injuries that could be prevented through the application of a few basic athletic principles is staggeringly high. Get your horse fit slowly, months before you plan on engaging in whatever activity you enjoy, and always warm it and yourself up and cool down slowly. That animal underneath you is not a machine that can be started up willy nilly, but is something that needs and deserves a bit more care and attention. That routine maintenance will make all the difference.

Be realistic!

Another quite frequent cause for disappointment in a stable yard is the overly high opinion riders have of their actual riding ability. Be realistic, and err on the side of caution. Confidence and even bravery are to be admired, but blindness to your limitations is foolish. One of the leading causes of broken legs in skiing comes from individuals overestimating their abilities and setting their bindings to 'expert' level: when they fall, the ski stays on and their leg breaks instead. Your choice of the animal you ride is just as crucial.

Recently, I was called to examine a horse belonging to a new client. After greeting the horse, I turned towards the owner to see that she had tears streaming down her face. 'What's wrong?' I asked.

'As you can see, I'm a bit h… h… hormonal,' she sniffed. 'And so is my horse!'

I was thunderstruck. How do you react to something like that? I bit my lip. 'And what's wrong with your horse, madam?' She dried her eyes and looked at me. 'It's uncontrollable, and I would like you to give me some hormones to calm it down.'

My head reeled. A quick calculation in my mind reckoned £60 a month for 12 months…. I took a deep breath: 'What kind of rider are you, madam?' I asked, looking at the five foot five young lady in front of me.

'I'm a n.. n… novice,' she sniffed. And turning to her horse, all 16.2hh of it, I asked, 'And what did this mare do before you bought it?'

A rider must help her horse to perform each task

The reply was just as stunning as the opening salvo had been: 'It was a huntsman's horse.'

'Then I'm afraid it is the wrong horse for you. What you need is a 15hh cob to hack around on, not a horse that's used to get up and go.' And so I departed that yard, knowing full well that although I had tried to help her the best I could, I had probably lost a client who would be looking for a more understanding vet!

The point is simple: one of the most common errors that novice riders make is to over-horse themselves. Certainly a 17hh horse is flashier – but flashy doesn't matter if you don't have the strength of leg to ride it, and it takes you where it fancies: the fun wears out of that really quickly and with it your confidence. That's not the way forward for you or the horse. So analyse your skills honestly, and buy a horse that you can ride; that way, both of you will stay safe and enjoy yourselves.

Be circumspect!

A final comment on horses and riders: *do not* work young animals too hard – let them mature or they'll never last the course. Be careful of buying that four-year-old Irish Sport Horse that has been hunting for two years, or that six-year-old dressage horse that can piaffe. Those joints are not mature yet, and the chances are that damage has already been done: it might not have, but it is more than likely.

Proper care has made this horse's 27th birthday a happy one

Indicators of Lameness

Before we see our horse move, we should all know what characteristics in a horse's movement are significant indicators of lameness. If you are in any doubt about how a sound horse moves, re-read The Horse in Movement (pp.20–25) before going on to read this section.

In the forelimb

Vertical head movement

In trot, a horse's head moves up and down twice between each stride: it reaches a maximum height just before the foot is about to bear weight, and a minimum height as the same leg reaches midstance. The head then moves back up to the maximum position as the opposite leg begins to bear weight. The head maximum and minimum heights are the same for both limbs.

A deviation from these heights is readily seen as a 'head nod', with the maximum height decreased on the sound leg. To put it in simpler terms: if you were walking along and suddenly I kicked you hard on your left shin, what would happen? Your gait would change! First you would be reluctant to bear any weight at all on that leg; then you would gingerly put your foot to the floor, all the while leaning as hard as you could on your right leg. To

LEFT REIN

RIGHT REIN

44

take a step forwards, your head would automatically lift higher as your sore leg began to bear weight in an effort to reduce that weight (and therefore the pain), all the while attempting to bring the good leg as fast forward as possible to take the next step. As soon as the right foot hit the ground, your head, neck and shoulders would relax in order to maximize the load on the good leg. It's no different in horses, though luckily, the lamenesses are often more subtle than the shin kick I have described.

I find it easiest to remember that as the good leg bears the horse's weight, the head goes down: thus *down on sound*. Therefore, *the horse is lame on the opposite forelimb!*

Subtle lamenesses can frequently be seen more easily during acceleration or deceleration – that is, at the beginning or end of the trot.

Changes in the stride

A stride consists of a swing phase in which the leg is moved forwards, a stance phase in which the limb is weight-bearing, before the breakover period and move into another swing phase. Obviously the weight-bearing phase in the horse that is too lame to bear weight will be drastically shortened on the affected limb. However, it is important to know that in more subtle lameness, the stance phase is actually increased on the affected limb; this is because the horse endeavours to decrease the peak load on that limb, thereby reducing the intensity of the emitted pain, and so it tries shifting the weight on to the contralateral hindlimb – but this is ineffective, so the only thing to do is to 'spread the total load over a longer period of time'.

However, the changes described are often too quick and too subtle to see and quantify using our eyes alone. What may become apparent is the decreased swing phase of the affected limb: the step may appear to be shortened, and not as high as the opposite limb. Note that both the lengthened stance phase and shortened swing phases only become apparent if the horse's speed remains the same. Again, under normal circumstances, this can be difficult to achieve.

In the hindlimb

→ Right: This horse is not being naughty...that back hurts!

Vertical pelvic movement

The vertical movement of the pelvis is similar to the movement of the head, though it is more subtle and difficult to see. A lameness on one hindlimb (unilateral) does change the symmetry of pelvic movement, in that the pelvis is lowered less during the stance phase, and lifted less at the end of the stance.

↓ Below: Viewing the horse from behind is essential when assessing pelvic and tuber coxae movement

Tuber coxae movement

The movement of the tuber coxae is similar to that of the entire pelvis, but it is more exaggerated and therefore easier to see. In general, there is an increase in movement of the tuber coxae opposite the affected limb, particularly in an upward direction at the end of the stance phase of the sound limb; this is known as 'hip hike'.

Hindlimb protraction

An easier parameter to evaluate is the willingness of the horse to 'step under' in walk and trot. This is easily quantified by observing the distance between the hooves of the fore- and hindlimbs of the same side (ipsilateral). In order to reduce weight on the affected limb, a horse will be unwilling to step under the body nearer the centre of gravity. This in turn will increase the distance between the foot of the maximally extended hindlimb and the protracted ipsilateral forelimb.

Bilateral lameness

The single most complicating factor is that many horses have a bilateral lameness. This will make assessment and diagnosis even more difficult, because horses that are bilaterally lame will often show only subtle signs of lameness, and that lameness can often switch from leg to leg during the course of an examination. Getting back to our analogy: after being viciously kicked in the left shin, you stumble and knock the shin of your right leg on the corner of your coffee table. What happens now? Both legs hurt, and your head no longer favours the right limb. So you can slow down a bit in the hope that the pain may recede with time, and you can increase the stance

phase of both legs, thereby decreasing the swing phase pattern in both. But you are no longer blatantly lame to the outside observer, just slow. And so it is with horses, who often display no more than a stumbling gait.

Grading system for degree of lameness

In order to quantify and communicate the degree of lameness to others, the following grading system has been recommended by the American Association of Equine Practitioners (AAEP) and is in widespread use today.

Grade	Lameness Observed
0	No lameness. Horse is sound.
1	Inconsistent lameness which is difficult to discern under any circumstance.
2	Lameness is difficult to observe at walk or trot on a straight line, but is consistently apparent under special circumstances: these include manipulation, hard surface, circling, riding, incline.
3	Lameness is consistently observed at a trot under all circumstances.
4	Lameness is obvious with marked nodding, hitching and/or shortened stride without manipulation.
5	Horse is reluctant to move, with little or no weight-bearing.

Lameness Evaluation

We have looked at the fundamentals that are necessary for us to conduct a thorough lameness investigation; now we must be consistent in our evaluation, and the easiest way to do this is to conduct the examination in the same way, NO MATTER WHAT. In that way, you will avoid making silly errors of judgement, or jumping to unnecessary conclusions. I have included a sample lameness investigation form that we, as veterinarians, use: make a copy of it and, armed with a clipboard, let's set to work!

Whistlejacket
Equine Veterinary Surgery
A Modern Professional Team Approach

LAMENESS WORK UP

Oliver C. Davis BA, MRCVS
Charlotte Shepherd BVetMed, BSc, MRCVS
Kirsten Storack BVM&S, BSc, MRCVS

Horse........................ Owner.................... Vet....................
Age......... Use.. Date....................
Insured Yes/no .... Farrier....................
BIOP.. Pre-purchase examination....................
Primary complaint ....

History..
....
....

Conformation
Feet..
LF..
RF..
LH..
RH..

Palpation
Limbs..
LF..
RF..
LH..
RH..

Neck/shoulder ....
Hindquarters ....
Back ....

Examination

	LF	RF	LH	RH
Digital pulse				
Hoof testers				
Palpation and examination				
Flexion tests				
Wedge test				

Fishmore Hill Farm, Milton Abbas, Blandford, Dorset DT11 0DL
Tel: 01258 881777 Fax: 01258 881778 EMERGENCY NUMBER: 07000 944785 (W9-H4-I4-S7-T8-L5)
VAT Reg: 754 8687 74

Whistlejacket
Equine Veterinary Surgery
A Modern Professional Team Approach

Oliver C. Davis BA, MRCVS
Charlotte Shepherd BVetMed, BSc, MRCVS
Kirsten Storack BVM&S, BSc, MRCVS

Walk..
Trot..
L circle..
R circle..
Ridden..

Nerve/joint block	Response at 10 minutes	Response at 20 minutes	Response at 30 minutes

Further diagnostics and results ....
Diagnosis..
Treatment plan..
Management..
Medication..
Supplements..
Dressings..
Shoeing..
Next appointment..

Fishmore Hill Farm, Milton Abbas, Blandford, Dorset DT11 0DL
Tel: 01258 881777 Fax: 01258 881778 EMERGENCY NUMBER: 07000 944785 (W9-H4-I4-S7-T8-L5)
VAT Reg: 754 8687 74

The lameness work-up form used by our surgery

Even if it is your own horse, the importance of a thorough clinical history cannot be over-emphasized, as it may give you clues as to what the problem may be. Just as importantly, it may also indicate what things are less likely to be at the root of a problem. For instance, a five-year-old pony with a bilateral forelimb lameness is less likely to be lame due to navicular disease than a 12-year-old showjumper. However, I would check those feet carefully to make sure it is not suffering from laminitis. Has it been out in the field all day? Is it overweight? Never be afraid of asking too many questions, but be sure that you pose them in a neutral fashion without trying to sway the answer, and never question as to force an answer; 'I don't know' is far more helpful than an answer that is given in duress.

Following the clinical history, your evaluation both visually and physically should be carried out as detailed in the previous chapters. Are you starting to amass some clues yet? Does that pony seem tight in the lower neck? Does it have an increased pulse in both of its front feet? If it does, you have a pretty good idea as to how it is going to move. If it doesn't, then the laminitis theory doesn't seem as probable.

Always be sceptical of your diagnosis, and continue to examine the horse in order to find more clues which will either corroborate or disprove your diagnosis.

Now finally, let's have a look at the pony moving!

Evaluating the horse in walk

To begin your evaluation, choose a hard, flat and straight surface. Place yourself towards one end of the stretch, and ask the person leading the horse to simply walk up and down past you. It is important that the horse is kept on a loose rein so that the head movement is unrestricted and therefore not influenced by the handler.

> Resist the temptation to trot the horse: you can gain a lot of valuable information by carefully observing the movement at the slower pace of walk.

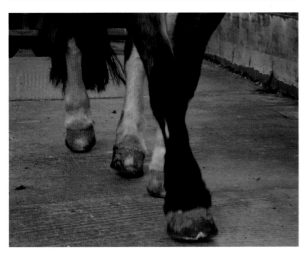
This horse is unbalanced!

Adopt a system of observation as the horse walks by you. Begin by observing the animal as a whole: does the body langauge show that it is comfortable? Is it happy to move freely? Listen to the cadence of the walk: is it regular and rhythmic? Finally, observe whether the horse is overly nervous or excited: if it is, is there anything you can do to put its anxiety to rest? Perhaps it needs a few minutes to adapt to its surroundings. Perhaps the horse is afraid because it can't see any of its field companions. Whatever it is, try to figure it out. *You must try to think like a horse, since it will certainly never be able to think like you.* Remember, *a nervous or excited horse will never show mild lameness.* Your best chance to observe obscure lameness problems is in a calm and relaxed atmosphere.

As the animal walks back and forth past you, focus your eyes on the tell-tale signs of lameness.

As the horse moves away from you, stand directly behind it; from this vantage point you are best able to observe the hindlimb movement. Are the hind hooves landing flat on the ground? Are the hindlimbs following a straight arc pattern, or do they land too far under or away from the body of the horse? As the horse continues to move away from you, let your eyes travel up the legs. Do the fetlocks roughly show the same amount of flexion – that is, do they descend roughly the same distance? Observe the point of the hocks for a few strides: do both seem to be moving in roughly the same way?

Finally, move your eyes up towards the pelvis and tuber coxae: does the pelvis move in a symmetrical fashion, or is it tilted to one side? Is the tail carried symmetrically behind? Can you observe any sign of the infamous 'hip hitching'? Finally, observe the neck and head from behind: does the head bob evenly and loosely from side to side as the horse casually watches its surroundings as it walks?

By this time the horse should be some thirty or so yards from you, and the handler should be turning it round to begin walking back towards you. You will not have had time enough to observe all of the above points accurately, but it doesn't matter because you will proceed with your observations the next time it walks by. *Continue to have the horse walked in front of you until you are satisfied that you have accurately observed all the points mentioned.*

As it begins to turn back towards you, watch the horse's front legs and head: does it seem comfortable, or did the stride shorten? Did its head movement change?

Now the horse is walking back towards you, you can observe the forelimb movement better. Begin with the hooves again: do they land flat? Are the legs straight, or do we have a toe in or out conformation? Do the limbs follow a straight arc pattern, or do they have a tendency to arc out and then in again (dish)? You will not be able to judge the fetlocks from this position, but must wait until the horse passes. For now, continue moving your eyes up the horse: does the shoulder movement appear symmetrical? Is there any sign of uneven head nodding?

A blatant dishing movement with the near fore

By this time the animal should be fairly close in front of you, so it's time to take two or three steps to one side so as not to impede its movement: remember the importance of keeping it at the same constant speed!

As the horse moves by, observe the protraction of the hindlimbs: are they the same, or is one increased over the other? Do the flexions of the joints all appear to be similar to one another? A quick glimpse as the horse moves away from you, then quickly retrace your steps to stand directly behind the horse again as it continues in walk. Begin observing where you left off last time.

Mimicking the horse's movement helps you to notice what your eye may find difficult to see

Continue in this manner, observing the horse's walk, up and down, until you are satisfied that you have seen all you are going to see. The next time it is led past you, begin walking next to it level with the head: watching the front legs all the time, begin to pace yourself exactly with the horse's movement, so when the near fore lands, your foot strikes the ground level with it, when the off fore lands, so does your other foot. Do you have to stretch your stride out more on one leg than the other? Continue walking in this manner, until you are satisfied you know the answer.

Now do the same with the horse's hindlimbs, so you mimic its stride exactly: do you notice any difference between the steps?

Write down your observations. Are you able to see a pattern yet? Do the findings for your initial examination of the horse match your findings of how it walks? They may not, but don't despair just yet if they don't, because we still need to collect a wealth of information. And remember, the horse may be lame not on one, but on two, three or four legs!

Evaluating the horse in a turn

We have seen the horse walk in a straight line on a hard surface, turning only to change direction back towards us again. Perhaps we observed an uncomfortableness in the horse during the turn: now is the time to make certain. Choose a large concreted area and ask the handler to lead the horse around in a circle roughly 10m in diameter. Choose a vantage point roughly another 5m away from the perimeter of the circle, and observe the horse's movement, carefully observing all the points mentioned before. Do not stand in the middle of the circle as you will only get dizzy trying to concentrate on the horse moving around you. After a few rounds, ask the handler to gradually decrease the size of the circle. This will begin to place more strain on the legs, particularly the inside ones. As the circle narrows, does a head bob or a hip hitch become more apparent?

When the circle cannot get any tighter, ask the handler to stop, and bringing the horse's neck around towards him with one hand, place his other hand on the horse's hip and push. In order to evade the pressure on

the hip, the horse will be forced to cross over its legs behind. Ask the handler to continue to apply pressure to the hip so that several cross-overs can be observed. At the same time, note the flexibility in the neck: does the neck arch gracefully around, or does it appear stiff and inflexible? Does this corroborate the observations made when you palpated the horse's muscles? *It is important that the handler brings the horse's head towards him whilst pushing on the hip at the same time*, or else the animal simply will not understand what you are trying to ask it to do.

Repeat the procedure on the other rein and be sure to note any differences.

At this point, I usually ask the handler to back the horse up several steps so that I can observe any signs of stiffness, weakness or lack of coordination.

Another test for weak hindquarters is to hold the end of the horse's tail to one side while it is being walked, pulling it gently towards you. A normal reaction for a horse is to resist being pulled over. A weaker horse will be pulled one, two or even three steps in your direction. Repeat the procedure on the other side. (Only perform this test on a calm horse. If you are in any doubt, leave it. It is not worth getting your head kicked in.)

Finally, and if possible, watch the horse being led up and down a hill or incline so that you can observe any change in its movement.

Evaluating the horse in trot

We now return to where we can observe the horse's movement in a straight line. Ask the handler to trot it up in a controlled, brisk trot, on a long lead so as not to hinder its natural movement. We wish to monitor the acceleration and deceleration at the beginning and end of the trot-up, so we don't want the horse skipping about and overly excited in between. And avoid circumstances that will encourage excitement – trotting towards the field where it is usually let out, for example: *try to anticipate how it might react,* and pick a suitable place where you can observe the horse trot up naturally.

Try to observe all the points as you did in the walk. *You will find things more difficult to see simply because they are happening faster!* Compare your observations with the ones you made at walk. Remember that there will be more jarring on those limbs at a trot, so this can exacerbate the pain for the horse. Listen for the two-beat trit-trot, trit-trot: does it remain rhythmic? Observe the hooves landing, the joints flexing, the legs moving, before watching for the head, hip and pelvis movement. Are there any tell-tale signs of uncomfortableness? Record your findings.

I personally do not trot horses on a circle on the concrete as not only can this be slippery and therefore dangerous for the horse, but I believe that most horses find it uncomfortable, even when they are sound. The reader may disagree, and other experienced equine veterinary practitioners do find this test valuable.

This horse is showing a balanced trot

↑→ When trotting up a horse for lameness evaluation it is important to allow free movement of the head (as at right). A tightly held head (as at left) will mask subtle head movements!

Investigating subtle lameness

Until now we have not needed any special facilities to conduct our investigation; however, in order to investigate subtle lamenesses, a modern school with a drained, all-weather surface is essential. A paddock or sand pit is no substitute and should not be used.

I prefer to observe a horse lunged in walk, trot and canter on a 15m circle on both reins at least once before ridden work; that way it is possible to see if the additional weight on the horse's back has a negative influence on its gait. Furthermore, the influence of the rider on a horse's movement should not be underestimated, an important factor to consider, particularly during a pre-purchase examination. So, does moving in a circle negatively affect the horse's gait? Carefully note the position of the head whilst it is being trotted and cantered; often a horse will move its head and neck to the outside of the circle if it is trying to avoid putting undue pressure on a bad limb.

A sound horse will have a regular, two-beat 'trit-trot' movement in trot. This is most easily heard on tarmac

Subtle lameness can often be exacerbated by very low doses of sedative, particularly in excited or nervous horses

Evaluating the horse in canter

We are able to observe a canter now for the first time; in particular the transition from trot to canter or vice versa will often exacerbate a hindlimb problem. If so, change gaits frequently, all the while trying to observe what exactly is going on. Always observe things critically. Often that little buck of a horse going into canter, or the initial frantic 'bunny hop' gait, is misinterpreted by the owner as being down to friskiness. In reality, this 'naughty' behaviour is often a symptom of a low grade hindlimb or back problem.

Another feature to note is the amount of tension the horse places on the lunge rein. An unbalanced or lame horse will often place undue strain upon the lunge rein, as it uses the person lungeing to help it balance or take the strain off a part that hurts. The rope is taut, often necessitating the person lungeing to move with the horse in an attempt to keep in balance.

Provided the surface is good, another important feature to note is the willingness of the horse to pick up its feet rather than drag them on the ground. In forelimbs it is a clear indication of lameness, whilst in hindlimbs it may also indicate a weak or unfit horse, or even a back or sacroiliac problem. Note that it is impossible to observe hoof placement on a soft surface.

Always note on which rein, the inside or outside one, the lameness is exacerbated. *As a general rule, lamenesses have certain characteristics according to which areas are affected.* (See opposite a table of common types of low-grade lameness, though you should use it as a guideline only.)

Working in a circle often exacerbates a subtle lameness. The horse in this photograph is going disunited

Evaluating the ridden horse

Finally, observe the horse ridden on a circle in walk, trot and canter, on both reins. Keep the rider involved, and ask for their input. What does it feel like to ride this horse? Remember however, not to influence the answer in any way, and bear in mind that only very experienced riders will be able to pinpoint irregularities, more than simply postulating that 'It doesn't feel quite right'.

Sometimes it is helpful if the rider uses the whole school, so that from a vantage point in the corner you can assess the horse's movement in a straight line.

Always compare a horse's movement with and without a rider as a rider can exacerbate a problem

Characteristics of Common Forelimb Lameness

Problem	Unilateral/Bilateral	In-/Outside Rein Exacerbation	Characteristic Appearance
Coffin Joint DJD	Unilateral	Inside rein	Better on soft ground
Navicular syndrome	Bilateral	Inside rein	Better on soft ground, stumbling, no extension in trot
Fetlock DJD	Unilateral	Inside rein	Fetlock joint slightly swollen
Suspensory ligament	Unilateral	No exacerbation	Obvious lameness even on straight
Carpal DJD	Unilateral	Outside rein	Carpus slightly swollen

Characteristics of Common Hindlimb Lameness

Problem	Unilateral/Bilateral	In-/Outside Rein Exacerbation	Characteristic Appearance
Fetlock DJD	Unilateral	Inside rein	Fetlock joint slightly swollen
High suspensory desmitis	Uni or bi	Inside rein	Toe dragging, poor transition, often disunited
Bone spavin	Bilateral	Inside rein	Bunny hop, unable to step under on inside rein, bucking, bone formation
Stifle	Both	No exacerbation	Toe dragging, poor transitions, no power from outside leg. Swelling possible
Sacro-iliac disease	Both, usually fluctuating	Outside rein	Poor performance, dragging toes

Flexion Tests

Perhaps no other test used in the course of a lameness investigation can stimulate as much controversy as a flexion test. The theory behind the test is simple: if you place enough pressure on a damaged joint through flexion, it will exacerbate the lameness. A difficulty arises however, when a horse that is perceived to be sound, goes lame on a flexion test. Particularly during a pre-purchase examination (vetting), emotions can run high when it comes to the 'dreaded' flexion tests.

One of the difficulties is that there is no standardization for the test: that is, each person uses varying amounts of pressure for a variable amount of time. Another difficulty is that there is no standardization for the interpretation of the results of the test. In other words, if a horse trots off lame for two steps, some consider that to be a negative, others a positive result.

There is no doubt, however, that flexion tests can be helpful when used correctly. Over the years, I have developed the following guidelines for myself.

1. I can flex most horses lame. However, that is not the purpose of the test: its purpose is to ascertain if a horse behaves abnormally to a reasonable amount of pressure on the joints.
2. While it is difficult to quantify the amount of pressure used during flexion tests, it is possible to quantify the time used for the test. For all forelimb flexions, and hindlimb fetlock flexions, pressure is applied for 30 seconds. For upper hindlimb flexion tests, the limb is flexed for 90 seconds.
3. Care should be used to apply only pressure to that part of the limb that is currently being evaluated.
4. In conducting lower limb flexions, I define reasonable pressure as pressure that strains my fingers – causes them to turn white without placing strain on the knuckles of my hand.
5. Generally, I do not consider horses that take one or two steps of mild lameness following flexion to have significant lameness problems.
6. *Always evaluate the results of flexion tests in the light of the horse's clinical history and the findings of your examination thus far.* For instance, if a five-year-old horse that I have been examining has been reluctant to turn on the near forelimb, and for which I have found quite a lot of muscle tension in the lower half of the neck, trots off lame for three to four steps following flexion, I would at least be suspicious that the area flexed may be the

cause for its lameness. If, however, I was examining a 12-year-old horse that showed no reluctance to turn and otherwise seemed fine muscularly, I would consider those few steps of lameness to be normal, given the age of the horse.

↓ **Lower forelimb flexion test:** Stand beside the limb you wish to flex, facing in the opposite direction of the horse, and pick up the forelimb. With the inside hand hold the leg at the level of mid-cannon, with the other hand, place the fingertips and thumb over the toe of the hoof and gently pull back until enough tension is placed on the fingers to cause the tips to go white but without straining the knuckles. Hold for 30 seconds and ask the horse to be trotted off immediately. Repeat the test for the opposite limb.

→ **Carpal (knee) flexion test:** Pick up the leg and bend it at the knee whilst supporting the upper cannon and fetlock areas. Pull the flexed limb upwards but not outwards. The normal range of movement for a carpus is past the horizontal, so carefully note any painful reactions of the horse to your manipulations. Hold the limb with its carpus flexed maximally for 30 seconds while continuing to support the lower limb. The horse should be trotted off immediately. Repeat the test on the opposite side in order to make a comparison.

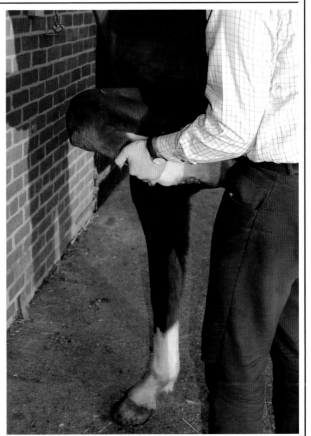

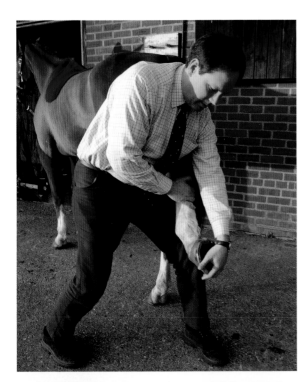

← **Lower hindlimb flexion test:** This should be performed in the same manner as for the forelimbs. However, first you must pick up the limb and stretch it away from the horse to near maximal extension; then step underneath it, allowing the front (dorsal) part of the cannon bone to rest on the thigh and knee of your inner leg. This is your safest position when examining a hindlimb, because like this it is possible to secure the limb effectively – as the leg is already in a stretched position, it will have little or no power to kick with. Now place your hand over the toe of the horse's foot and pull the fetlock towards you. Flex the limb in the same manner as you did for the forelimb.

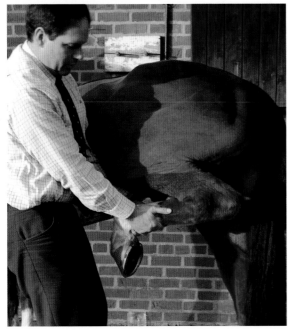

← **Tarsal (hock) flexion test:** Face in the opposite direction of the horse and pick up the hindlimb. Hold the cannon bone with both hands and flex the limb upwards, ensuring that it remains relatively close to the body and does not stretch out away from it. As the hock has a large range of movement, flexion should bring the cannon bone nearly parallel with the ground. This position should be held longer than for the other tests, generally 90 seconds. As the hock is released from flexion the horse should be trotted off immediately.

SECTION 2 VETERINARY DIAGNOSTICS

(THE PROCEDURES DESCRIBED IN THIS SECTION SHOULD ONLY BE UNDERTAKEN BY A QUALIFIED VETERINARIAN.)

Nerve Blocks

Until now, we have relied solely on the power of observation and our knowledge of a horse's anatomy and movement to aid us in our examination. Perhaps we think we have a pretty good idea of where the problem lies. But only in exceptional circumstances is it right to grab that x-ray machine or ultrasound scanner, for two very good reasons:

1. We may have made a mistake and the problem is not in that particular area at all.
2. Finding structural abnormalities with the use of modern technology does not prove that these are the actual cause of the horse's lameness.

Take a 12-year-old point-to-pointer, for instance. Even if it is sound, it is bound to have wear and tear on its joints – that is what it means to get older! But for the most part, the body is amazingly adept at coping with changes and adapting to new circumstances. So, finding radiographic or ultrasonographic changes does not prove that they are the actual cause of the problem. We must prove first where the area of lameness is before we can begin relying on high tech to come to our aid. But how?

The answer to this problem came in with the use of perineural nerve blocks. The theory behind this most important diagnostic feature is simple enough. Dissection of cadavers revealed that the anatomical structures within the horse, while not 100 per cent accurate, each followed very similar patterns, and from these it became possible to map out the nerves within the horse's leg. Nerves transmit information from the brain to the rest of the body, where information is collected and sent back again to the brain. In a lame horse, part of this information is sensory information – in other words, painful stimuli. The brain reacts by sending out signals to try and minimize the pain, and the horse begins to limp. Therefore, if we inject local anaesthetic along a known nerve, this will alleviate the pain *from that point downwards* and the horse will become sound, indicating to us that the pain is in the affected area.

Once the analgesia of the nerve blocks wears down, we can then try to pinpoint the area even more accurately. If this is not necessary, we can focus our attention on the area, usually with the use of radiography.

Shown here is a photograph of the nerves within a horse's limb. Although the fore- and hindlimb nerves are similar, there are some important differences to consider. These are pointed out in the description of the individual nerve blocks.

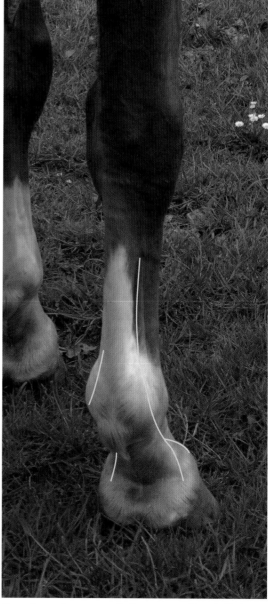

Every horse has a very similar nerve pattern in their limbs. Pictured here is the distal limb nerve pattern

Preliminary procedures to nerve blocking

In deference to clients' wishes, I do not employ a sterile technique when nerve blocking except for the four-point nerve block in the forelimb, or the six-point nerve block in the hind leg. A sterile technique requires the removal of hair around the injection site before surgical scrubbing, giving the legs a moth-eaten appearance (I have thankfully never experienced any negative reactions to nerve blocks without clipping).

The choice of local anaesthetic is an important one. Mepivicaine, though more expensive than Lignocaine, is far less likely to cause an inflammatory reaction within the leg's tissues, and should always be employed over its cheaper counterpart.

While most horses tolerate nerve blocks reasonably well, some animals can be difficult to block. One useful tactic is to *use much smaller needles* than generally described in most literature. Most of our blocks are routinely performed using 25-guage, ¼in long needles, rather than the much larger 21-guage needles. Another useful technique is to *lift the skin* well away from the underlying tissue (and nerve) you are trying to inject; this reduces the chances of the needle actually piercing the nerve, which is unnecessarily more painful than simply injecting under the skin. It will also reduce the amount of bleeding, as the main nerves always travel in the company of a vein and an artery.

It is *useful to distract the animal* somewhat while the nerve blocking injections are being performed. I find it helpful to have the owner pat continually and firmly on the horse's neck so that it will be focusing its attention there, rather than thinking about its leg. Bribery with food can also prove a useful diversionary tactic. I rarely employ the use of a twitch, as some animals can become unpredictable, exploding from a tranquil state without any warning. Better the devil you know than the devil you don't!

Safety considerations should always be at the forefront of your mind. As a young assistant I spent countless afternoons dodging hooves in order to finish a nerve block, but now I just give the horse a little sedative! Yes, it takes a little bit longer and there is a greater risk of diffusion – the local anaesthetic travelling further up the leg and blocking out more than it normally would – but it makes life so much easier, and you don't have a horse that is left traumatized by the experience. *So if things are getting a bit dangerous, sedate the horse!*

Remember to give the horse at least ten minutes for the nerve block to take effect before watching it trot up. It is helpful to have the horse walk up and down a few times in order for it to get used to the numb sensation in its leg before assessing it.

When not to nerve block

There are certain instances in which nerve blocks should not be employed – if a fracture is likely for instance, as the horse will then weight-bear on the injured leg, thereby increasing the risk of a disastrous fracture. It is also worth noting that although nerve blocks are an extremely valuable diagnostic tool, they are not foolproof, and certain conditions will only partially respond to treatment, if at all. This is where an analytical mind and intuition must guide the examiner. In my experience, three conditions can be (but are not always) difficult to block:

1. Infections, particularly infected hooves
2. Deep-seated conditions involving bone, such as some cases of navicular disease
3. Fractures

Some nerve-blocking anomalies

As we have said, a nerve block is not foolproof – and remember that horses have similar, but not duplicate nerve patterns, so each block should be tested before the lameness is assessed. This can usually be done easily with a ball-point pen: standing on the opposite side of the injected leg, reach across to prod the area which should be effectively blocked. The horse should not feel the pen on the surface of its skin, nor the deeper pressure when the pen is pushed harder. If no reaction occurs, that is a good sign. But always compare your findings to the other, *unblocked* leg: if the horse doesn't move when you poke your pen into *that* leg, it is quite clear that you still don't know much about the quality of your block; what you *do* know is that you are dealing with one easy-going horse!

One further point worthy of consideration is the issue of a *reversal in lameness*. Frequently, lameness can be bilateral, in other words in both limbs, either front or hind. A classic example of this is a horse suffering with navicular syndrome. Often the animal has a history of suddenly going lame; a precursory examination reveals moderate lameness on one leg, and a palmar digital nerve block alleviates the pain – but instead of going sound, the animal goes lame on the opposite leg! It now becomes clear that the horse did not go suddenly lame, but has been experiencing pain in both front legs for quite some time. Careful observation of the animal's gait over a period of years will reveal that it has coped with its problem by gradually shortening the length of its stride in both legs. The owner hasn't noticed this gradual and subtle difference until the day the animal is no longer able to cope with the pain in one of its limbs and goes 'suddenly' lame. It is therefore a common feature for horses with this affliction to exhibit a short, choppy gait, shifting lameness and painful turning.

Following nerve blocks, a clean dry bandage should be applied over the leg in order to minimize any swelling to that area. The effects of the nerve block should wear off within four to eight hours. If a local reaction is noted, it is important to treat this as soon as possible; cold hosing and bandaging the affected area should be sufficient. In some cases anti-inflammatory drugs can be used.

Commonly employed limb nerve blocks

Below is a list of commonly employed limb nerve blocks, in the order in which they are used in a standard lameness investigation. Thus the first nerve block anaesthetizes the heel of the foot; if the lameness does not improve after 15 minutes, the entire hoof is blocked with the abaxial nerve block; and so the process continues up the leg until the animal does finally become sound.

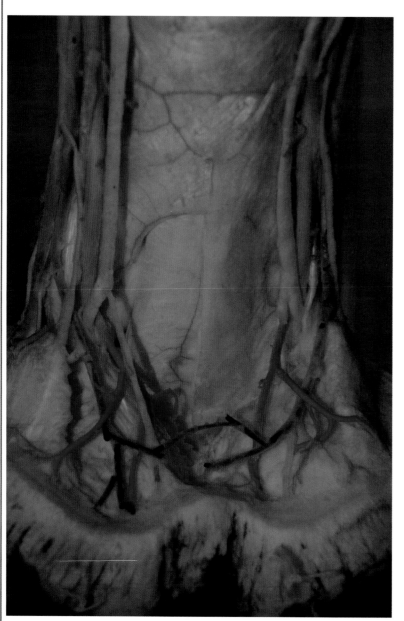

Close-up view of the palmar digital vein, artery and nerve

Palmar digital nerve block

The leg should be held in a comfortably bent position. Approximately 3ml of local anaesthetic is injected under the skin (subcutaneously) on either side of the flexor tendons and just proximal to the level of the lateral cartilage. The area anaesthetized is the heel of the foot and all the structures contained within it: navicular bone, navicular bursa, tendon sheath and a small portion of the coffin joint.

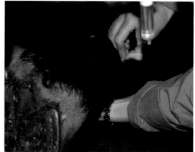

Even the largest horse has a similar nerve pattern. In this photograph, an abaxial nerve block is being performed on a Shire

Abaxial nerve block

Holding the leg up as before, the nerve and vascular bundle can be easily felt on either side of the sesamoid bones; it feels like a straw under the skin. Inject 3ml of local anaesthetic over each nerve. It is best to avoid pricking either the nerve or the blood vessels; I find it helpful to push the skin up with the thumb from my left hand, which is holding the leg.

Note that if you nerve block first with a palmar digital nerve block, and then move on to an abaxial nerve block, there is a problem which is not usually described:

Imagine a forelimb lameness work-up in which a palmar digital nerve block is negative, but an abaxial nerve block is positive. But if we look carefully at the nerves affected by the abaxial nerve block, it is apparent that not only is the entire hoof and its structures blocked out, but so too is the *proximal interphalangeal joint*, as well as the distal parts of the pastern *and* a portion of the fetlock joint, including the sesamoid bones. In other words, we are uncertain at this stage whether the problem is in the foot, the pastern or even the fetlock joint! Given the difficulty of using x-rays to determine what is diagnostic, it is no wonder that many a practitioner has made a mistake at this juncture.

P3 ring block

Whilst working in Germany, Dr Dörte Böhm taught me the following nerve block. Given the amount of lameness that occurs in the foot, I regard it as the single most important nerve block available. It has been called a 'P3 ring block', meaning a block which places a ring of local anaesthetic around P3, or the pedal bone.

Following the negative result of a palmar digital nerve block, a longer (21-guage, 1½in) needle is inserted within the bleb of local anaesthetic left by the block; the horse should therefore not feel this procedure. The needle should be angled carefully just under the skin and slowly pushed forwards, depending on the size of the horse's leg, but usually until its full length is inserted. A 2ml bleb of local anaesthetic should be injected. I prefer to continue depositing 1 to 2ml of anaesthetic as I slowly retract the needle, thereby ensuring that a ring of local anaesthetic has been deposited on that side. Repeat the procedure for the other side.

A positive result on a ring block will prove beyond a reasonable doubt that the problem you are seeking to locate lies within the hoof and its structures.

Four-point nerve block

To effectively block out everything from the fetlock down, it is necessary to anaesthetize four different sites instead of two: hence the name. The block may be performed either with the leg held up, or with it weight-bearing, depending on preference.

Given the close proximity to the joint and tendon sheath, the area for this block should be clipped out and surgically scrubbed before injection. The procedure for this aseptic technique is described fully in the following chapter covering joint injections. In this instance, two nerves are to be anaesthetized:

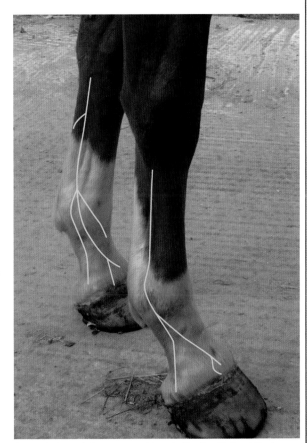

Lateral view of the nerve pattern in the forelimb of the horse

Palmar nerves: These are simply the continuation of the nerves blocked previously in the palmar digital and abaxial nerve blocks as they head up the leg. The injection sites are between the deep flexor tendon and the suspensory ligament approximately half way up the cannon but above the digital sheath and below the communicating branch of the palmar nerve, which runs superficially around the superficial flexor tendon. Both of these structures can be easily felt. Although technically it is necessary to inject both the lateral and medial branches, given their close proximity, it is possible to simply inject the lateral side only and push the needle over to the medial side to anaesthetize it at the same time. I prefer to use a 23-guage, ½in needle, which seems to work fine on all but the largest of limbs. Using this procedure also has the advantage of not needing to inject the medial aspect of the cannon, which can be awkward. In essence, you are blocking four nerves with three needles.

Palmar metacarpal nerves: These originate from the lateral palmar nerve at the height of the distal carpus, and run distally, axial to the lateral and medial splint bones where they emerge from the distal button of the splint bone to supply the dorsal aspect of the fetlock joint. Using the button as a marker for the site, inject 3ml of local anaesthesia using a 23-guage, ½in needle; this should be inserted fully up to the hilt in order to achieve a deep enough placement.

Subcarpal nerve block
This injection blocks out all the structures on the palmar aspect to the cannon, as well as the fetlock and foot structures. Pick up the leg and, keeping it flexed, palpate just under the carpus and on either side of the margin of the deep flexor tendon. If you angle your finger at 45 degrees pointing inwards, a noticeable V-shape can be felt. Using a 23-guage, 1in needle inserted at the same angle into the recess, inject 5–7ml of local anaesthetic into either side; medially this will block the medial palmar nerve, and laterally the lateral palmar nerve. It may be beneficial to block out the palmar metacarpal nerves which originate off the lateral palmar nerve. It is possible to do this by injecting slightly more proximally midway along the distal edge of the accessario-metacarpal ligament, which attaches the accessory carpal bone to the head of the splint bone. Slightly more local anaesthetic (10ml) can be injected here.

Median and ulnar nerve block
Anaesthesia of these nerves will result in the desensitization of the entire carpus and everything distal to it. However, skin desensitization may be patchy. I am not keen on using this block for a couple of reasons. Firstly, I have found that many horses find it more difficult to adjust to having a leg that is numb from above the knee down. They can stumble frequently, making it difficult to determine whether the block has been successful or not. Secondly, the injection site is more prone to error: unlike most lower-limb nerve blocks, it is not possible to palpate the nerves, and so a greater volume of local anaesthetic must be injected into the area – if you are slightly off the mark, enough local anaesthetic should diffuse in order to achieve nerve desensitization. Given the difficulty of proving full anaesthesia due to the patchy skin desensitization, I always allow up to 30 minutes before considering whether or not these blocks have worked or not.

There is another practical consideration. If the entire leg has been blocked up to a subcarpal nerve block with negative results, the horse has been through a great deal of local anaesthesia (and needles!) and is usually ready

to have the rest of the day off. After allowing the local anaesthesia to wear off over the course of a day or two, you can return with a fresh mind to a 'normal' – that is, a non-anaesthetized – limb. As the carpus is the main structure to be blocked between a sub-carpal and the median and ulnar nerve blocks, it is worth considering blocking this joint if it is suspect.

The site of injection for the median nerve lies just distally to the superficial pectoral muscle, just cranial to the median artery and vein on the caudomedial border of the radius. Using a 21-guage, 1½in needle, inject 15 to 20ml into the area at a depth of approximately 4cm (1¼in). Skin desensitization will only involve the medial aspect of the pastern.

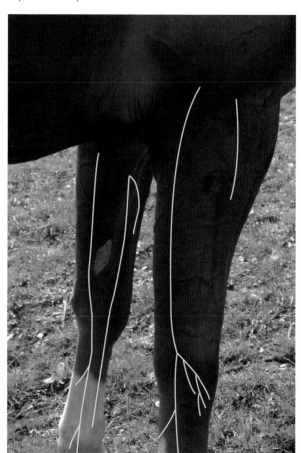

The nerve pattern in the proximal limb

The injection site for the ulnar nerve lies on the palmar aspect in the groove that is formed by the ulnaris lateralis and flexor carpi ulnaris, approximately 10cm (4in) proximal to the accessory bone. Using a 23-guage, 1in needle, inject 10–15ml of local anaesthetic at a depth of approximately 1–2cm (¼–¾in). Skin desensitization occurs on the dorsolateral aspect of the proximal metacarpus.

Hindlimb nerve blocks

The lower limb nerve blocks for the hindlimb are performed in much the same way as for the forelimb. There are nevertheless important differences.

Six-point nerve block

The desensitization of the fetlock joint, and all the structures distally to it in the hindlimb, is carried out in the same manner as for the forelimb, but with two variations:

1. The deep peroneal nerve sends out medial and lateral branches to innervate the dorsal aspect of the fetlock. In order to desensitize these structures, perform the injection of the palmar metatarsal nerves as if you were doing a forelimb, that is, just below the button of the splint bone, then slowly pull the needle out and redirect it several centimetres dorsally under the skin and leave a 3ml bleb of local anaesthetic there. In essence, you are still only using three needles, but you are blocking a total of six nerves!

2. The communicating nerve branch which runs around the plantar aspect of the tendons is located more distally in the hindlimb. Given its close proximity to the tendon sheath, it is advisable in this case to inject the palmar nerves proximal rather than distal to this marker.

Tibial and peroneal nerve blocks

Blocking these nerves has the same negative features as has been mentioned for the median and ulnar nerve blocks; in particular, the horse's inability to cope with such a large proportion of its leg being desensitized can play a negative role when you are trying to assess the effectiveness of the block.

The injection site for the tibial nerve is located approximately 10cm (4in) proximal to the top of the tuber calcaneus on the medial aspect of the limb, just caudal to the deep flexor tendon and cranial to the Achilles tendon. Using a 23-guage, 1in needle, inject 15–20ml of local anaesthetic into the area.

The injection site for the peroneal nerve lies about 10cm (4in) proximal to the lateral malleolus on the lateral aspect of the tibia. As the peroneal nerve possesses both superficial and deep branches, using a 21-guage, 1½in needle, deposit first 15ml of local anaesthetic to the deep branch, and slowly retract the needle before injecting the final 5ml.

The nerve pattern in the distal hindlimb is similar, but not identical to that of the forelimb. Most importantly an additonal nerve innervates the dorsal fetlock area

Joint Injections

Joint injections in the horse can serve many important functions:

1. In conjunction with nerve blocks, they serve as an invaluable tool in the diagnosis of lameness.
2. As a way into the joint, they can assist in obtaining joint fluid so that it may be analysed for signs of inflammation or infection.
3. In conjunction with therapeutic drugs, they can be one of the most effective means for treating joint disease.

There are dangers however, and the *decision to inject into a joint should not be taken lightly*. The hygienic procedures listed below should be followed scrupulously. The possibility of introducing a joint sepsis, which is potentially a life-threatening condition, should always be recognized.

1. The hair should be clipped generously around the area to be injected using a fine clipper blade. Following this, I prefer to use a scalpel blade and a surgical scrub (Hibiscrub) to remove the hair stubble, leaving a smooth surface which can be easily cleaned.
2. Any hair that might overhang the site should be cut off – feathers on a cob, for instance. When injecting a hindlimb, it may be necessary to apply a tail bandage to keep it out of the way.
3. The shaved area should be cleaned thoroughly using gauze swabs soaked in a Hibiscrub or similar surgical disinfectant wash. The scrubbing should be thorough and conducted in circular motions, from the cleaner inside area towards the less hygienic outward area, never the other way round.
4. The area should now be degreased using swabs soaked in surgical spirit.
5. The same scrubbing procedure using a surgical scrub followed by surgical spirit should be repeated, only this time, sterile gloves and swabs should be employed to ensure minimal contamination of the site. The drugs to be employed should be taken from a new container and should be aspirated in a sterile fashion.
6. Be aware that injections into the joint can be painful, and sedation may be an option for difficult horses. If circumstances will not allow this, then a thin bleb of sterile local anaesthetic, administered with a 25-gauge, 16mm (⅝in) needle into the site where the injection is to take place, can be a useful way to minimize unexpected reactions during the injection. Twitching some horses can also be beneficial.
7. Try to imagine the landmarks you are feeling. Sometimes slowly rocking the affected leg can help you pinpoint the joint better under your thumb. Stab the needle through quickly, as it is the piercing of the skin that horses seem to object to the most.
8. If no synovial fluid appears, it does not mean that the needle placement is incorrect. Some joints simply do not produce much synovial fluid. In other cases, the needle may be blocked. Twisting the needle around or repositioning it may unblock it. Using a sterile syringe to inflate the area with a small amount of air is another handy way of checking yourself. Whenever possible, obtain a synovial fluid sample which you can examine.
9. Injection into a joint should be easy. If it is not, the placement of the needle is probably incorrect.
10. While the progress of the block can be checked every ten minutes post injection, a block should not be considered negative until 30 minutes have elapsed.
11. Following the injection into the joint, the area should be covered with a sterile Melanin pad and bandage. For added security, I prefer the bandage to be changed after two days, keeping the injection site covered for a total of four days. During this time the horse should be stable rested and kept quiet. I realize that this is a conservative approach, but given the ramifications of a joint infection, to my mind it is a minor inconvenience.
12. The horse should be monitored over the next week for any signs of increased lameness or inappetance. When in doubt, his temperature should be checked.

Starting again with the forelimb and working our way up the leg, the following joint injections are possible.

Pressing the thumb firmly against the leg is very helpful in detecting the position of narrow joint margins

Coffin joint (distal interphalangeal joint)

The coffin joint is one of the most frequently injected joints, not only because it is a joint frequently affected with degenerative joint disease, but because it may be used as a means to anaesthetize and treat the navicular bursa which it usually communicates with. Direct treatment of the bursa is more difficult, and requires more assistance and facilities, which will be discussed at greater length later.

Much has been written about the amount of diffusion of local anaesthetic from the anaesthetized joint into neighbouring structures of the foot, rendering the block inaccurate. However, as a site for the diagnosis and treatment of degenerative joint disease in the foot, it remains invaluable.

There are several approaches to the coffin joint, including dorsolateral, lateral and even palmar; however, I have only ever had to perform the dorsal approach, deemed to be the most accurate. It should be carried out with the horse standing squarely on the affected limb. In many lameness situations, it is not advisable to use a sedative, but in this case, the unsedated horse should be twitched. Do not carry things to an extreme, however, as my experience has been that some horses absolutely loathe this injection. If sparks start flying, sedate the horse anyway and get on with things. There is no need for anyone to risk their life – there is plenty of information which can be gleaned from a coffin joint injection with or without the use of a sedative.

Here is one helpful hint: inject a small amount of sterile local anaesthetic under the skin where the injection is intended, using a small 25-gauge needle. Mask even the entrance to this needle by tapping the area rapidly with the outside edge of your gloved hand whilst holding the needle between thumb and forefinger; then pop the needle in place. This will be 1.5cm (⅝in) above the coronary band and about 1.5cm (⅝in) off the midline, either medial or lateral. Wait a few minutes for the local anaesthetic to take effect, then using a 21-gauge, 1½in needle, *direct it 90 degrees to the angle of the pastern into the coffin joint*, punching it through quickly. You may feel a small popping sensation when the needle enters the joint capsule. Some joint fluid may escape from the needle hub, which indicates it is in place. If not, try injecting a small amount of air (2–3ml): if the needle is in place the syringe plunger bounces back, often with a tiny amount of synovial fluid.

I have found that the position of the needle is not quite as steep as described in most literature. And another thing: coffin joints are funny

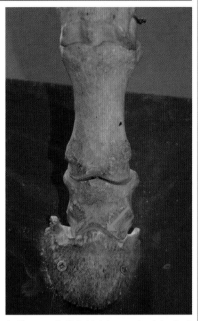

In theory all distal joints can be injected using a dorsal approach, but practically only the coffin joint is wide enough. The pastern and fetlock can be injected more easily using other approaches

creatures – some are found with the first needle, others require serious toil to locate. If blood enters the hub of the needle it will mask any sign of synovial fluid, and it is then best simply to retract the needle and start yet again with a fresh one. If you are having difficulties, an x-ray is invaluable in assessing the accuracy of your needle placement, which is invariably placed too steeply.

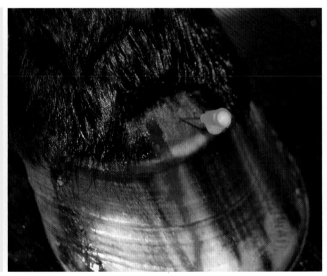

The needle has punctured the coffin joint and synovial fluid can now be aspirated

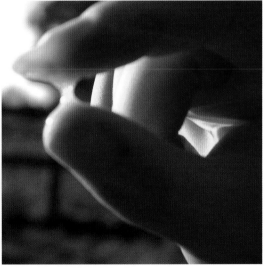

Testing the synovial fluid for viscosity

Navicular bursa

The navicular bursa is located deep inside the heel, so there are no landmarks to be felt. A radiograph should be made immediately following the placement of the needle to ensure the accuracy of the positioning. This does require the aid of a couple of assistants, but given the size of the needle employed (19-gauge spinal needle) and the need for a sterile environment and radiographic facilities, this injection is usually carried out in a hospital environment anyway.

Carefully prepare the leg you intend to inject: clip out the back of the pastern, paying close attention to the juncture between the horn and skin. At the midline of this juncture, I like to take a small scalpel blade and shave the hair and outer horn layer. Now place a Vetrap over the cannon, fetlock and hoof, ensuring that the back of the pastern remains open. After careful surgical scrubbing and prior sedation, ask an assistant to hold the leg with one hand, while flexing the toe as far as possible. With the point of the needle turned upwards, pierce the skin perpendicular to the axis of the pastern. Continue to push the needle forwards, ensuring that it travels completely perpendicular or even slightly towards the foot, but never upwards! Once the needle meets a resistance, retract it just a millimetre or so, and take a radiograph to ensure that the position is correct.

Pastern joint (proximal interphalangeal joint)

This block is rarely used, as the pastern joint is rarely seen as a primary cause of lameness. There are two approaches to the joint, though I find the frequently described dorsal approach difficult, bordering on

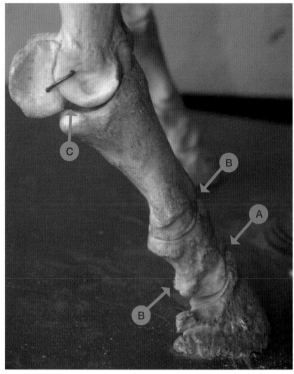

A lateral view of the recommended injection points in a skeletal model: A) coffin joint; B) pastern joint; C) fetlock joint

unusable. 5 to 10ml of local anaesthetic is used when blocking the pastern.

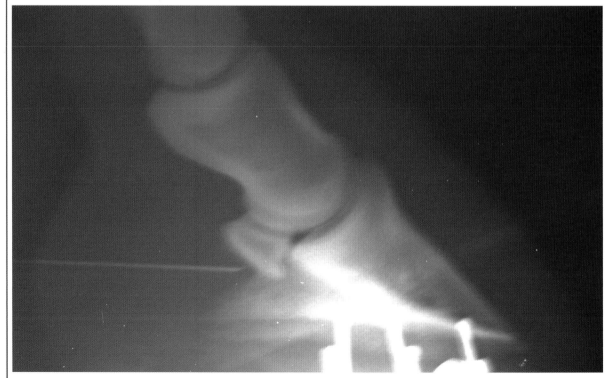

Navicular bursa injection. Note that the point of the needle is turned upwards

64

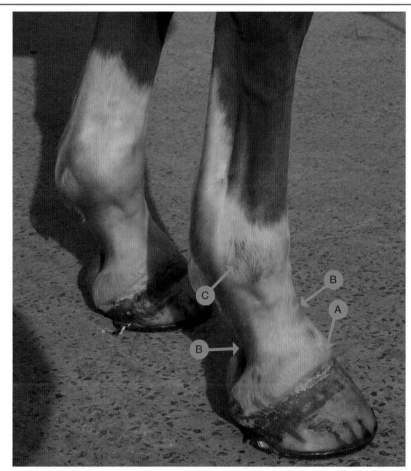

Lateral view of the same recommended joint injection sites: A) coffin joint; B) pastern joint; C) fetlock joint

the axis of the leg. Synovial fluid will always be tapped.

Carpal joint

There are two joints to block within the carpus, but they are probably the easiest: the radiocarpal joint, and the intercarpal joint which communicates with the carpo-metacarpal joint. Holding the leg flexed with one hand, carefully feel the indentation of these joints either to the middle or side of the extensor carpii radialis tendon. Then insert a 21-gauge, 1½in needle. Synovial fluid is readily aspirated.

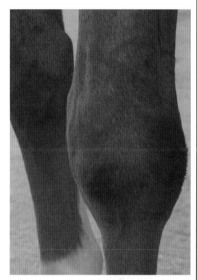

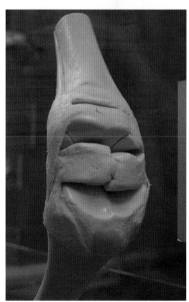

↑ Top and above: Although not as apparent when weight-bearing simple flexion of the carpus widens the joint injection site palpably when flexed

In the dorsal approach, with the leg weight-bearing, feel the medial and lateral eminences of the proximal aspect of the middle phalanx (P2). The entrance to the joint lies slightly higher between the two. Using your thumb to probe deeply, the joint margins can be felt. Direct a 21-gauge (1½in) needle through the common digital extensor tendon into the joint.

Injecting the limb in a non-weight-bearing position with the leg extended forwards and the foot resting on the bent knee of the examiner has the advantage of opening up the joint somewhat. A dorsolateral approach can be used by inserting the needle under the common digital extensor tendon into the joint, using the lateral condylar eminence of the distal proximal phalanx as a marker.

The simplest technique is the palmar approach. The needle is directed into the depression formed by the proximal phalanx, the distal eminence of the same, and the insertion of the lateral branch of the superficial flexor tendon.

Fetlock joint

There are several techniques described for the arthrocentesis of the fetlock joint. Again, the main explanation you find is the dorsal approach, through the extensor tendon – and similar to the one explained for the pastern joint, I find it equally as dissatisfactory. A far simpler approach is the lateral/medial one: flex the limb to displace the sesamoids caudally, opening a space between the lateral sesamoid bone and the cannon bone. Hold the leg with one hand, or in the case of a hindlimb rest it on your knee. With a 21-gauge, 1½in needle, penetrate the joint by inserting it through the lateral collateral sesamoid ligament at 90 degrees – perpendicular – to

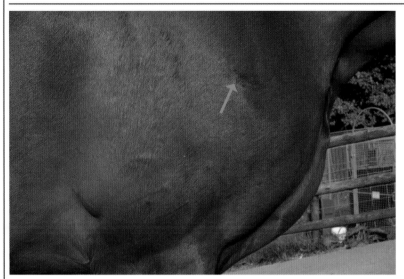

Given the muscle mass surrounding it, the shoulder joint is located relatively deep

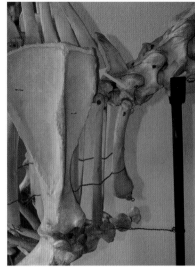

The approach to the shoulder on a skeletal model

Elbow joint (humeroradial)

Neither the elbow nor the shoulder joint is injected with any amount of frequency to become really proficient at it; only one approach is necessary. With the horse weight-bearing, grasp the elbow on either side between your forefingers and thumb. Using the thumb, find the lateral humeral epicondyle and the radial tuberosity, and place it between the two. Now gently rock the elbow a few millimetres from side to side until you can feel it easily under your thumb. The 21-gauge, 1½in needle should be inserted just in front of the edge of the lateral collateral ligament, straight into the joint. Approximately 20ml of local anaesthetic is needed to block the joint. It is important that local anaesthetic is not injected into the surrounding tissue as this can anaesthetize the distal branches of the radial nerves, causing a temporary paralysis of the limb. As the horse will be unable to lock its carpus in extension, a splint bandage should be applied until the effect wears off.

Shoulder joint (scapulohumeral)

The shoulder joint is difficult to inject due to the relative depth at which it lies. The injection should be performed in the standing horse, which should be sufficiently sedated to avoid the needle breaking. The point of the shoulder (lateral humeral tuberosity) is large, and divided into the cranial and the more easily palpable caudal prominences. Pressing your thumb firmly so as to palpate deeply, move forwards until you find the cranial prominence. A depression should be noted between the two. A tiny bleb of local anaesthetic administered subcutaneously (under the skin) should minimize reactions to the joint injection. An 18-gauge, 3½in spinal needle should be inserted into this notch and directed parallel to the floor and somewhat caudally (towards the tail), aiming towards the

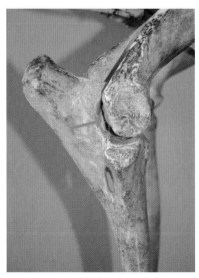

↑ → The approach to the elbow joint on a live and skeletal model

opposite elbow. The depth needed to penetrate the joint may vary, but may be as deep as 13cm (5in). It is not advisable to administer more than 10ml of local anaesthetic into the joint, as diffusion into surrounding areas could cause anaesthesia of the suprascapular nerve, which would in turn result in a temporary paralysis of both the infraspinatus and the supraspinatus muscles.

Always use flexible needles that bend easily to prevent the needle from damaging underlying tissue. It is a common occurrence for limb motion or muscle contraction to bend a positioned needle.

In some horses, the shoulder joint communicates with the bicipital bursa; therefore, be aware that local anaesthesia to the shoulder joint may improve lameness associated with this structure.

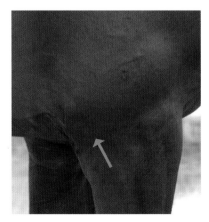

Tarsal joint

The tarsal joint is actually made of three different compartments which can be accessed separately. All three should be approached in the standing horse with the animal weight-bearing. Unsedated horses should be twitched, and an assistant should also help hold a front leg. Fractious horses should be sedated.

The tibiotarsal joint is the easiest joint to inject, and can be approached either medially or laterally. If injecting medially, care should be taken to avoid injuring the large saphenous vein which crosses the joint vertically. As the joint capsule lies directly beneath the skin, the penetration depth need only be 13mm (½in). Therefore, a 21-gauge,1in needle is sufficient to administer the 10ml of local anaesthetic that is necessary to block the joint. Synovial fluid will always be present. (Remember that the tibiotarsal joint communicates with the proximal intertarsal joint.)

The approach for the distal intertarsal joint is medial. Locate with your hand, the distal tubercle of the talus and the head of the splint bone. Approximately half way between the two there is a palpable small indentation in the gap between the third tarsal bone and the central tarsal bone. This is usually just distad to the distal border of the cunean tendon. Once you have located the position, place your thumb firmly

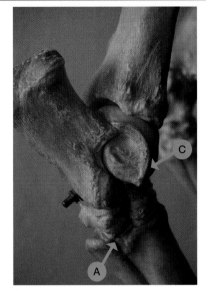
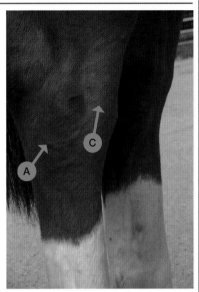

↑ → Lateral views of the hock joint in a skeletal and a live model: A) tarsometatarsal; C) tibiotarsal

over it and ask for an assistant to gently rock the leg a few millimetres. You should now be able to feel the joint margins clearly, and using a 25-gauge, 1in needle, aim it horizontally into this margin.

The *tarso-metatarsal* joint is injected on the lateral aspect. Feel the inner prominence of the head of the splint bone (4th metatarsal), and follow the curvature of the head around until you can feel the bony prominence of the 4th tarsal bone. Between the two structures there is a palpable indentation which is the joint space. Using a 23-gauge,

1in needle, inject 4 to 6ml of local anaesthetic into the joint. This will usually inject easily. As the tarso-metatarsal joint may communicate with the distal intertarsal joint in some horses, some practitioners believe that injecting a further 2 to 4ml under pressure increases the chance of anaesthetizing that joint too. This cannot be relied upon.

Studies have shown that a great amount of diffusion occurs after injection of the tarso-metatarsal joint. This should be kept in mind, as this diffusion may also anaesthetize other lesions in the area of the joint.

67

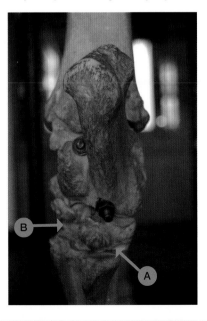
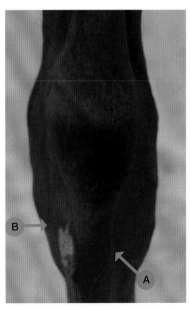

→ → Anterior (plantar) views of the hock joint in a skeletal and a live model: A) tarsometatarsal; B) distal intertarsal

Stifle joint

The stifle joint is made up of three synovial compartments: the lateral and medial femorotibial sacs, and the femoropatellar sac. There is communication between the femoropatellar and medial femorotibial sacs in approximately 65 per cent of horses. Interestingly, it has been observed that communication between the two occurs more frequently if the medial femorotibial sac is injected rather than the femoropatellar joint (one-way system). There is no communication between the lateral and medial femorotibial sacs.

The femoropatellar sac is approached most easily with the leg bearing weight in a slightly flexed position. An 18-gauge, 3½in needle is inserted either to the side of or central to the middle patellar ligament, far enough away from the apex of the patella to be directed underneath

it into the trochlear groove; 20ml of local anaesthetic should be administered.

For the lateral femorotibial sac, palpate the caudal (tail-side) edge of the lateral patellar ligament. A 19-gauge, 1.5in needle should be inserted along the caudal edge of the lateral patellar ligament, approximately 1cm (¼in) from the tibia. If in doubt about the exact margins of the joint, ask an assistant to rock the horse's leg softly as you palpate the area with your thumb. Penetration depth is generally about 2.5cm (1in), and 20ml of local anaesthetic should be administered.

The medial femorotibial sac should be entered in the space between the medial patellar ligament and the medial collateral ligaments just above the inner edge of the tibia. Again, 20ml of local anaesthetic should be administered at an approximate depth of 2.5cm (1in).

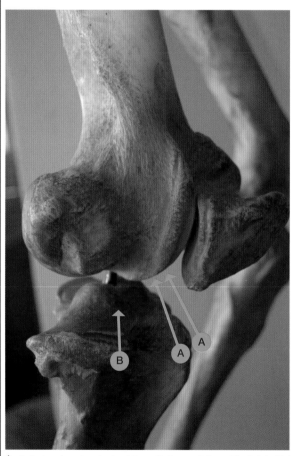
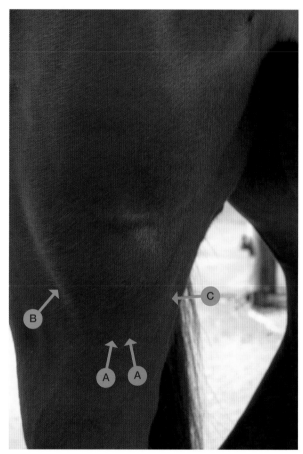

↑ → Lateral and anterior (dorsal) views of the stifle joint; A) femoropatellar; B) lateral femorotibial; C) medial femorotibial

Hip joint (coxofemoral)

This is the most difficult joint to enter, but it is the joint least frequently encountered in everyday practice. The horse should be sedated and standing squarely in a set of stocks, as movement during the procedure could cause the needle to fracture. The important landmarks to identify are the paired summits of the greater trochanter of the femur, and the notch between them. Particularly the lesser cranial protruberance can be difficult to feel. The site for injection is at the caudal aspect of the lesser trochanter and 1cm (¼in) from it. A small bleb of local anaesthetic should first be administered subcutaneously under the site, using a 25-gauge needle. An 18-gauge, 6in spinal needle is inserted in the site and guided, pointing slightly downwards, staying close to the femoral neck. On entry into the joint, some 10cm (4in) deep, the point of the needle should be approximately 13mm (½in) lower than the point of entry. Advancement of the needle may be difficult at this point, as firm fibrous tissue may be felt before entering the joint. Joint fluid can usually be aspirated before injecting 20ml of local anaesthetic.

If the needle does not enter the joint, it is best to correct the angle by drawing the needle back out to within ½in or less of the skin, before redirecting it.

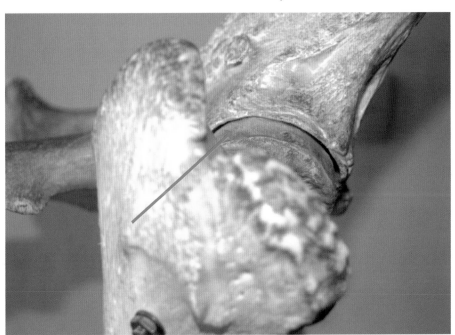

↑↓ The hip joint is a very difficult joint to approach given the muscle mass surrounding it. The notch between the paired summits of the greater trochanter, and the summits themselves, are important landmarks to identify

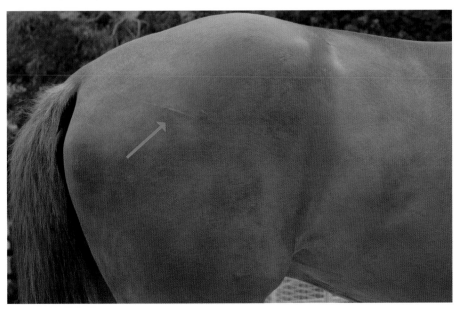

The Marvels of Modern Technology

Technology today allows us a variety of ways to image areas of interest to help us arrive at a diagnosis. These techniques are not to be seen as a replacement for a proper lameness work-up: 'whole leg' investigations are both prohibitively expensive and time-consuming, and are also fraught with anatomical anomalies of unknown significance. That little closure in a hock joint, or that little spur on a coffin joint – how do I know that they are actually the cause of the horse's problem? There are really no shortcuts in finding the answer. Before you reach for this sort of assistance, the approximate seat of pain must be identified with the help of local anaesthesia.

The most commonly employed diagnostic imaging techniques today are radiography and ultrasonography. Larger hospitals also make use of scintigraphy, and more recently MRI and CT scanning.

The type of investigation you choose depends on the type of material you wish to image. For instance, radiography can make some wonderful images of bone, but for soft tissue it is of no diagnostic value whatsoever. Ultrasonography, on the other hand, is a good method for examining soft tissue, and at times even the outline of bone, when searching for a pelvic fracture, for instance. For investigating the entire joint for signs of DJD however, it makes sense to use the x-ray machine.

Radiography

The x-ray remains the oldest yet most commonly employed imaging device in the veterinary field. The x-rays are produced in an x-ray tube, and on exiting one end of the tube, a collimator there restricts the size of the x-rays and allows these to be focused on the object to be imaged. An x-ray cassette is placed directly behind the imaged object. These cassettes contain screens which amplify the effect of each x-ray passing through them on to the x-ray sensitive film directly against them. This allows far less radiation to be produced than would otherwise be necessary. Each film must then, similar to 'normal' photography, be brought into a dark room where it is developed, fixed and dried before it is ready to be examined.

It is of vital importance that standard angles are used so that the results can be compared to the 'normal' image. In the limbs, these usually include the lateromedial, dorsopalmar or plantar views. In some cases, such as the imaging of hocks, it is necessary to take oblique views. Finally, specialized views are also needed in certain instances – this might be a 'skyline' view of a navicular bone, for example.

But like all technology, radiography does have its limitations. It should always be remembered that radiography images bone and not cartilage, so it is not possible to diagnose acute arthritis using radiography. In addition, given the sheer mass of the horse, only extremely powerful high-frequency machines are able to penetrate the depths of the spine and pelvis: 'normal' hand-held units are simply not powerful enough.

It is important to have the horse stand on a block in order to obtain good lateral views of the distal limb

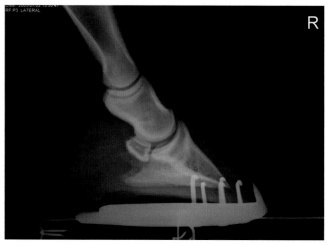

A radiograph of the distal limb

Radiographic Main Views

FOOT	A complete radiographic examination of the equine foot usually consists of four different views. • Lateromedial (LM) • Two dorsoproximal-palmarodistal oblique (DPr-PaDiO) (upright pedal or high coronary route) – centred and exposed for the distal phalanx – centred and exposed for the navicular bone. • Palmaroproximal-palmarodistal oblique (PaPr-PaDiO) (flexor or skyline view). Other oblique views can be useful when fractures of the wings of the third phalanx are suspected, or abnormalities of the hoof wall are investigated.
PASTERN	• Lateromedial (LM) • Dorsopalmar (DPa) Oblique views are occasionally obtained to highlight the palmarolateral and palmaromedial borders of the first phalanx, on to which the distal sesamoidean ligaments insert.
FETLOCK	• Dorsopalmar(DPa) • Lateromedial (LM) • Dorsolateral-palmaromedial oblique (DL-PaMO) • Palmarolateral-dorsomedial oblique (PaL-DMO) These four standard projections can be supplemented with different specialized views if a particular area of the fetlock requires further highlighting.
CARPUS	• Lateromedial (LM) • Dorsopalmar (DPa) • Dorsolateral-palmaromedial oblique (DL-PaMO) • Palmarolateral-dorsomedial oblique (PaL-DMO) • Flexed lateromedial (flexed LM) • Dorsoproximal-dorsodistal oblique (skyline) (DPr-DDiO) taken at varying angles to skyline the distal radius or proximal or distal rows of carpal bones.
ELBOW	• Flexed mediolateral (flexed ML) • Craniocaudal (CrCa)
SHOULDER	• Extended mediolateral (extended ML) • Craniomedial-caudolateral oblique (CrM-CaLO)
HOCK	• Lateromedial (LM) • Dorsoplantar (DPl) • Dorsolateral-plantaromedial oblique (DL-PlMO) • Plantarolateral-dorsomedial oblique (PlL-DMO) Additional view: Plantaroproximal-plantarodistal oblique (PlPr-PlDiO) skyline of the sustentaculum tali.
STIFLE	• Lateromedial (LM) • Caudocranial (CaCr) Additional views: Cranioproximal-craniodistal oblique (CrPr-CrDiO) skyline of the patella and oblique variations of the CaCr.
HIP	• Ventrodorsal

71

Ultrasonography

Ultrasound waves are produced by piezo-electric crystals inside the head of a probe (transducer). This transducer is placed above the area to be imaged. In order for the waves to penetrate deeply into the tissue without scattering, it is necessary for the transducer to touch the skin as snugly as possible. This 'coupling' is achieved by the prior clipping and cleaning of the area, which is then covered with a generous layer of ultrasonographic gel. The sound frequency penetrates the tissue and is reflected back to the transducer in varying degrees, depending on the type of tissue and its refractive properties. This is not unlike the sound waves that we are used to. If you stand in a cave, the sound waves of your voice will be carried by the air until they are reflected back by the hard walls of the rock, producing a sound. In ultrasound, these sound waves are then translated into a visual signal.

High frequency (10 MHz) transducers have a poor depth of penetration but good resolution, while low frequency (3.5 MHz) transducers penetrate deeply but with a poor resolution. Transducer types are classified as sector, linear and phased array scanners, depending on the image penetration pattern.

The images produced by the transducer are therefore markers of echogenicity. This is generally graded as being:

- anechoic: echo free, generally black on the ultrasound screen
- hypoechoic: low echogenicity
- medium echogenicity
- hyperechoic: high echogenicity, generally white on the ultrasound screen

Proper preparation and technique are the key to producing quality images; the following is a guide to proper scanning preparation:

1. Whenever possible, use the opposite limb as a comparison.
2. Clip out the area generously with a pair of fine clippers.
3. If necessary, shave the area with a safety razor.
4. Clean with a surgical scrub.
5. Degrease with surgical spirit.
6. Apply scanning gel and let it soak in for 10 minutes. This is the perfect time to set up the scanner.
7. Sedate lightly if necessary.
8. Always hold the transducer tightly to the skin at an angle of 90 degrees to the area to be imaged. If in doubt as to whether something is an artefact or not – that is, whether it is being artificially produced by the ultrasound waves, usually through insufficient coupling – carefully move the transducer back and forth across the image.
9. Take your time, scan both limbs, make a general assessment, and then take your pictures.
10. Take pictures systematically and label them.
11. Finally, always use measurements in order to quantify your assessment.

A thorough anatomical knowledge of the area is essential for correct interpretation of these images. In orthopaedics, the most commonly employed use for an ultrasonographic examination is the imaging of the suspensory apparatus. An example image is included below. A more detailed interpretation of the anatomy in this area can be found on page 130.

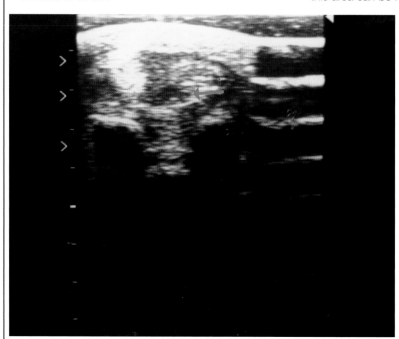

This ultrasonagraphic picture reveals a complete picture of a ruptured tendon

Scintigraphy

Nuclear scintigraphy consists of injecting a radiopharmaceutical substance, usually technetium-99m-labelled methylene diphosphonate (MDP), into the bloodstream of the patient to be examined. A gamma camera captures the source of radiation and produces an image of its intensity. MDP binds selectively to all tissues in which phosphorus exchange is active, that is, calcified soft tissues, but primarily bone. There are therefore three phases which can be imaged: the flow phase, the soft tissue phase, and the bone phase, and the only difference is in how much time is allotted for the radiopharmaceutical to travel and accumulate within the horse's body.

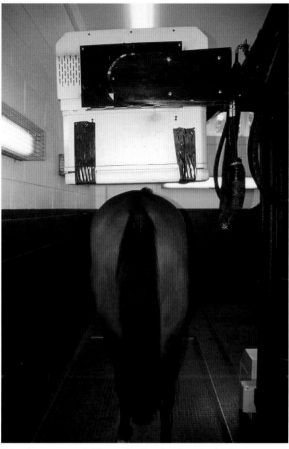

It is also very useful in evaluating back pathologies

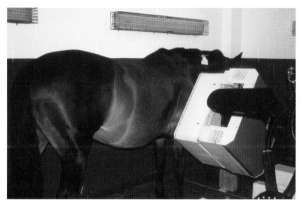

A scintigraphic examination is particularly useful in diagnosing a fracture

In equine orthopaedics, the bone phase is the most commonly employed investigation and is conducted approximately two to three hours post injection. Since MDP accumulates in areas that have an increased activity, it is particularly useful in localizing bone fractures or lesions which are not apparent in radiography or which haven't blocked out using local anaesthesia. It is also useful in horses suffering from a multitude of problems, as it images the entire horse. Neck, back and hip problems are particularly beneficial to image using scintigraphy as they are difficult to image otherwise. Furthermore, as scintigraphy measures the actual inflammatory response of the body, suspicious lesions found in the neck, for example, can be assessed to see if they are indeed a source of pain for the horse. This is useful in ascertaining low-grade 'wobblers'.

Because the horse's body has natural 'hot spots' of radiopharmaceutical uptake, it is important that the sometimes subtle changes in the scan area are assessed by an experienced evaluator.

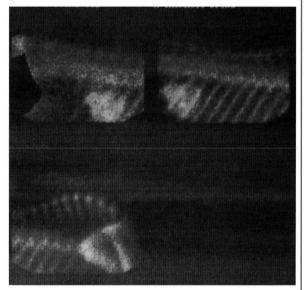

Scintigraphic readouts can be very subtle. It is important, therefore, to have an experienced interpreter to read the results

Magnetic resonance imaging

Until recently, MRI investigations were limited to various 'closed system'-type imaging devices intended for the human market. In these systems, the patient is physically placed into a cylindrical, superconducting magnet. The image is produced by the energy recorded by the excitation and relaxation of hydrogen nuclei by the strong magnetic field produced within the scanner. By varying the magnetic variation, an image can be produced. Hydrogen is abundant in water and fat tissues.

The obvious disadvantage in using a closed system is that due to size constraints, investigations are limited to limbs and the head and neck. The animal also has to undergo a general anaesthesia, making the entire process not only

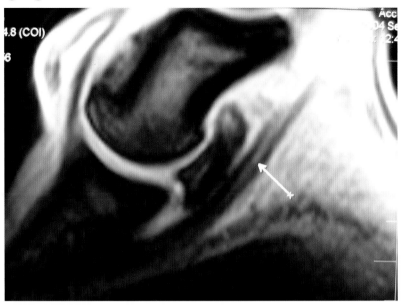

MRI allows us to locate pathologies which previously could not be imaged. This photo shows a tear in the insertion of the deep flexor tendon

cumbersome, expensive and time-consuming, but risky for the patient as well.

The advent of open magnets capable of producing a quality image has changed things drastically. Requiring only a sedated, standing horse, these machines spin around the limb of the horse, finally making these areas freely accessible for investigation. As it is possible to obtain an image at millimetre intervals, even the tiniest of lesions becomes apparent. However, to date it is not possible to fully image a horse's back and internal organs with this method.

Computer tomography

Similar to the MRI, the CT scanner is able to produce a three-dimensional image. However, it does this through the use of an x-ray tube within a circular gantry. But similar to the problems with human MRI devices, the size of the CT gantry limits investigations to the limbs. The extent of the head and cervical studies are limited to the size of the animal, although usually images up to C5 can be produced. Again, the animal must be given a general anaesthesia to obtain an image.

MRI cameras are very sophisticated pieces of equipment

Thermography

Thermography is a technology used primarily in the building and defence industry sectors, but it has been incorporated into the veterinary medical field. Its use to date has been fraught with controversy, mainly due to the lack of objective, reproducible studies and the sometimes sensational claims made by its proponents.

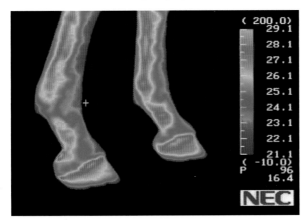

Thermography images the physiological anatomy of a patient based upon fine surface temperature differences

As in nuclear scintigraphy, thermography does not produce an anatomical image, but a physiological image of its subject. Sensitive, portable units are able to detect the smallest temperature differences. Aimed at a horse, it is hoped that areas of inflammation or circulation anomalies can be detected in this manner.

A multitude of difficulties must be overcome in order to eliminate certain factors that will render the image undiagnostic. Horses must be stabled in a draught-free environment set at an ambient temperature. They must not sweat, so at least 30 minutes should be allowed for them to acclimatize to their surroundings following transport. They should not be exercised before, nor is sedation advisable as this may cause vasodilation panting and/or sweating. It is essential that they are clean, and that they have had their hooves picked out prior to an investigation.

It is clear then, that travelling thermography units are unsuitable for giving any accurate diagnosis. However, there are instances in which the use of thermography in a controlled hospital environment may be of use.

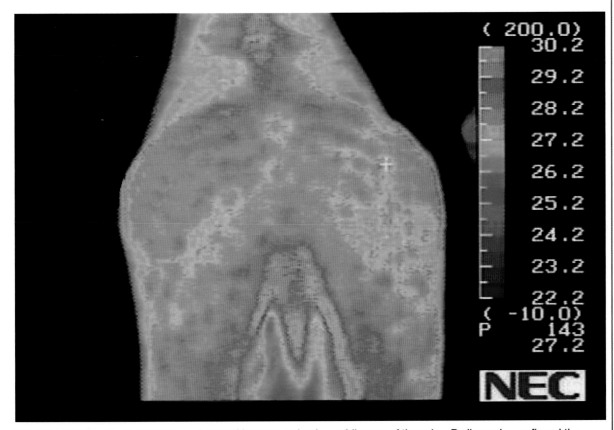

Thermogram of the back showing an abnormal hotspot under the saddle area of the spine. Radiographs confirmed the diagnosis of a kissing spine

Arthroscopy

The single greatest improvement to equine orthopaedics in the last thirty years has been the wide-scale acceptance and use of arthroscopy (keyhole surgery). It has the huge advantage that it can be used diagnostically as well as therapeutically, in the removal of an OCD lesion, for example, without the joint having to be traumatized by a large incision (arthrotomy).

The joint or synovial cavity is distended with sterile fluid injected via a needle. A small stab incision is made to produce a portal, and the narrow, rigid fibreoptic scope is inserted into the joint. This scope is coupled to a light source and a video camera, which displays the projected image on to a television monitor. A continual flow of sterile fluid is pumped through the joint in order to keep it distended and therefore easy to visualize, and to flush out unnecessary debris and/or bacteria. As the area is examined systematically, additional portals can be cut to allow for the various surgical tasks, such as grasping, resecting and burring to be performed under the supervision of the arthroscope.

The obvious disadvantages of this procedure are the high costs involved, and the anaesthetic risk to the patient. Still, it remains the single most effective way of influencing joint and tendon sheath pathologies.

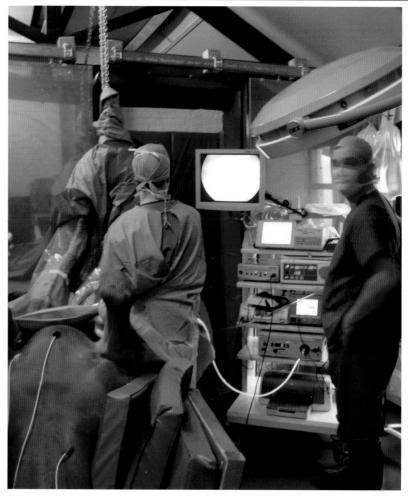

Arthroscopy remains one of the most useful diagnostic and therapeutic methods available in equine orthapaedics

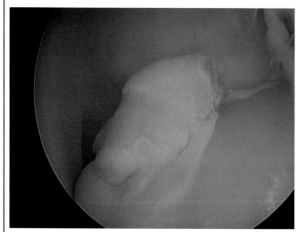

An OCD 'chip' lesion in the hock joint as viewed through an arthroscopic camera. Note the cartilage surrounding it has been eroded

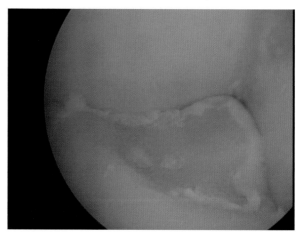

The same area of hock after the chip has been arthroscopically removed and the damaged cartilage around it debrided

Kinematic Analysis

Already in the early 1900s, photography was used to help analyse the movement of animals. With the advent of high speed cameras (500 images per second) and powerful computers to assess the produced images, an increasing amount of information can be gleaned from this methodology.

Markers are glued on to the skin at standard anatomical positions, generally over a joint. The animal is then moved past a series of cameras, which record its gait; depending on the location and quantity of the cameras, a two-dimensional or three-dimensional image of their movement is produced. Using the markers as reference points, the computer is able to analyse the angle, velocity and rotation of the individual joints as well as the linear acceleration of the limb.

A major difficulty of kinematic assessment is the limited field of vision, generally no more than five metres. This is often overcome by using a treadmill, although it is then necessary to ensure that the velocity of the animal remains constant, as a change in velocity will have an effect on limb and joint angles.

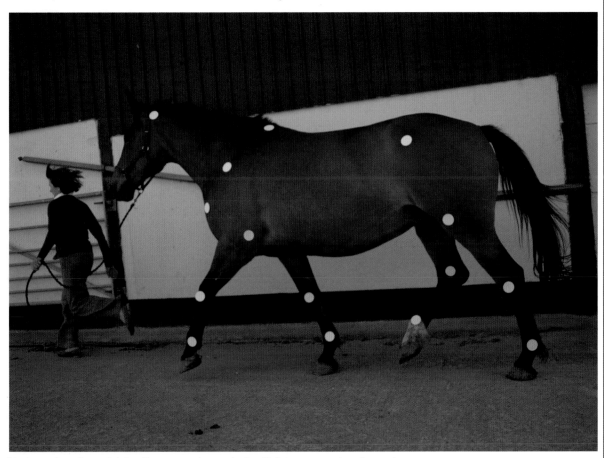

Markers placed over joints allow computer analysis of joint movement and speed

SECTION 3 FIRST AID AND INJURY MANAGEMENT

Essential First Aid

Skin laceration to the limbs is a commonly seen problem in horses and is often caused by fencing, particularly loose barbed or even straight wire. Although the use of it is banned in some European countries, fencing horse paddocks with barbed wire is still widespread in the United Kingdom. As a direct consequence to this inadequate husbandry, both severe and fatal accidents occur with relative frequency.

Maximizing wound healing

When dealing with extensive injuries, often involving excited horses and owners, it is important to concentrate on the essential matters at hand and instil a sense of calm to the situation.

1. Stem the bleeding: given the large blood vessels in the leg and their relative proximity to the skin surface, it is possible that these become injured, resulting in substantial blood loss. However, always remember that horses can lose over two buckets of blood without problems. That's a lot of blood, and it is important to think about this when surveying the amount of blood on the floor. Usually it isn't anywhere near that amount. In truth, I have only ever seen one horse bleed to death from a laceration. This poor creature badly damaged his heel when he stepped on some old tin – there was blood everywhere. Still, he would have survived this ordeal, had he not stood in the stream nearby, effectively hindering any form of blood clotting.

    Usually bleeding can at least be slowed down enough to effectively clot by applying a pressure bandage directly over the wound. In particularly severe circumstances, it may be necessary to tie a tourniquet around the area above the wound. Of course none of us carry tourniquets around, so be resourceful! A torn bit of cloth, a bicycle inner tube – anything you can get your hands on will suffice.

2. If possible, move the horse to a safe environment and take steps to calm it. This will often entail bringing it back to the stable to give it a bit of hay or a bran-mash to eat. A little bit of honey or molasses in the feed is helpful for particularly weakened horses. Always offer plenty of water. Depending on the elements, affected horses should be cooled or offered stable rugs to help stabilize them. Veterinary treatment for shock will be necessary in some cases.

3. Clean the wound and surrounding area. Once the bleeding has subsided, it is of paramount importance to clean the area sufficiently not only to prevent infection, but to obtain a clear idea as to the extent of the injury. This will always involve the removal of all hair surrounding the wound edges. This can easily be done using a scalpel blade, or for the more feeble-hearted, a plastic gentlemen's razor can be usurped by cutting off the safety bar in front of the blades. Clippers can also be used, but only fine blades will remove enough hair. There is one simple rule to remember: do not ever *not* remove hair from

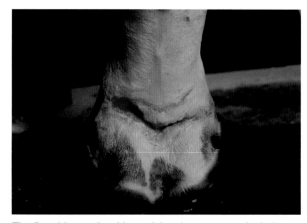

The first thing to do with any injury is to remove the hair around it to prevent contamination of the wound

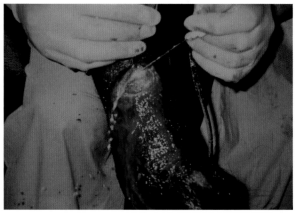

Flushing for contaminated wounds is essential for proper wound management

around a wound, regardless of how insignificant the injury appears! If you don't, the scab will form in dirty, bacteria-laden hair, and over a few days, the bacteria will multiply within the blood clot, leading to wound infection and/or a cellulitis of the leg.

Following hair removal, a gentle cleansing of the area using a surgical disinfectant is recommended.

4. A decision should be made as to whether further medical treatment is needed. This should be based on the position of the injury and the depth of the wound. Even small punctures can have drastic effects! Therefore, any injury to the area overlying a joint, tendon or tendon sheath should be examined by a veterinary surgeon.

5. The area directly over the wound and below it should be bandaged using a sterile dressing. Where this is not possible, the dressing should be taped on and a stable bandage placed on the lower limb. This will reduce swelling to those areas.

6. Wounds in areas undergoing constant movement will not heal effectively unless movement is reduced considerably. This will often necessitate the placement of a Robert-Jones splint bandage or even a cast for complete immobilization.

Wound healing can occur in two distinctly different ways:

1. Primary or first intention wound healing: this occurs when the wound edges are repositioned together, i.e. with the use of suturing, within the first 6 to 8 hours following the injury.

2. Second intention or delayed wound healing occurs when the wound edges do not meet. The body compensates for this by filling the wound with granulation tissue. Epithelialization occurs from the wound edges, which gradually begin to contract until the wound is closed.

The difficulty in the healing of the distal equine limb occurs primarily for three reasons:

1. Wound contraction is difficult as there is no loose skin as on the torso.

2. The blood supply is reduced.

3. There is often high movement in the distal limbs.

A delay in wound healing to the distal limb will result in the formation of an excessive amount of granulation tissue. It is therefore important that injuries to the limbs are dealt with properly and as soon as possible.

Once an area is affected by an excess of hypergranulation tissue, it will never heal, unless it is removed and healing is allowed to begin from the wound edges again.

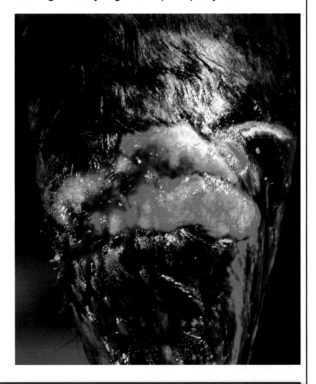

Two examples where injuries have occurred in high movement areas and have not been cared for properly, allowing the body to granulate poor quality tissue

Injury Management

Bandaging

Bandaging is invaluable in giving support and reducing mobility in affected limbs. It also provides an effective barrier to contamination, and in the healing phase of a larger flesh wound it counteracts the tendency of the body to produce hypergranulomatous material (proud flesh). In short, *most injuries and swellings to the lower limbs will benefit from bandaging.*

Bandages applied incorrectly, however, can and will lead to serious problems by constricting the blood supply. Bandages applied too tightly or with not enough wrapping material underneath will inevitably lead to localized skin necrosis, and if not corrected in time will begin affecting deeper structures such as tendon and bone. Similarly, bandages applied too loosely will not only be ineffective, but by 'scrunching up' will inevitably place a constriction upon the blood supply further down the limb. I can remember as a young assistant being told by my boss to rebandage a horse three times in front of a client, and I can still feel the tingle of embarrassment on my cheeks as I unwrapped my poorly designed bandage. But I learned a crucial lesson: if you need to bandage, *always bandage well.*

As a general rule, *horses that are bandaged should be stable rested,* as too much movement is contra-indicated and inevitably will lead to rub sores. An exception to this is the hoof bandage applied for hoof infections, as there is little possibility of constriction or rubbing. Dirt and debris that work their way into the bandage will also enhance rubbing, which is yet another reason for the necessity of stable rest.

In animals that are suffering from acute lameness, the contra-lateral limbs are forced to bear all or most of the horse's weight, and these weight-bearing limbs should be provided with support bandages. Usually a piece of gamgee or fibergee wrapped with a crêpe or stable bandage will suffice.

If the bandaged limb is swollen, the bandage should be changed daily, as it will naturally loosen. In some instances it is possible to extend the time period to every other day.

Bandaging materials

A variety of bandaging material is available on the commercial market; those that are particularly recommended are described below. It is useful to have these at hand to cater for different situations.

Self-adhesive bandage (Vetrap): Although comparatively expensive as it can only be used once effectively, the advantages of Vetrap bandage are that it is difficult to put on too tightly, and it forms a relatively tight barrier against infection, particularly when it is used in conjunction with duct tape.

Crêpe bandage: These elasticized cloth bandages have two distinct advantages over the more modern self-adhesive: they can be applied more tightly, thus giving the limb more support; and they can be washed and used again. Their danger, particularly to the novice, is the greater possibility of causing sores by applying too tightly. They are indispensable when making a Robert Jones bandage.

Rolled cotton wool: Cotton wool is the least expensive of the cushioning materials. It is important to obtain evenly rolled cotton wool so that the bandage can be applied evenly. Cosmetic cotton wool balls should not be used. One thing to remember about cotton wool is that it adheres to cuts, therefore any skin lesions should be covered with a non-adhesive bandage first.

Rolled synthetic cotton wool (Soffban): Essentially a synthetic cotton wool, it has the advantage that it is rolled very thinly and evenly, and does not stick to itself like cotton wool; it is therefore easy to use, particularly when applying a hoof bandage. It is sold in various widths, the 10cm (4in) and in particular the 15cm (6in) rolls being the ones to purchase. Although it is more expensive, it is highly recommended.

'Gamgee': Gamgee is the commercial name for cotton wool sandwiched by either a gauze or synthetic non-adhering layer. It is sold in wide rolls, approximately 30 to 60cm (12–24in) in length. When it is being wrapped around the lower limb, it has a tendency to wrinkle, thus making it more prone to causing a bandage rub.

Nappies: An inexpensive alternative that can be used to bandage the hoof is the disposable nappy. It is sterile, absorbent, and its outer plastic layer is fairly impermeable,

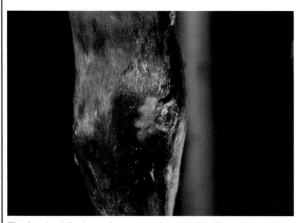

The back of the knee is an area frequently affected by poor bandaging

particularly when subsequently wrapped with duct tape.

Non adhesive dressing (Melanin, or Rhondopad): An inexpensive dressing pad used to place over a limb wound before bandaging. It usually has a shiny side that does not adhere to a wound surface. The most useful size is the 10cm (4in) square pad.

'Allevyn' pad: Affectionately called a 'mouse mat' by my colleagues, these thick, soft pads do not adhere to wounds, and 'wick away' moisture from suppurating wounds; they are therefore valuable in cases of highly contaminated wounds. They are, however, very expensive.

Duct tape: Invaluable to all walks of life from the armed forces to the plumbing industry, duct tape provides a most effective waterproof barrier over a bandage. Tape should not be placed directly on a limb unless it is being used to seal the proximal edge of a bandage to keep shavings and dirt from getting into the bandage. In this case, a strip of tape should be torn from the roll and placed *loosely* over the edge of the bandages and taped on; it should not be taped on whilst unrolling it.

Commercial poultice (Animalintex): Given its ease of use, this has become a favourite in the home stable. It is certainly easier than poulticing with bran and Epsom salts, but horse keepers should be careful not to poultice too much, as this will cause the skin and in the case of the foot, the hoof to become too wet and soft; in particular thin-soled animals such as Thoroughbreds are prone to go lame through too much poulticing. Many people then mistakenly believe that it is still the initial problem that is the cause of the lameness, and diligently continue to poultice. As a general rule, do not poultice more than three days in a row, then dry bandage for a couple of days in order to dry the hoof out. If there is still infection in the hoof, it probably warrants cutting out further.

Other useful bandaging aids are a pair of scissors and a scalpel blade. A large piece of thick inner-tube rubber can also come in handy, particularly when bandaging the hoof of a shod horse, as the rubber is resistant to the usual wear in the toe area. Owners with ponies that are prone to bouts of laminitis should have several frog supports already made up in their first aid kit. A guide on how these can be made can be found in the laminitis section (see page 115).

There are all sorts of other commercially available products, ranging from equine boots to frog supports, but in my experience these tend to be unnecessarily pricey and in many cases they are less effective than the materials that are mentioned above.

Bandaging methods

Hoof bandage

This bandage is helpful when poulticing for a hoof infection or as a method of keeping exposed tissue from coming into contact with stable contaminants. If possible, the shoe should be removed as it will cause greater wear of the bandage, particularly in the toe area. Always wash the hoof off carefully with soapy water (Hibiscrub, for example) and a brush. Any loose bits of frog should be trimmed off with a knife: that way, you aren't locking in a large amount of bacteria with your bandage. If the shoe is being left on, I like to tear off a strip of cotton wool and then double it over so that it covers the sole of the foot and provides more of a cushion for the bandage against the metal of the shoe.

Next, wrap a 15cm (6in) synthetic cotton roll (Soffban) around the hoof, heels and lower portion of the pastern; cross the bandaging material over the heels as it will then be less likely to slip. Using the same method, wrap a Vetrap over the synthetic cotton, leaving just a little (5mm/¼in) sticking out at the top of the pastern; like this you can be sure that it won't rub. Finally, use duct tape to seal the entire bandage completely.

Always bandage 'looking into' the material, and apply all the materials used in the same direction; that way, they will not loosen each other.

The great advantage of bandaging in this fashion is that the foot is completely protected, and it is therefore possible to let a horse out on to a limited paddock, provided it is not ankle deep in mud.

Severe injuries for which hygiene is essential – for example, cuts to the lower palmar aspect of the pastern – should always be bandaged with both a hoof and a lower limb bandage. This will make contamination from outside impossible. For cases that do not require quite as much attention to hygiene, or if the animal is on stable rest anyway, a less expensive way of bandaging is to use a disposable nappy to cover up the foot, followed by a Vetrap and/or tape combination.

Lower limb bandage

Although it is possible to begin the bandage at the pastern area, bandaging down to below the coronary band will help to prevent rubbing. It also makes it possible to seal the bandage more effectively. Be careful to hook the bandage below the heels of the foot to prevent it from slipping upwards.

The key to all bandaging is to provide enough material under the bandage to minimize the chances of restricting blood flow and creating bandage sores. Two 15cm (6in) rolls of Soffban are generally sufficient to provide good cover from just below the knee to the hoof, followed by a Vetrap bandaged over it. If extra support is desired, a crêpe bandage can be applied in between. Duct tape should be used to tape the bandage directly on to the hoof wall.

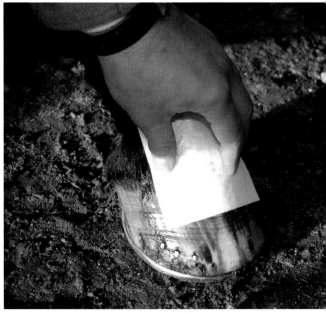

1. Field bandaging should only be performed when absolutely necessary and will necessitate frequent bandage changes. First, a sterile pad is placed over the wound

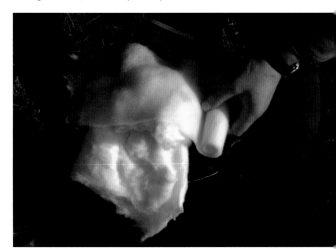

4. Pick up the leg and place a thick layer of cotton wool over the hoof. Bandage the entire hoof with a Vetrap or other water-resistant bandage

Upper limb bandage

The same procedure applies to either a knee (front leg) or a hock (hind leg). First apply a lower limb bandage, as described above: this will help to prevent the upper limb bandage from slipping down. Secondly, it will prevent swelling from the affected proximal regions of the limb from sinking downwards. In certain instances it may be possible to apply just a piece of fibergee and a stable bandage to the lower limb, like a support bandage. The most likely sites for bandage sores are the palmar aspect of the accessory carpal bone in the front, and the point of the hock on the hindlimb.

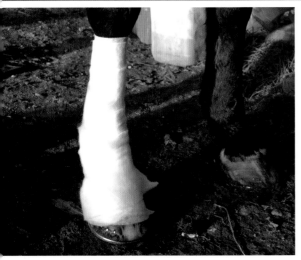

2. A cotton wool layer is applied to the distal limb

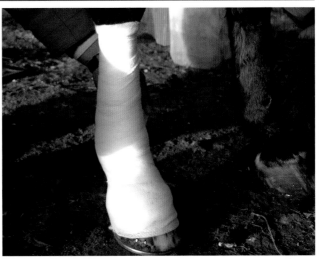

3. Now a crêpe bandage is placed over the cotton wool to hold it in place and add stability

5. An old inner tube and some duct tape are good for adding durability and water resistancy to your bandage

6. This bandage should effectively prevent outside contamination

Many books stress the importance of producing a neat figure-of-eight pattern, but if you wind the bandage in a widely spaced spiral up the leg, wrap it once around the top of the limb, and then spiral back down again in the opposite direction, this pattern will be formed automatically. If you use 15cm (6in) synthetic cotton rolls, avoid bandaging the likely rub sites, the back of the knee or hock. If you are using cotton wool, tear a large hole out of these areas so that the points peep through the cotton; if using gamgee, cut a circular hole into the area over the point.

Apply a self-adhesive bandage (Vetrap) and/or crêpe bandage in the same manner. Finally, a strip of wide duct tape should be applied over the top of the bandage to seal it off, and to help prevent it from slipping. Again, this should be applied as a strip, and not wrapped around the leg.

The carpus in particular is prone to swelling, so bandages will naturally go loose and slip down as the limb begins to reduce in size as the swelling goes down. For this reason, in the acute swollen phase, upper limb bandages should be changed daily.

Robert Jones bandage

A Robert Jones bandage is an excellent bandage if more support is needed – for instance, if a limb fracture is suspected. It also has the advantage of not being permanent like a cast. This is important if there is a wound on the leg that needs regular attention. The disadvantage of a Robert Jones bandage is that it is relatively expensive and very time-consuming to fit.

It basically consists of four or five layers of cotton, each tightened firmly with a crêpe bandage. In order to keep the bandage clean, the outer layer is covered with a layer of Vetrap. Plastic guttering cut to size or wooden splints (such as broomstick handles) can be used to strengthen the bandage further. These should only be added after several layers have been applied to the limb.

Depending on the location of the injury, a Robert Jones bandage can be applied either as a low or a high bandage. In addition to using the techniques that are described above, it is also helpful to remember the following pointers:

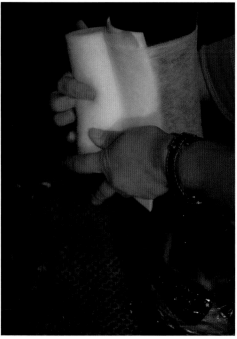

1. A sterile pad is placed over the injured tendon. Note that the heel has been wedged to reduce strain on the injured area

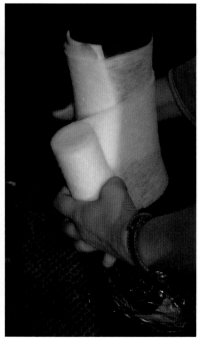

2. A synthetic cotton bandage is progressively unrolled down the limb...

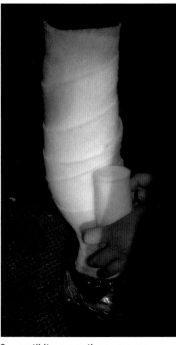

3. ...until it covers the coronary band and back of the heel

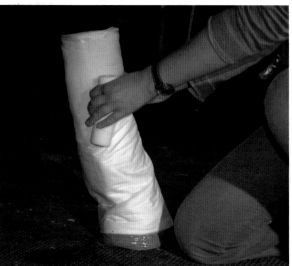

6. A layer of gamgee is now placed over the limb and the proximal and distal areas are padded perfectly to accommodate...

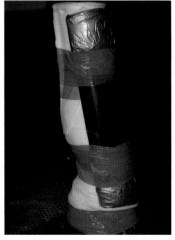

7. ...a drainpipe down the dorsal limb. Both ends of the drainpipe have been padded with gauze strips and duct tape to prevent injury. The drainpipe is taped on tightly before...

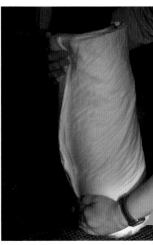

8. ...another layer of gamgee is placed over it...

- Try not to produce any wrinkles in your bandage. This is especially true of the layer closest to the skin.
- Apply the bandage evenly. For the first couple of layers, pad the palmar/plantar aspect of the pastern with a folded up piece of cotton, for instance, in addition to your bandaging material. This will ensure that over the course of a few layers, the bandage looks straighter and straighter.
- Always cushion well, and then tighten the material with the crêpe bandage. A properly completed Robert Jones bandage should give a satisfying 'thump thump' sound like a ripe watermelon when you flick your index finger against it.
- In order to reduce the amount of pressure on the point at the back of the knee, it may be helpful to cut a hole in an Allevyn bandage and place it over the area before bandaging over it.

A Robert Jones bandage should be changed at least once a week.

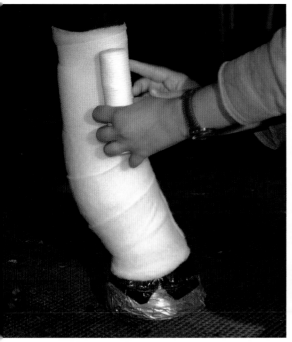

4. Two rolls are applied to provide a soft padding

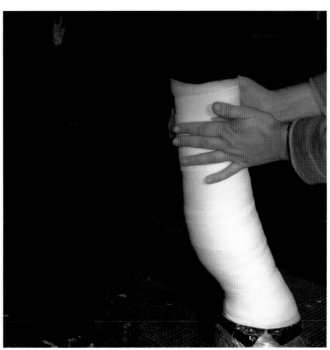

5. A crêpe bandage is appled firmly over the cotton wool

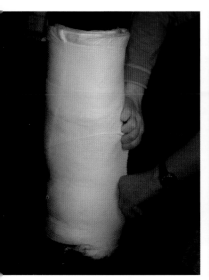

9. ...and secured with another crêpe bandage

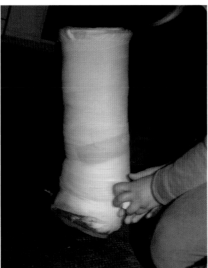

10. A Vetrap is applied over the crêpe bandage to hinder contamination

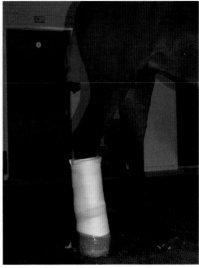

11. The finished product after a layer of tape has been applied to the bottom. The limb is now fully supported

Stabilizing bandages

These will vary somewhat, depending on the location and type of fracture. Although it is not always possible to know immediately what lesions are present, the clinician should bandage according to the best knowledge available. A table of fracture location and Robert Jones bandage technique is included here as a reference:

FRACTURE LOCATION AND BANDAGE TECHNIQUE

Region limb	Type of Robert Jones bandage	Position of splints	Length of splints (cm)
Forelimb			
Phalanges and distal MC	Half limb	Dorsal	35–40
Mid MC to radius	Full limb	Lateral and caudal	70–80
Mid to proximal radius	Full limb	Lateral	140–150
Above proximal radius	Full limb	Caudal	70–80
Hindlimb			
Phalanges and distal MT	Half limb	Dorsal	35–40
Mid to proximal MT	Full limb	Lateral and caudal	55–60
MC= Third metacarpal bone, MT= Third metatarsal bone			

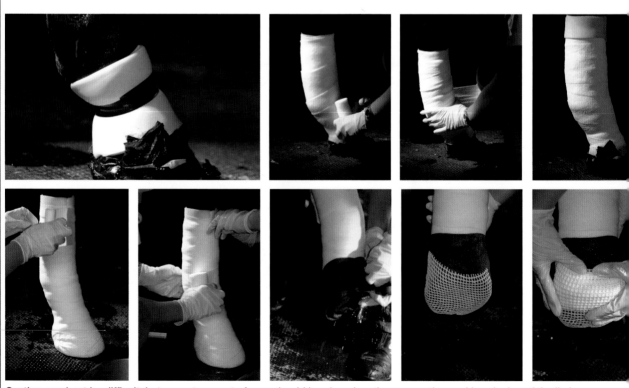

Casting need not be difficult, but a great amount of care should be placed on the preparation and bandaging of the limb beforehand. An Allevyn bandage is cut in half and taped over the pastern to prevent rubbing. Two rolls of synthetic cotton are applied, followed by a Vetrap. A strip of polsterplast is cut to fit exactly around the proximal end of the bandage. The leg is lifted and a bandage of synthetic cotton and Vetrap is applied. It is helpful to place a very thin layer of synthetic cotton around the bandaged weight-bearing leg as this will keep the casting material from sticking – a useful thing when it comes

Casting

Not too many years ago, I attended a course to learn as much as I could about how to cast the limb of a horse. All morning I listened to the explanations of temperature and technique, along with countless photographs of horses lying on an operating table. Finally, I raised my hand to ask a question: 'But how do you apply a cast in a standing horse?' The reply was: 'You can't. It just isn't possible without producing dangerous rub wounds.' I was stunned. I knew for a fact that my boss had been casting horses standing for over 15 years! But that was the attitude of academia not too long ago.

The obvious problem with applying a cast to a fully anaesthetized horse, is that the animal is usually suffering from a fracture to one bone or the other, and the last thing you want to do is place an unbelievable amount of strain on that fracture by knocking one ton of horse flesh down and then watch it get back up again. If there's one recipe for disaster, that's it! However, the problem of applying a lower limb cast on a standing horse was seen by many to be two-fold:

1. It was not possible to have an assistant help to pull the toe forwards as the cast was applied.
2. It was not possible to cast the entire leg in one piece, as the horse was naturally standing on it.

But the clever thing that some practitioners figured out for themselves, no doubt through the simple but brave procedure of trial and error, was that:

1. It wasn't necessary to pull the toe forwards at all. Through simple sedation and correct weight placement on the limb, the correct hoof-pastern-fetlock axis would be achieved naturally.
2. While it wasn't possible to cast the limb all in one go, a two-procedure technique could be used: first, as much of the limb as possible was cast with the horse standing. After waiting for the cast to cure, the limb was picked up and the hoof was cast. In this way it was possible to produce a strong and supportive cast all the same.

Of course, each practitioner favours slightly different materials or techniques, but as a general rule, they only vary slightly. The fact of the matter is, that the application of a limb cast that is tight enough to support, but not so tight as to create pressure sores, is difficult and based on personal experience and preference. The procedure our practice employs is shown below.

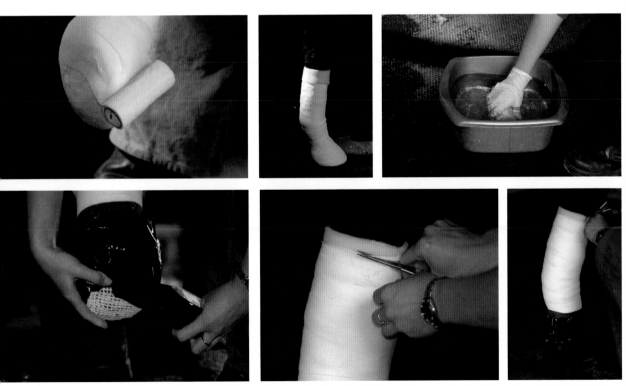

to removing the cast. The casting material is applied evenly down the limb, making sure to hook it underneath the heel of the foot. Once this is allowed to cure, the foot can be picked up and the hoof is cast. Strips of hot 'grid' (Vet-lite) are then placed over the foot to prevent the cast from rubbing through. A final layer of duct tape is added, and the proximal edge of the bandage is inspected and trimmed to prevent rubbing to the canon

Procedure for applying a cast to a lower limb

■ APPLYING THE BANDAGE ■

1. Remove the shoe.
2. Sedate the horse. Ensure that it is standing as squarely as possible on the injured limb.
3. Cut a 10 x 10cm (4 x 4in) square piece of Allevyn in half; place one half behind the pastern and the other half in front, ensuring that they overlap, and tape them to each other with electrical tape. This will make the leg more of an even size all the way up, and will help prevent rubbing at this most vulnerable site.
4. Apply two Soffbans a good inch below the point of the carpus, and 7cm (3in) below the point of the hock, extending to the hoof. It is essential that the bandaging material hooks over the back of the heel.
5. Apply a crêpe bandage over the Soffban, again making sure that there are no wrinkles.
6. Apply a Vetrap.
7. Ensure the bandage is not too high up the leg or it will rub against the back of the point of the leg as the horse walks. At the top of the bandage, place a strip of Allevyn approximately 7cm (3in) wide over the Vetrap. Always let your cast end halfway up this strip.
8. Pick up the foot.
9. Apply a thick enough layer of Soffban over the hoof to ensure the oscillating saw will not cut into it when the cast is removed, and bandage the foot with a Vetrap.
10. Apply as thin a layer of Soffban as possible over the finished bandage. This will prevent the cast sticking to the Vetrap, again making it much easier to remove.

■ APPLYING THE CAST ■

Though expensive, modern synthetic casting material is strong and sets very quickly. It is essential that the cast is applied as quickly as possible so that the different layers cure into one piece. In order to accomplish this, ask someone to help you by activating the casting material while you are applying the last third of the roll, and time it exactly so they hand you the newly activated roll the instant the one before is completed. And be sure that you wear gloves!

1. Open the package and place the first roll of synthetic casting material (Dynacast) in a bucket of warm (37°C/98.6°F) water.
2. With the cast completely immersed in the water, *gently* squeeze while turning it. Count to five, then start applying from the top of the bandage.
3. Keep the cast smooth, using handfuls of warm water as you go.
4. Once half of the first roll is used, the seal should be broken on the next and placed in the water as before.
5. Extend the cast as far down as possible, hooking it under the heels of the foot.
6. A total of four to five rolls are needed on the cannon.

7. Once all the rolls have been applied, bend the top edge of the cast slightly away from the leg to decrease the chance of rubbing.
8. Once the cast is cured (this takes approximately five minutes), pick up the leg and apply the foot cast using one to two rolls of cast material.
9. While you hold the foot, the assistant should cut a piece of synthetic grid (Vet-lite) approximately 2.5 times the length of the bandaged foot. It should be folded in half and boiling hot water poured over it. Apply the grid quickly over the foot, ensuring that the entire toe and heel is covered with it. The material will set within seconds. It provides a slip-resistant, extremely durable protective layer that will not rub through.
10. A Vetrap can be placed over the top of the cast to keep it clean. A layer of duct tape over the foot is also a good idea.
11. It is preferable to keep the horse on straw instead of shavings, as this will limit the amount of debris likely to work its way in from the top of the cast. If this is not practical, the Vetrap can extend slightly over the lip of the cast to help seal it off better.

Procedure for the application of a foot cast

A hoof cast is invaluable in the treatment of heel bulb lacerations. This is a common injury in horses, and is often due to forging, although lacerations due to flint stones and other foreign bodies can also occur. Deeply lacerated heels tend to heal only very slowly due to the amount of movement in the heels, and hypergranulation and scarring are common complications. Pressure bandaging is difficult to achieve, costly and also time-consuming, and as long as no vital structures – namely the tendon sheath – have been exposed, a hoof cast will achieve the best cosmetic result with a minimum of time and money invested.

1. Remove the shoe and trim the foot. Spray the sole with an antiseptic spray.
2. Trim away any infected or proud flesh.
3. Place a non-adhesive dressing over the wound, and apply a foot bandage using one Soffban and one Vetrap.
4. Using the technique described above, apply one to two rolls of casting material to the foot, making sure that only the heel and not the pastern is covered with the casting material.
5. Apply a synthetic grid (Vet-lite) to the sole of the foot, and tape duct tape over it.
6. Place a stable bandage over the affected leg and extend it as low as possible. This will ensure that no material falls down the back of the heel.
7. The stable bandage should be checked daily. The cast should stay on two to four weeks, depending on the size of the lesion.

Despite all efforts, casts can rub. If there are any signs of lameness or swelling, the cast should be removed immediately and the leg inspected for possible rubbing.

Removing a cast

Although it is possible to place fetotome wire between the bandage and cast extending the full length of the cast laterally and medially, synthetic casts can still be difficult to remove in this manner. It is far easier to use an oscillating saw to cut through this portion of the leg, and peel the cast back. However, always take care because although these marvellous saws will not cut through flesh, they will go right through anything hard, including the hoof. It is imperative, therefore, that enough soft material is used when bandaging the leg.

Minor cast or bandage rubs should be treated with the use of systemic NSAIDs. Deeper wounds should be cleaned carefully, and the horse given systemic antibiotics. Corticosteroids can be useful for the treatment of localized dermatitis.

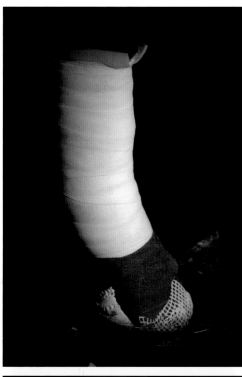

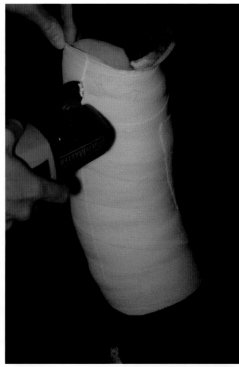

When removing a cast, it is best to use an oscillating saw that will not cut the soft underlying bandage. Cut through the entire length of cast medially and laterally. This will allow you to then peel it away from the leg

89

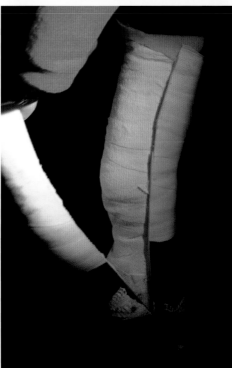

SECTION 4 TREATMENT OF THE LAME HORSE

The Principles of Joint Disease and Treatment

Joint disease is one of the leading causes of lameness in horses, and provokes consternation in all horse owners, however professional. This little understood process is commonly described as 'arthritis'.

Inflammation is the common thread in the development of joint disease. The classic signs of *rubor* (redness), *calor* (heat), *dolor* (pain), *tumour* (swelling) and loss of function were first described in Roman times, and they are still applicable today.

The role of inflammation

Inflammation is a protective mechanism of the body following injury, designed to instigate healing. On a microscopic level, the blood vessels dilate, bringing more blood into the area. When this occurs, the distance between the individual cells of the blood vessel walls increases, allowing cells and fluid to leak out into the periphery. A lot of these cells are white blood cells, and these form a vital part of the body's defence mechanism, designed to remove unwanted bacteria or damaged tissue from an area so that healing can take place. In doing so, they release a variety of enzymes into the surrounding tissues. Unfortunately, these can also have

a detrimental effect on surrounding tissue. Another unwanted effect of severe or continual inflammation is the formation of fibrous bands, which appear as adhesions between the various tissues. These bands are actually congealed bits of built-up protein, and they restrict normal movement.

There are two different types of inflammation, acute and chronic.

Acute inflammation: This type of inflammation occurs suddenly, as a result of a sprain or fracture, or in the early stages of bacterial infection. Acute joint inflammations may be correctly termed arthritic conditions ('arthrose' meaning 'joint', and '-itis' a medical suffix meaning 'inflammation').

Chronic inflammation: If the initial acute inflammation is minor and the body is able to heal itself, the acute inflammation will go away. However, if it remains unchecked, chronic inflammation will set in. This process always initiates new tissue formation and usually causes irreversible and permanent damage to the joint. Once this occurs, it is called osteoarthritis or degenerative joint disease. All of the joint structures can be affected.

The effects of inflammation

Certain changes may be observed in body structures that are affected by inflammation.

Joint capsule: An inflammation of the joint capsule (capsulitis) can cause it to become very swollen and painful. If the inflammation persists, a permanent thickening of the capsule wall will occur, and this in turn will reduce the natural range of movement of the joint.

Synovial membrane: Given their close proximity to each other, it is not surprising that an inflammation of the synovial membrane (synovitis) always coincides with a capsulitis. The nerve endings within the thin-walled synovial membrane become stimulated, producing not only pain, but also themselves releasing substances into

Bone

Periosteum

Marrow Cavity

Collateral Ligament

Joint Capsule

Subchondral Plate

Synovial Space

Articular Cartilage

Increased Intramedullary Pressure

Periosteal Elevation

Trebecular Remodeling

Chemical/ Physical Capsulitis

Osteophyte

Erosion Channel

Desmitis

Enthesiophyte

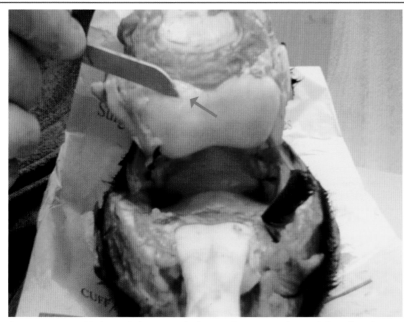

A necropsy on this horse's foot revealed a small amount of pus sitting directly on the navicular bone

the joint, which can damage the cartilage. In addition, the synovial membrane loses its permeability, while at the same time producing more synovial fluid; this causes the pressure in the joint to increase, which in turn stimulates pain within bone tissue. Extensive or repeated trauma to the synovial membrane will result in the formation of fibrous scar tissue. This tissue is of inferior quality, and cannot replace the functions of the normal synovial membrane. It also lacks elasticity, and thus contributes to stiffness in the joint.

Cartilage: All inflammation affects cartilage, which unfortunately has a limited ability to heal itself. The success of this healing process is determined by the size, depth and location of the cartilage injury (whether or not it is located in a weight-bearing area), and the age of the horse. It is not clear when the first changes within diseased cartilage take place; however, what *is* known is that small chip fractures occur spontaneously in areas with undiagnosed pre-existing cartilaginous damage. Another early change is collagen breakdown coupled with a loss of proteoglycans within the cartilage surface. As this occurs, the cartilage becomes softer and less robust to outside forces. The diagnosis and treatment of this low-grade damaged cartilage is an important question to answer in the continuing search for answers to the treatment of joint disease.

Synovial fluid: The products of inflammation that are released by the synovial membrane into the joint cause physical changes to the thick, oily joint fluid, most notably a loss of viscosity.

Bone: Bone inflammation always results in the formation of new bone. Depending on where the bone is, this will have varying effects:

- Continual wear and tear injuries on the bone underlying the cartilage caused by overloading, will cause the bone to scar and thicken. This is called **sclerosis**, and while serving to support the bone better, it has a detrimental effect on the overlying cartilage due to its decreased shock-absorbing capabilities.
- Inflammation of a joint capsule, ligament or tendon will cause the formation of new bone tissue at their attachment to the bone. This is called an enthesiophyte, after *enthesis* ('attachment') and *phyte* ('cell'). However, these enthesiophytes do not always mean that the affected joint will develop osteoarthritis, since they are located outside the joint.
- If inflammation within a joint causes an erosion of the cartilage thereby exposing the underlying bone, new bone spurs will be produced. These osteophytes (*osteo* meaning 'bone' and *phyte*, 'cell') are a definite sign of osteoarthritis.

91

The byproducts of inflammation reduce the viscosity of fluid in the joint

Specific joint diseases

Joints may suffer from a variety of specific diseases, as described below.

Osteoarthritis is another term applied to degenerative joint disease. It is characterized by a continued deterioration of the articular cartilage and change within the bone and soft tissues of the joint. Osteoarthritis in the horse can be divided into five categories:

1. Acute osteoarthritis characterized by synovitis and capsulitis. This initial inflammatory response to an injury will instigate further degeneration if not treated. Usually high motion joints such as fetlocks and knees are affected.
2. Insidious osteoarthritis which involves high load/low motion joints such as ringbone formation in the interphalangeal joint or bone spavin in the intertarsal joints.
3. Incidental or nonprogressive osteoarthritis usually not associated with lameness.
4. Secondary osteoarthritis due to intra-articular fractures or luxations, sepsis, or osteochondrosis.
5. Chondromalacia of the patella.

Osteochondrosis is a multifactorial developmental abnormality of the articular cartilage and subchondral bone affecting young horses. Three specific diseases are attributed to osteochondrosis:

1. Osteochondritis dissecans (OCD): The common term applied for OCD is 'chip fracture'. Both chondral fragments affecting cartilage and osteochondral fragments affecting bone and cartilage are possible. The most commonly affected sites are the lateral trochlear ridge of the femur, the intermediate ridge of the tibia, and the caudal aspect of the humeral head. Lesions are frequently bilateral.

2. Subchondral bone cysts: These occur in high weight-bearing areas of the joint. Although predominantly articular, non-articular ones do occur. These do not usually cause lameness and often go undiagnosed. The exact aetiology of subchondral bone cysts is unknown – whether by a defect in the endochondral bone or by intra-articular trauma of the same. The resultant breaking through of abnormal cartilage into the weaker underlying bone forms the cystic lining of the bone cyst.

3. Physitis: This condition is characterized by an enlargement of the growth plates in the long bones of affected foals; larger, well nourished foals are the most affected. Joint swelling and lameness in a young horse are the presenting signs; usually more than one joint is affected. Radiography is essential to establish the exact nature and extent of the problem. Arthroscopy is then necessary in order to remove the lesions. Where there is extensive damage to the joint cartilage, the prognosis for a return to soundness is poor.

High energy diets and calcium–phosphorus imbalances have been implicated in the development of the disease. Another important factor is a low copper diet (15 ppm or less). Finally, a genetic disposition for rapid growth also plays a role. In all cases, the immature joints simply cannot carry the weight of the animal.

Osteitis refers to an infection of the cortical bone, and this usually occurs in the distal extremities of the limb following trauma to the area. The underlying periosteum and the outer layers of the bone may eventually die, but the deeper cortical layers of bone remain intact due to the internal vascularization. Sequestrum formation is possible. The necrotic tissue must be debrided in order for healing to take place.

Osteomyelitis is a term applied to an infection of the bone and its marrow. Osteitis is an infection of cortical bone only. The most common cause is due to local trauma, which subsequently becomes infected. In chronic cases, the affected horses are not lame, but present with an intermittently discharging wound. Antibiotics are of limited value in these cases and surgical excision of the necrotic material is necessary.

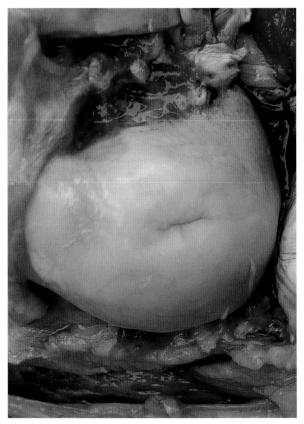

A subchondral bone cyst in a stifle. Note the sunken appearance of the overlying cartilage. A radiograph of the cyst is included on page 141

Given the multiple causes for degenerative joint disease, medical treatment for the condition is just as varied. Where there is an underlying cause, an OCD lesion or subchondral bone cyst for example, this must be removed first. It should be emphasized that not all of these underlying causes need be surgical issues – the same rule applies for conformational defects which predispose to arthritic conditions. The limb and/or hoof must be realigned in addition to the implementation of expensive medical treatment.

Medication can be used to treat systemically or locally:

1. **Non-steroidal anti-inflammatories (NSAIDs):** In addition to anti-inflammatory capabilities, these drugs have a pain-killing effect. They can be injected, usually in intravenous form, or given orally in the feed. These drugs are very useful in the management of osteoarthritis. However, their misuse can lead to other internal issues, including ulceration of the stomach mucosa. Commonly used drugs include phenylbutazone, also known as 'bute'; flunixin meglumin (Finadyne, Binixin); meclofenamic acid (Arquel); ketoprofen (Ketofen); and carprofen (Zenecarp, Rimadyl).

2. **Corticosteroids:** These are the most powerful anti-inflammatories: administered in low doses within a joint, these can reduce inflammation. In high doses or with continued use, however, these drugs encourage the breakdown of cartilage; this is why they remain the drug of choice in the treatment of bone spavin. Systemic injections of corticosteroids always carry the risk of inducing laminitis. The exact reason for this side effect is unknown. Oral administration of prednisolone appears not to induce this drastic side effect. The injectable form is usually methyprednisolone acetate 40mg per ml (Depo-Medrone V) or triamcinolone acetonide 10mg per ml (Adcortyl).

3. **Hyaluronate (HA):** Injection of HA into the joint is supposed to increase the synthesis of endogenous HA by synovial cells as well as to increase the viscosity of the inflamed endogenous synovial fluid. Intra-articular medications are marketed as Hyalovet 20, Hy-50 and Hylartil. There remains a controversy as to whether higher molecular HA increases the efficacy of treatment. An intravenous formulation (Hyonate) also appears to be effective in achieving therapeutic levels of HA within the joint.

4. **Polysulfated polysaccharides:** This group of drugs includes polysulfated glycosaminoglycan (Adequan) and pentosan polysulfate (Cartrophen). They are referred to as disease-modifying osteoarthritic drugs: that is, they are meant to prevent and even reverse cartilage damage. Both formulations are injected intra-muscularly, although intra-articular injection of Adequan can also be beneficial.

5. A vast array of commercially is available neutraceuticals. More expensive products such as Synequin and Cosequin include a combination of glucosamine hydrochloride and chondroitin sulphate. Oral glucosamine is also available commercially as a pure product (Newmarket Joint Supplement). Less expensive glucosamine products contain glucosamine sulphate, but this has a much poorer uptake. Glucosamine has a marked anti-inflammatory effect, reducing joint pain and increasing range of motion, as well as stimulating the synthesis of proteoglycan and collagen by chondrocytes.

Other drugs that deserve mention are:

- **Isoxsuprine hydrochloride (Navilox)** is used as a vasodilator to increase the circulation in the hooves of horses suffering from navicular disease.

- **P2G solution (a phenol and glycerol solution)** is used as a sclerosing agent, mainly for inflamed sacroiliac joints.

- **Dimethylsulfoxide (DMSO)** is a free-radical scavenger and can be applied topically or infused intravenously.

- **(Tiluronidate) Tildren** is relatively new on the market. Given as an infusion, it is meant to have a depressive effect on osteoclastic activity, thereby inhibiting bone resorption and indirectly new bone formation.

- Another new product for equine use is an **interleukin-1 receptor antagonist (Orthokine)**. It is recommended for injection into the distal intertarsal or tarsometatarsal joint every 14 days for three treatments. More research is needed to test its efficacy.

- Chemical ankylosis using **alcohol** is currently being tested as an alternative to sodium monoiodoacetatef (MIA). MIA is known to cause an extremely painful reaction when injected intra-articularly. Its use cannot be recommended for ethical reasons.

- Autologous Condition Serum (ACS) is currently marketed as 'irap'; ACS consists of a syringe containing specially coated glass spheres which encourage white cell growth once mixed with the patient's blood. White blood cells in turn produce cytokines which inhibit interleukin-1, a major mediator of joint disease. Initial studies indicate potent anti-arthritic effects of irap with no side effects.

93

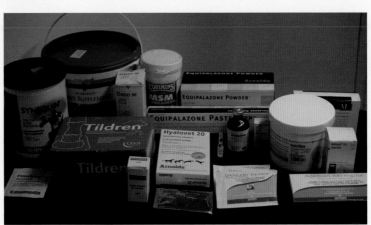

The principles of joint disease treatment revolve around the symptomatic treatment of inflammation and the hindrance of osteoarthritis

Radiography is essential in order to ascertain the extent of the infection. If a sequestrum of bone is present, this will present as less dense than the bone surrounding it. Usually in cases of osteomyelitits there are marked areas of bone lysis and sclerosis.

A hematogenous osteomyelitis does occur in young foals, usually combined with a septic arthritis.

Idiopathic synovitis

Here we come across my favourite word in the medical dictionary: idiopathic, meaning 'of unknown origin'. An idiopathic synovitis is therefore an inflammation of the synovium, for which we do not know the origin. This occurs, for instance, in bog spavin of the tarsocrural (tibiotarsal) joint and in the windgalls of the fetlock. In these cases, the inflammation is low grade and generally does not affect the gait of the horse. It is seen more often in horses with poor conformation, and the condition is self-perpetuating. Treatment is not generally necessary.

Traumatic arthritis

This category includes a diverse collection of conditions that develop after a single episode, or repetitive episodes, of trauma.

Traumatic synovitis/capsulitis: These are usually referred to as 'type I injuries', meaning injuries that do not affect the articular cartilage.

Sprain: A sprain occurs when a supporting ligament of a joint is stretched beyond its normal range of movement. A minor sprain can be treated by rest and support alone. Moderate to severe sprains are always accompanied by a laxity in the ligament. Severe sprains cause a complete loss of ligament function, and this may lead to a complete displacement (luxation) or a partial displacement (subluxation) of the joint. The joint instability caused by these luxations will almost always lead to the development of osteoarthritis.

Meniscal tears

The menisci are located in the stifle joint, and the most common area of injury is a sagittal tear through the axial portion. Meniscal tear injuries are often accompanied by injury to the cranial ligaments of the meniscus and the cruciate ligaments. Treatment is based on arthroscopic resection of the damaged tissue. The prognosis is guarded to poor.

Intra-articular fractures

Fractures which extend into the joint always carry a poor prognosis. Immediate fixation of the bones is paramount. Otherwise deterioration of the joint surrounding occurs rapidly.

Joint and tendon sheath sepsis

Symptoms

When bacteria or other foreign organisms are introduced into the synovial membrane or synovial fluid, it triggers the most exaggerated response possible. Just how rapid and severe that response is depends on a number of factors, ranging from the amount of bacteria introduced, the virulence of the bacteria, and the overall immunity status of the individual horse or pony.

Although the synovial membrane is relatively effective against infection, the inoculation (entry) of virulent bacteria resistant to its defences stimulates the body to produce a large number of inflammatory cells, mostly neutrophils, to ward off the infection. These cells contain enzymes designed to kill bacteria. These enzymes and other mediators are able to enter the joint environment through the damaged blood-synovial barrier, and trigger off a series of reactions which activate, amongst other things, the coagulation and fibrinolytic systems, and further continue to stimulate the inflammatory environment. The bacteria and cellular debris release interleukins and free radicals, amongst other things, which in turn attack the joint environment.

This whole infective process is extremely painful, and if not treated quickly and aggressively, can destroy the joint environment and even be life-threatening.

The earliest clinical signs are swelling, heat and pain within the affected area, with the horse reluctant to place weight on the affected leg. If the infection is already systemic (known as septicaemia), the animal becomes febrile and will show an increase in both heart and breathing rates.

It is strongly advisable to take a sterile synovial fluid sample prior to treatment so that an accurate culture and sensitivity test can be obtained. Further useful diagnostic techniques include a total and differential white cell count, and a total protein measurement; both an EDTA and sterile sample containers are therefore necessary.

Treatment

- Broad-spectrum antibiotic therapy should be commenced immediately. The most commonly used treatment is a systemically injected combination of penicillin and gentamicin, and this should be continued for at least one week after sepsis (with a synovial fluid cell count of less than 5,000 x 10 6/L).
- In most cases, it is also advisable to irrigate the synovial joint or sheath with up to 5 or 6 litres of sterile electrolyte solution. This is ideally performed via arthroscopic surgery in order to allow for visualization and surface debridement. In some instances, particularly if antibiotic therapy has been initiated without obtaining synovial fluid samples beforehand, it is advisable to take a biopsy of the synovial membrane.
- It is possible to successfully lavage most areas in the standing horse effectively, provided that the infection is in the early stages with little fibrin or cartilage debris accumulation. The lavage should be repeated after 48 hours if there is no improvement of clinical symptoms. The use of a 10 per cent DMSO solution, or for particularly septic joints, a 0.01 povidone-iodine solution, has been advocated in the use of joint lavage. There is little evidence to support this theory.
- Antibiotics such as gentamicin or amicin should also be injected into the joint. Systemic NSAIDs to reduce pain and inflammation are also indicated.

Prognosis

The prognosis for septic arthritis depends upon the duration of the sepsis, because this in turn determines the amount of articular damage. Degenerative joint disease is often a long-term complication of joint sepsis.

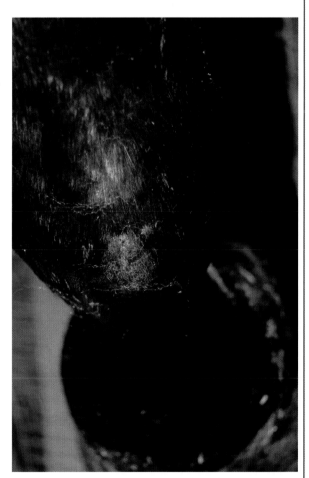

The small puncture wound has entered the fetlock joint. If not treated immediately it may prove fatal

Adhesions are a common complication of tendon sheath infection. As a general statistic, of horses that are treated for lower limb tendon sheath infections, one third will remain lameness free, one third will suffer from chronic low-grade lameness, and one third will need to be destroyed on humane grounds.

The Equine Back

There is no topic in equine medicine that generates more controversy than the diagnosis and treatment of dysfunction of the equine back. Veterinarians, physiotherapists, chiropractors, massage therapists and any number of pseudo-scientists and con-artists have competing and often contradictory opinions which they propagate amongst themselves and their clients. In fact, many practitioners still do not recognize primary back problems to date. How can this be in the 21st century?

The major stumbling block thus far has been a lack of scientific study in this field. In part this has been due to a focus on joint and limb pathology as the culprit of all lameness: 'Fix the problem in the leg, and the back difficulties will go away naturally'-type attitude. In fact, many practitioners still do not recognize primary back problems to date. This has undoubtedly been exacerbated not only by the constant barrage of anatomically imprecise and incorrect explanations made by more adventurous laymen to equine practitioners, but also by the difficulty of producing quantifiable and repeatable studies upon the equine back.

After all, the horse is unable to tell the examiner how much and where things hurt. That is the challenge!

Nevertheless, attention to the equine back has begun to increase lately, with a rise in popularity of a 'whole horse' approach to equine lameness and medicine. Technology is helping to close the gap of misunderstanding with an ever-increasing array of medical diagnostic instrumentation available to even the general practitioner. Initial results using algometry to quantify muscular pain in the back are promising. The next few years will undoubtedly be exciting for study in this area.

A useful method of categorizing back problems is in the following way:
1. Primary back problems.
2. Secondary back problems that arise through other problems in the skeleton, usually the limbs.
3. Back problems which, despite popular opinion, have limited anatomical or medical evidence to support them.
In order to understand and accept this categorization, let us consider the anatomy of the equine neck and back.

The anatomy of the equine neck and back

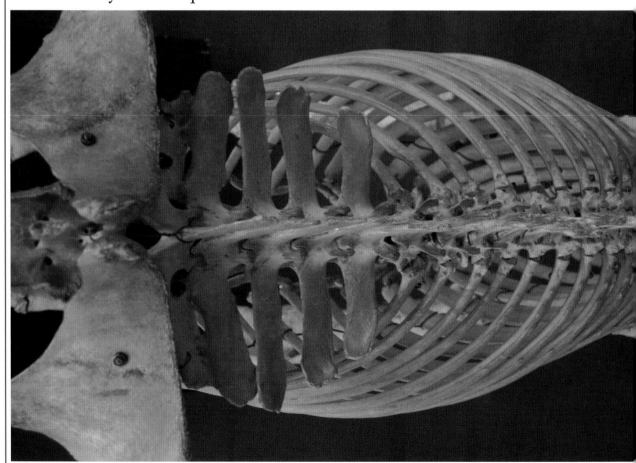

Vertebral structure

The head is held by the first cervical (neck) vertebra, the atlas; this is followed by the axis, which in turn is followed by five more cervical vertebrae, which in their entirety make up the skeletal neck of the animal. Both the atlas and the axis have unique shapes, while the remaining five cervical vertebrae have a basic rectangular appearance with small surfaces upon which they articulate with each other. All of these vertebrae house and protect the spinal cord, which transmits neural information from the brain to the periphery of the body and back.

The seventh cervical vertebra is followed by 18 thoracic vertebrae.

These help form the thorax, hence the name; in general shape they are like an inverted capital T. Again, they house the spinal column. They also have small areas of articulation which allow them to move semi-independently with one another, and where the ribs are attached. Their large spinal processes radiate upwards and slightly towards the back of the horse, the latter vertebrae becoming more and more vertical. It is these processes that make up the withers, and it is precisely the tips of these, and the space between them, which can be palpated in the standing horse.

The six lumbar vertebrae follow on. These have shorter processes, but much larger wings which help

protect the vital organs, giving the upside-down T image a more squashed effect.

The five sacral bones that follow usually fuse together between the ages of four or five years, forming a sturdy support for the pelvis.

Finally, the smaller and ever-narrowing cover for the spine ends with the tail or coccygeae vertebrae, which gradually lose their canal formation in favour of a groove which is open on top.

It is this multi-piece construction, with each individual vertebra articulating with the other, that gives the back its flexibility. However, let us consider the structures which counteract that flexibility and stabilize it.

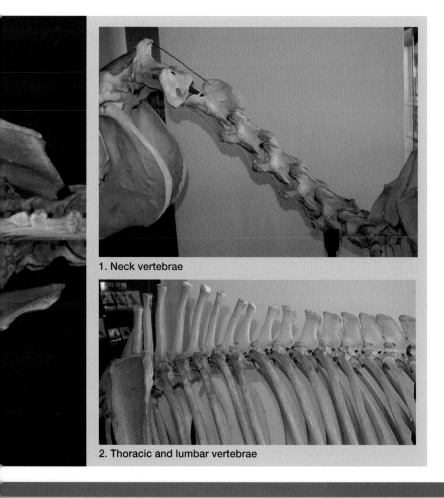

1. Neck vertebrae

2. Thoracic and lumbar vertebrae

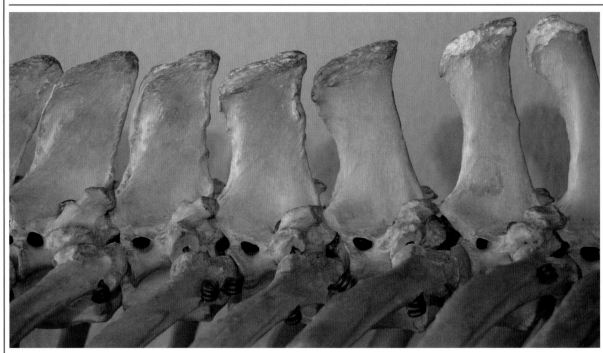

Notice the distal interlocking of the spinal vertebrae

Muscle and ligamentous structure of the back

Stretching from its broad origins on the tops of the cervical vertebrae down the entire length of the spinal processes until it finally inserts into the sacral vertebrae, the flexible nuchal and inelastic supraspinous ligaments have been compared to the powerful cables on a suspension bridge. Further support for the vertebrae is found in the form of very short, tough interspinous ligaments which stretch from vertebra to vertebra. Large muscles fill the hollow area created by the vertebral spines and transverse processes, most notably the serratus and longissimus muscles. Covering these two in turn are the trapezius, rhomboideus and latissimus dorsi muscles.

Many have postulated, and still do, that it is the largest muscle in the back, the longissimus dorsi muscle that holds the back up and doesn't allow it to sag.

This may be the case in a cow, but not in a horse! The longissimus dorsi muscle on either side of the spine is segmentally structured and innervated, thereby giving the back a rippling effect as it acts to transmit power from the horse's hindquarters, in particular the lumbosacral joint.

In the late 1880s Gustav Steinbrecht first proposed the 'ring of muscles' theory to explain all movement of horses, including such terms as 'impulsion', 'collection' and 'engagement'. This has been expanded upon since then, but the concept is the same: the power and suppleness of a horse's movement is dependent upon a system of bones, ligaments and tendons which interconnect with each other to form a ring. Thus, from the insertion of the dorsal spinous ligament in the croup, the ring is carried on by the sacrosciatic ligaments and a part of the semitendinosus muscle, which continues down to the tibia and hock and attaches there in the form of a fibrous ligament. The possession of a cable-like

This interlocking combined with the ligaments and musculature surrounding it...

...make moving single vertebrae impossible

98

structure from poll to hock is unique in the horse, where a pull on either end of the cable will raise the centre of the back.

The circle is continued from the pelvis through the rectus abdominus muscle, which inserts to the sternum. Finally, the scalenus muscle closes the ring by connecting the first rib to the neck.

In this model, the importance of a well developed neck and, in particular, the scalenus muscles becomes clear: with a well set neck, when the horse lowers his head, through the ligamentous system, his back will automatically rise; whereas a horse with a ewe neck will achieve little or no effect in his back when he raises his head.

The importance of the abdominal muscles is also clear, because it is the rectus abdominus muscle, more than any other, which must be strong in order to carry a rider. Dressage therefore does not strengthen a horse's back, but its belly!

Gustav Steinbrecht's ideas were popularized by the publication of *System der Reiterausbildung* by his devoted pupil Paul Plinizer. Little did Plinizer, who became Head of Horses for Kaiser Wilhelm II, realize how much of an impact his book was to have upon dressage even to this day

Pathologies affecting the equine back

In the light of our anatomical knowledge, we may now consider the various pathologies which may affect the equine back. In general, the difficulty in the diagnosis and treatment of back problems can be strictly viewed as a problem of size. The horse's limb is readily accessible from most sides, and when necessary, the deeper portions of the leg can be viewed with the use of radiography or ultrasonography. This is not the case with the back of the horse, however, where access is only readily available from the top (dorsally). Even with the use of ultrasonography and radiography, only the top 15cm (6in) or so is readily open to scrutiny. Although specialized techniques are able to access the more complex, deeper parts of the horse's back, their use is limited given their high cost.

An added difficulty is that primary back problems cause no lameness, or only a low-grade hindlimb lameness that is often bilateral. Frequently the case history will include a reluctance to perform; jumping in particular will be affected, and bucking, resentment to the rider's weight or to girthing may also be evident. This usually subsides with exercise. Horses with an excitable temperament are more prone to back problems due to the increased tension of the muscles.

Many back problems are chronic, therefore treatments should be continued over a longer period of time. NSAIDs are useful to alleviate inflammation, while oral carbamol (15–44mg/kg) will help relieve muscular tension. Many horses improve spontaneously.

It is important to keep these difficulties in mind when examining and treating the back. Even if one thing has been diagnosed, kissing spines for example, remember that there are probably other things wrong with the back that you can't diagnose. Therefore the only thing you can rely on, again, are your eyes and your hands to tell you if treatment is meeting with success.

99

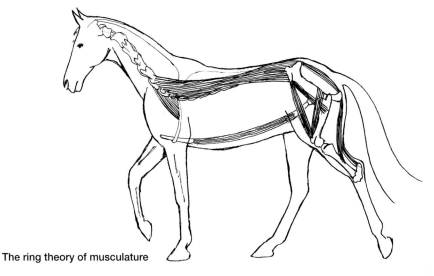

The ring theory of musculature

Vertebral deformities

As in humans, an abnormal curvature of the spine is usually the result of an abnormality at birth (a congenital defect). The curvature is named according to its misshape:
1. Kyphosis, better known as 'roach back';
2. Lordosis, or 'dipped' or 'sway back';
3. Scoliosis: a deviation in the skeletal vertebrae from right to left.

Diagnosis: These conformational conditions can be readily diagnosed by an examination of the back, and radiographs can be helpful in confirming the extent of the problem.

Supraspinous ligament damage

This may appear to be thickened, and is painful on palpation. Latero-medial flexion is reduced in one or more directions. The lumbar area is most commonly affected.
Diagnosis: An ultrasonographic examination, though low-exposure radiographs may be useful in determining abnormal ligamentous thickening. As in any ligament, healing is slow, and re-injury to the area is common; the prognosis must therefore be guarded.

Impinging spinous processes (kissing spines)

Over time, the long spinal processes upon which the supraspinous ligament rests, may thicken, gradually closing the intervertebral space until they touch. This condition occurs most frequently between the 13th to the 18th thoracic vertebrae, which is the area where the saddle usually rests. Although this has given rise to discussions regarding the role that tack plays in the morphology of this disease, this disease has also been found in long-extinct equine species. It occurs most frequently in Thoroughbreds. Pain presumably results from the continual rubbing of the two opposing vertebrae to each other, resulting in inflammatory processes of the bone and surrounding tissue.

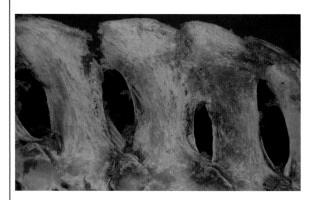

Kissing spines in a point-to-pointer. Two spinal processes have fused together. Although this would have been painful initially, the lack of extra bone points to a resolution of the problem. The remainder of the spinal skeleton was free from other pathologies

Diagnosis: Impinging spinous processes can usually be readily palpated. Given the width of the back, standard radiography can only picture the first 10 to 15cm (4 to 6in) of the back – though this will suffice to see the impingement. Another difficulty is that some horses with kissing spines have no clinical symptoms: thus, the mere presence of kissing spines is not sufficient to diagnose the disease. It may be helpful to inject local anaesthetic into the affected area in order to see whether or not there is an improvement in the horse's gait or demeanour (inter-vertebral nerve blocks). I find that clinically significant kissing spines will always be accompanied by painful muscular tissue in the surrounding area, and the back will be stiff and painful to manipulate.

Treatment: The treatment of kissing spines is varied, and is mostly aimed at the treatment of the symptoms only. This includes injection of the area with a long-acting corticosteroid and regular physiotherapy. The surgical excision of kissing spines is of questionable efficacy, and should only be undertaken when symptomatic treatments prove ineffective.

Degenerative joint disease of the articular processes

This is a fairly common feature in older horses, as the articular processes between vertebrae (zygaphophyseal joints) undergo the same degenerative pathology as other joints of the body. The initial dysfunction of the joint is accompanied by a reduction in joint motion, localized pain and hypertonicity of the surrounding muscles. Internally, inflammation mediators begin altering the internal structures of the joint, including the joint fluid and cartilage. If unchecked, this decrease in joint motion will lead to the formation of joint capsule adhesions, bone demineralization, and loss of surrounding muscular and ligamentous strength. Finally, intra-articular adhesions form as the interior cartilage is eroded, leading to osteophyte (bone) formation and irreparable capsular and ligamentous damage. The final stage of this process is ankylosis, which is the complete fusion of the joint. These processes are known to be extremely painful in humans, however, more studies are needed in order to prove their significance in horses.

The cycle is therefore: reduction in joint motion—adhesions—bone formation—complete joint fusion (ankylosis).

Treatment: As in limb joints, prevention plays a far greater role than treatment. This includes correct husbandry, appropriate tack, riding and training. The use of oral glucosamines is beneficial. NSAIDs and physiotherapy provide symptomatic relief only.

Spondylosis

This is a condition when the degenerative joint processes described for the articular processes affect the ventral vertebral bodies themselves. New bone formation (osteophyte) begins to form on the ventral processes and eventually bridges the gap between the vertebrae. If unchecked, complete fusion of the joint can occur.

Increased bone formation will increase the chances of either impinging on the spinal cord itself or the many nerve roots coming out of the intervertebral foramen.

Treatment: None

Vertebral fractures

Stress fractures appear to occur more frequently than was previously thought. In a study involving thirty-six racehorses, 50 per cent of them had incomplete fractures of the vertebral lamina. The most usual site is near the cranial articular process, where particularly the caudal thoracic and lumbar vertebrae are slotted deeply

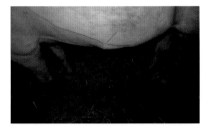

Not to be overlooked – a fractured rib

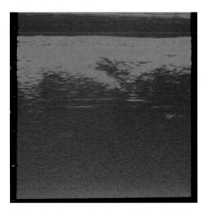

An ultrasound scan is helpful in determining damage to the supraspinous ligament

Ultrasound examination of the dorsal ligament and the tips of the spinal processes

within each other, severely restricting rotating motion. Other fractures usually involve the spinous processes of the withers. As these constitute the highest part of the back, falling over backwards is often part of the clinical history.

Treatment: is usually conservative as surgical intervention is not usually necessary.

Muscle strain

This is the most common type of back injury and usually involves the large back muscle, the longissimus dorsi. Frequently the injury is acute and happens whilst the horse is being exercised. The area usually shows the classic signs of inflammation: swelling, heat and painful to touch. The back may be held rigidly in an attempt to minder the pain. If these symptoms occur in the area of the saddle, a careful investigation of tack is wise as this frequently can be the cause for pain in this area. Another frequent cause is the inability of the owner to keep the horse properly fit. Riding skill and balance are a further important issue.

Treatment: Rest. Buy a saddle that fits properly.

Rhabdomyolysis (tying up syndrome, exertional myopathy)

Although this disease should not be viewed as a primary back problem but as a systemic disease, it is mentioned here because of the classic symptoms involving painful back muscles. Historically the condition was known as 'Monday morning disease', as it predominantly affected horses working after having had a day off. Originally this was attributed solely to the hard feed given to the horses. Recently, however, it has been shown to include a wide variety of factors, ranging from electrolyte imbalance to an inherited trait, particularly in Quarter Horse and heavy horse breeds in which type II muscle fibres store an increased amount of non-bioavailable polysaccharide and muscle glycogen.

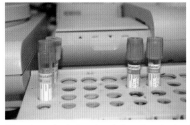

Blood analysis to check for elevated muscle enzymes is critical to diagnosing rhabdomyolysis

The acute symptoms of the condition include a reluctance to move, combined with excessive sweating and increased heart and breathing rates following or during exercise. The urine may be discoloured with the myoglobin from destroyed muscle cells (myoglobinuria). Horses may take a stance similar to the one adopted in acute laminitis. Chronic, less acute forms of the disease are also possible, particularly in horses suffering from polysaccharide storage myopathy.

Confirmation of the diagnosis can be obtained by collecting a blood sample and investigating the level of muscle enzymes, particularly CK, AST and LDH; these will be greatly elevated. It should be remembered that peak levels of CK and LDH occur only after approximately 14 to 24 hours after the onset of the problem, and do not return to baseline for seven days. AST does not peak until 24 hours after the incident, but takes up to four weeks to return to normal. A muscle biopsy can confirm the diagnosis in horses suspected of having a polysaccharide storage myopathy.

Treatment: Severe cases should be treated as medical emergencies. The animal should not be forced to move. For analgesia, NSAIDs or even butorphanol should be administered intravenously. Acepromazine (0.04–0.1mg/kg) can also be used for its promotion of circulation through the muscle cells. DMSO, Dantrolene sodium and corticosteroids have also been promoted. Intravenous electrolyes should be administered for dehydrated horses and those suffering from myoglobinuria in order to promote a dialysis of the kidneys. Recumbent horses should be placed on a deep bed and turned every few hours. The initial diet should be low in energy and high in fibre.

Horses that have suffered from bouts of rhabdomyolysis should be exercised regularly. A high fat diet should be used to replace the carbohydrates, which are to be avoided. Electrolytes and a vitamin E/selenium supplement may also be beneficial.

Sacroiliac disease

The sacroiliac joint is the area connecting the hind limbs to the spine. In order to assist propulsion, stability is essential. The joint surfaces between the sacrum and ilium are not smooth, but consist of reciprocating uneven surfaces that are covered by a thin cartilage layer. The inside of the joint is often held by fibrous bands. In addition ventral, dorsal and lateral sacroiliac ligaments assist in keeping the joint rigid.

Traumatic injury as well as low-grade repetitive trauma can induce a subluxation of the sacroiliac joint. The clinical signs are varied. Chronic cases usually include stiffness of the hindquarters, often shifting from limb to limb. This reluctance to step under can cause a squaring-off of the toe, and horses may resist being backed up a hill. Downward pressure on the tuber coxae causing a rotation of the pelvis may elicit a painful response by forcing movement into the sacroiliac joint. The overlying musculature is frequently held in spasm. The tuber sacrale may become more prominent, resulting in 'hunter's bumps'. Acute cases can present as an obvious lameness, though this is much rarer.

Diagnosis of the treatment is difficult, and even today is mainly reached by elimination of other lameness through nerve blocking. Anaesthesia of the sacroiliac joint is possible for diagnostic purposes. However, accidental anaesthesia of the surrounding nerves can cause a temporary paralysis of the hindquarters. Nuclear scintigraphy is the preferred method of diagnosing a sacroiliac problem.

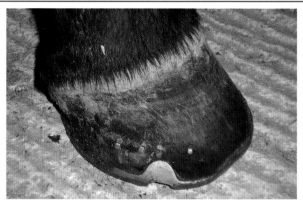

A squared-off toe in the hind feet is a sign of the horse not lifting its hindlimbs up properly, a symptom often associated with sacroiliac disease

Treatment: Treatment of this condition requires a considerable amount of time dedicated to stable rest, followed by months of controlled exercise. Weekly intravenous injections of sodium hyaluronate for one month, followed by monthly administration, have also been advocated.

Injections into the sacroiliac joint with corticosteroids or a sclerosing agent such as P2G can be beneficial. A large area (20 x 20cm/8 x 8in) should be clipped out over the tuber sacrale and prepared aseptically. A small amount of local anaesthesia should be injected along the cranial aspect of the opposite tuber sacrale to be injected. Using sterile gloves, insert an 18G 20cm/8in spinal needle into the anaesthetized area. It is helpful to pre-bend the needle! Directing the needle towards the cranial aspect of the greater trochanter on the affected side, advance it along the medial aspect of the affected ilial wing towards the caudomedial portion of the affected sacroiliac joint until contact is made with the bone. The injected medication will diffuse within the longissimus muscle or the interosseous sacroiliac ligament.

Horses suffering from sacroiliac disease frequently have obvious 'hunter's bumps' accompanied by spasm of the overlying musculature

Complementary therapy may include physiotherapy, or chiropractic manipulation can also be used in conjunction with NSAIDs to alleviate muscle spasm.

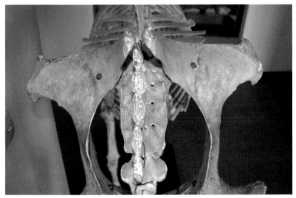

The sacroiliac joint (above) connects the hindquarters to the spine. When injecting the joint, it is helpful to pre-bend the needle (below)

Pelvic Fractures

The symptoms for pelvic fractures are highly variable, depending on the location. Most involve trauma, usually from a fall, though it has been shown that a high number of racehorses suffer from stress fractures. I have seen two cases in older horses where a traumatic fracture of the pelvis simply occurred during rolling; in both cases the razor-sharp bone fragments severed the internal femoral vessels, causing the animals to bleed to death internally within a matter of minutes. Osteoporosis may have been a factor in the relative weakness of the bones.

A fracture of the tuber coxae rarely causes lameness. In all other cases, manipulation of the limbs and/or a rocking of the pelvis will elicit a painful response. Acetabular fractures often occur when a horse 'does the splits'.

An internal examination is important if pelvic pathology is suspected, as instability may be palpable. The psoas major, psoas minor and iliacus muscles should be palpated for hypertonicity or swelling: these lie ventral to the lumbar spine. The pelvic canal should also be palpated whilst rocking the pelvis back and forth to assist in detecting any fractures. It may be helpful to use an ultrasound scan internally and externally to visualize the fracture.

Scintigraphy is helpful to diagnose fracture lines or to ascertain healing progress.

Treatment: Surgical treatment is not possible. The only treatment available is stable rest for up to a year, depending on the extent of the injury. For the first two months it may be necessary to sling the horse for support, or cross-tie it to prevent the animal lying down. Sequestrum of the bone may necessitate surgical removal. The prognosis is guarded, though again this is dependent upon the location of the injury and the age of the horse.

A internal examination is indispensable in diagnosing the extent of a pelvic fracture

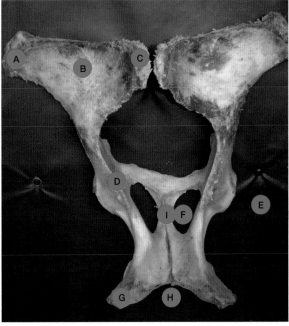

Fractures of the pelvis can cause a variety of symptoms depending on where the fracture is. A) Tuber coxae; B) ilium; C) tuber sacrale; D) ischiatic spine; E) acetabulum; F) Obturator foramen; G) tuber ischii; H) ischial arch; I) symphysis pelvis

103

The Neck

The neck is arguably the most overlooked feature in the evaluation of equine athleticism and movement. Its importance has been highlighted throughout this book as a way of evaluating chronic lameness, jumping ability and most importantly, as a key to engagement of the hindquarters in the horse.

A basic examination of the neck should always be performed on horses that are introduced with a history of lameness or uneven gait. This evaluation is outlined earlier (see Use Your Hands, page 14). Again, the importance of impartiality on the part of the examiner, and the repeatability of responses, cannot be over-emphasized: 'Can I induce that painful reaction every time I palpate here, or was that a one-off?' 'Is that really muscle tension I'm feeling?' This is the type of question that should come naturally to you as you carry out the examination.

Evaluating neck mobility

A useful method in the evaluation of neck mobility lies in the carrot-stretching exercise: by using food you can get a horse to stretch his neck and show you what range of motion he is capable of. But remember, proper stretching is painful, and the horse will learn to 'cheat' in order to lessen the pain, in the same way that you learned not to hold your legs quite straight in order to touch your toes!

Three basic stretches (or non-stretches, as the case may be) are possible. Stand beside a horse, preferably with an apple or a stick of carrot. Show the animal the carrot, and slowly lead its neck around until your hand rests on the shoulder of the horse. This will stretch mainly the middle portion of the neck. A horse with full range of movement in its neck will be able to eat the carrot without problem. But if it can't, it will think of other ways to get it – that is, it will cheat so that it can come close enough to eat it. Often, horses will literally step around the issue by moving their hindquarters back and to the opposite side of the neck stretch. This can easily be circumvented by standing the horse against a wall. And remember, just as you aren't as likely to be able to touch your toes as easily as you used to, do not expect the horse to be able to stretch all the way the first time around! Find the maximal amount of extension that the horse is capable of by holding the carrot just in front of its mouth. Hold it there for a second, allowing for the muscles to stretch, and then give the horse its well earned treat. Repeat the stretch on the opposite side. Are there blatant differences in the horse's flexibility?

The exercise can be varied slightly to stretch the lower neck more by feeding the carrot just forward off the point of the hip rather than the shoulder. Feeding the carrot from between the two front legs off the lower abdomen will flex the neck and stretch the back.

Be careful to note if the horse is actually stretching its neck fully, or simply resorting to trick mechanisms which it has learned in order to overcome its lack of neck movement. Study the pictures below carefully. The first horse shows full range of movement: it is comfortable in this position, and the neck is curled around gracefully. The photo of the grey horse clearly shows this horse's inability to bend its neck around – notice how stiff the middle section of that neck looks! This horse was also completely unable to stretch, but it had learned to corkscrew its neck in order to achieve its goal, fooling the owner into thinking that it had full range of movement.

Why do horses get a stiff neck in the first place? The causes are diverse, and, similar to the back, can be divided into primary neck problems and secondary neck problems, which are the result of other, primarily gait deficiencies within the horse.

Primary neck problems

The bone pathologies experienced in the neck are similar to those described for vertebrae in the back, and likewise range from no more than a reduction in the range of movement, to complete fusion (ankylosis). In rare cases, there can be a malformation of the cervical vertebrae,

Despite its size the bay horse has been trained to become very flexible. The grey horse, initially introduced for a primary neck problem, was eventually diagnosed with navicular disease

though sufferers of this condition tend to show symptoms early and are humanely destroyed. The advantage to the practitioner is that neck vertebrae are much more open to examination and analysis than the thoracic and lumbar vertebrae that are buried deep within the horse's body. This is particularly true for the first five cervical vertebrae, though the sixth and seventh vertebrae become obscured from palpation by the shoulder. Careful palpation should reveal even minor muscle swelling or atrophy, either symmetric or asymmetric. If cli\nical findings conclude only minor flexibility issues in the horse's neck, an initial course of treatment with anti-inflammatories and daily carrot stretching exercises may be in order. If the problem persists, or the range of motion within the neck is greatly reduced, ultrasonography and in particular radiography become invaluable for a diagnosis and treatment regime.

The difficulty in detecting primary neck lesions is that a broad spectrum of symptoms is possible, depending upon the involvement of the spinal cord. Compression of the spinal cord due either to injury or chronic inflammation will present a varied spectrum of central nervous system symptoms, depending on the location and extent of the lesion. It must be remembered that it is not at all uncommon for horses to suffer injuries to the spine; horses – very often youngsters – that rear up on their hindlimbs and fall over backwards can suffer fractures to the vertebrae, but show little or no clinical symptoms. Over time, symptoms can become more apparent as the maloccluded fractured area produces more and more bone, which can eventually impinge on the spinal cord.

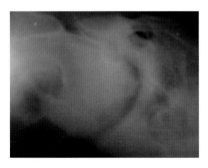

Below is an x-ray taken from a ten-year-old event horse with a reputation for 'going mental' every so often. He had won an intermediate event the week prior to this radiograph being taken. Whilst being lunged, he reared up suddenly for no apparent reason and fell. As he was unable to get up, the owner believed he had broken a leg, but careful examination revealed the troublesome area to be in the upper cervical area. Radiographs were taken and they revealed extensive remodelling to C1 and C2. The pain that this horse was suffering must have been excruciating; how he even allowed someone on his back to train him, compete and actually win, is an attest to his honest and willing nature.

This horse has mild rotation of the sixth cervical after suffering a fall. The area is painful

Mild arthritic conditions or muscular contraction can be treated with gentle manipulation of the neck, usually under sedation, and/or injections in the local area with long-acting corticosteroids. Calcification of the insertion of the nucal ligament has also been documented. If substantiated by radiography, injection into this area with the use of a spinal needle is warranted.

Depending on their severity, rotations of cervical vertebrae can elicit a variety of symptoms.

This radiograph reveals a nearly complete fusion (ankylosis) of C1 and C2. There is extensive bone proliferation around the articular facets with marked areas of sclerosis and a narrowing of the spinal canal. There is no treatment possible for this condition, and euthanasia of the animal was necessary

Initially there may be swelling in the area, and palpation can cause a painful response. Over time, the entire neck may stiffen and unusual sweat patches may appear in the general vicinity; this has been attributed to inflamed nerve fibres exiting the spinal cord, though there is little documented evidence for this. Mild rotations can heal spontaneously, though gentle manipulation of the area is beneficial. If nerval inflammation is suspected, long-term oral corticosteroids are recommended. Sudden or severe rotations can mimic fracture symptoms, with horses becoming ataxic. Well positioned radiographs with the neck held completely straight are essential in order to diagnose a cervical rotation.

A rotated sixth cervical in a 29-year-old pony suffering from sudden ataxia. After 24 hours of recumbency in which she was treated for shock with intravenous infusions of DMSO, corticosteroids, NSAIDs and adrenalin, she eventually managed to stand. Still unable to maintain balance, she was kept in a stable in which the walls were padded out with old mattresses; she used the corner of the box to prop up her back end. Gradually her condition improved and she made a full recovery

Maggie three years on at a ripe old age of 32

Secondary neck problems

Fortunately the number of drastic primary neck pathologies is rare compared to the number of horses that have dysfunctional necks due to some other lameness problem. These will often improve spontaneously once the actual cause of lameness is found and corrected. On occasion though, the dysfunction masks the severity of the lameness. In these cases, treatment of the neck problem first in order better to find the cause of lameness is advisable. However, these cases are rare. Only experience can assist in making this unorthodox decision.

'Wobbler' syndrome

'Wobbler' syndrome or cervical stenotic myelopathty refers to a condition in which there are malformation or malarticulation anomalies involving the cervical vertebrae. Affected horses suffer from ataxia or weakness due to the resulting compression on the spine. Hindlimbs are usually affected more severely than forelimbs. Predilection sites for constant or static compression occur mainly in the lower neck, C5-6 and C6-7, while intermittent or dynamic compression usually occurs in C3-4 and C4-5 where there is a lot of movement. Although malformation of C1 and C2 is possible, under normal circumstances the intervertebral space in these areas is very wide, making compression of the spine unlikely.

Symptoms can often be accentuated by making the horse walk up and down hills, step over obstacles, circle and back up. Although the symptoms are usually subtle to begin with, the condition is usually progressive. Acute paresis and ataxia usually arise from an accident which exacerbates the normally mild spinal compression. Older horses may demonstrate sweating and lack of sensation in the areas immediately adjacent to the affected cervical vertebrae.

This arises from a compression of the nerve roots in the area of the articular processes as they exit the vertebral canal.

Precise lateral radiographs of the cervical vertebrae should be made and then used to assess malformations, malalignments or abnormal ossification within the neck. Afterwards, the sagittal ratio should be calculated for each vertebra. This is obtained by measuring the narrowest sagittal diamenter of the vertebral canal (minimum sagittal diameter or MSD) by the widest point of the cranial vertebral body. If the sagittal ratio is below a certain level, then a stenosis of the vertebral canal must be suspected. Further investigation is then warranted, involving either a myelographic or scintigraphic examination.

Treatment: Horses suffering from 'Wobbler' syndrome should undergo conservative treatment including the use of corticosteroids, NSAIDs, and stable rest. Foals may additionally benefit from a strict diet involving less protein and energy intake, coupled with supplementation of vitamins, minerals and fibre. Surgery can be attempted to decompress the spinal cord via a dorsal laminectomy. Severely affected horses should be euthanased. Under no circumstances should any horse suffering from spinal compression be ridden.

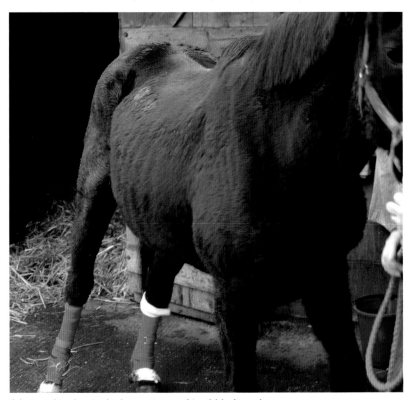

A horse showing typical symptoms of 'wobbler' syndrome

Systemic Diseases

Tick-borne disease

Lyme disease is a tick-borne neurological disorder which can cause a variety of symptoms ranging from lethargy to acute ataxia. Head pressing is sometimes seen. Horses are often febrile.

Treatment: A two-week course of antibiotic therapy using amoxicillin or tetracyclin. A blood test (ELISA) should be made to confirm the diagnosis.

Lymphangitis

Lymphangitis refers to an acute swelling of the limb caused by a restriction of the lymphatic circulation usually due to a bacterial infection. Most cases will involve the hindlimb. Affected horses will usually be lame. If the swelling affects the entire limb proximal to the stifle, this lameness will be severe.

Treatment: Broad spectrum systemic antibiotics and NSAIDs should be given quickly to prevent further swelling up the limb. Once adequate antibiotics are given, a short-acting corticosteroid injection can be beneficial. Pressure bandages should be used initially until the drugs take effect. This should be followed by cold hosing the limb and walking to further reduce leg swelling. If prompt treatment is not initiated, the lymph vessels can suffer permanent damage, causing the leg to be chronically filled. Although aesthetically not pleasing, this swelling will usually not cause lameness. Affected limbs tend to go down with exercise and swell again during inactivity. Horses suffering from chronic lymphangitis however, are more prone to further infective bouts. Abcessation in untreated legs can also occur, producing large septic wounds.

'Skippy' Although the lymph vessels have been damaged in this horse´s hind limb, it quite obviously is not suffering from the chronically swollen leg

Thrombophlebitis

This condition in the caudal aorta, iliac arteries or femoral artery can also cause the occasional hindlimb lameness in the horse. Strongylus vulgaris larvae may damage the intima layer of the arteries, leaving them prone to thrombus formation. Other aetiologies that cause damage to the interior of the artery are being researched. The lameness is always intermittent, disappearing with rest and reappearing with exercise. If a large thrombus is present, the affected leg may feel cooler; if both legs are affected, the horse may have difficulty supporting itself. The veins on the affected side are less noticeable. A rectal examination of the aorta and iliac arteries may reveal a decrease in pulsation on the affected side. An ultrasound examination can help reveal the extent of the thrombus.

Treatment: Many horses continue to deteriorate, and humane destruction may be necessary. Treatment using a 20 per cent solution of sodium gluconate (500mg/kg bwt) administered very slowly intravenously has been reported to have been successful in two cases.

THROMBOSIS

Blood clot formation in the distal aorta, usually just proximal to the origin of the external iliac artery, can cause intermittent hindlimb lameness in the horse as pieces of the thrombus detach and block smaller arteries in the hind legs. The actual cause of the embolism is unknown. As more arteries become blocked, the condition becomes more evident. Affected horses usually exhibit a normal gait at slower paces until a speed is reached after which they can no longer cope. Continued exercise at this rate may cause the animal to knuckle over or even fall. Another clinical sign is a stamping, kicking or even holding of the leg after exercise. Following rest, the lameness subsides. Examination of the limbs may reveal a regional coolness or absence of sweating. Pulse intensities in the limbs at various heights should be compared. An internal examination is useful for examining the pulse in the aorta and its major branches. Ultrasonography of suspect areas is useful in determining the extent of the obstruction.

Treatment: The condition is difficult to treat and it usually only includes symptomatic therapy. Sodium gluconate is only effective when administered in the first 24 hours while the thrombi are unorganized. Surgical excision may be performed in limited cases. Aspirin may limit further formation. Moderate exercise should be continued as both stable rest and high intensity work are contra-indicated.

Conditions of the Foot and Lower Limb

Conditions of the foot

Bruising (subsolar bruising)

Bruising of the foot occurs most frequently in horses suffering from thin soles and/or collapsed heels. Laminitic horses also suffer from subsolar bruising as the normally concave sole becomes flatter. Exercise on hard ground exacerbates the problem, but it is wrong to think that bruising is restricted solely to hard ground. Bruising often occurs under really soft, wet conditions in which the foot sinks in the mud on to exposed rock and gravel. Bruising that occurs at the heel is often referred to as 'corns'.

Clinically, the symptoms range from mild low-grade lameness to an acute onset of severe lameness. There may be a pulse in the foot. In mild cases, this pulse may be exacerbated by making the horse walk several steps, so check its intensity immediately after leading it. Hoof testers may also indicate the area of lameness, as may careful cleaning and paring of the foot to look for signs of discoloration.

Treatment: As a general rule, bruises need not be opened. Systemic use of NSAIDs can help in reducing the discomfort. Poultices are not recommended as they will only soften the foot further and make a secondary bacterial infection more likely. Hygiene is very important to prevent infection, and the hoof should be bandaged after first scrubbing it thoroughly with a surgical cleanser. It is advisable to remove the shoe if it is pressing on the sole, and to reduce the wear upon the applied bandage. When shoeing a flat foot prone to bruising, careful attention should be placed on seating out the inside of the shoe so that the weight of the leg rests on the wall of the hoof alone, and not the sole. Horses with corns may also benefit from the use of bar shoes in order to distribute the weight more evenly, or in severe cases, to suspend that particular heel off the shoe entirely. Regular trimming and shoeing will be necessary if conformational problems exist.

Canker

This refers to a condition in which the frog and related horn-producing structures of the horse's foot begin to hypertrophy, and exude a foul-smelling secretion.

Treatment: is usually prolonged and difficult, and consists of radical resection of the affected horn and treatment with astringents designed to dry and disinfect the bandaged foot. Systemic treatment with antibiotics may also be prescribed concurrently. The prognosis in these cases is guarded.

Club foot

A club foot refers to a hoof with an upright conformation and a concave hoof wall of 60 degrees or more. The condition is often congenital, and secondary to contracted flexor tendons. However, it may occur in horses of all ages suffering from chronic lameness. Radiographs often reveal periosteal new bone formation to the pedal bone.

Treatment: New-born foals suffering from contracted tendons should receive an infusion of Tetracycline. If given within the first few days post natum, this will relax the tendons. In chronic cases involving lameness, a check ligament desmotomy combined with aggressive heel trimming and extended toe shoes may be indicated. In theory, this allows the flexor tendons to stretch out further over time.

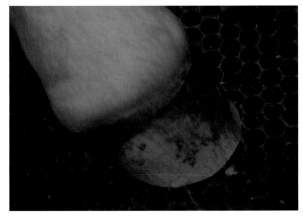

This foal has a congenital club foot due to a contracted tendon. Prompt treatment can still remedy this

Corns

This is a traditional term used for subsolar bruising in the heel area. (See Bruising, above.)

Coronitis

This is an inflammation of the coronary band, and is only seen rarely in laminitic horses and those suffering from systemic, often febrile illnesses. Clinical findings include swelling around the coronary band of the foot and an acute onset of lameness, with the horse reluctant to bear weight on one or more legs. Initially therefore, the disease is easy to mistake with abscessation or laminitis. Over a period of days, exudate development under the coronary band may increase until it finally bursts forth, causing a separation between the hoof wall and the coronary band.

A severe case of pastern dermatitis. The inflamed skin produces an exudate which eventually hardens to form a crust over the affected area

Treatment: is difficult, and usually limited to pain relief. The prognosis is poor. In many cases which do resolve, abnormal hoof growth can occur. When considering whether or not euthanasia is appropriate, it is important to consider the aetiology of the disease. Certain cases warrant prevailing with. I once treated a pony that had caught its hind pastern in straight wire. Unusually this did not do much damage initially, but in the coming week, the hoof slowly began separating from the coronary band: the wire had obviously cut off the blood supply to the foot. The entire hoof was removed, the exposed foot cleaned and carefully bandaged, and the pony placed on clean soft shavings. Surprisingly, it experienced only mild to moderate pain throughout its ordeal, convincing us to persevere. The satisfaction was immense when trimming the hoof eight months later revealed a completely normal hoof, and the pony was able to return to work.

Extensor process fracture

These fractures are often found incidentally following a radiographic investigation. Smaller fractures will show no presenting signs, while larger fractures may cause a swelling of the dorsal aspect of the coronary band. It is important to pinpoint the seat of lameness to the dorsal aspect of the hoof before assuming that the fractured extensor process is the cause of lameness.

Treatment: Smaller chips should be removed arthroscopically. Re-affixing larger fractures with the use of a lag screw has only met with moderate success, as secondary arthritis is a frequent result of surgery.

Grease heal (pastern dermatitis, scratches)

A plethora of remedies, home-made and commercial, is available for treating this condition Nevertheless, an old adage should be remembered when dealing with pastern dermatitis, namely that the more treatments there are, the less effective any of them are likely to be! However, it must also be realized that there are a number of completely different factors which may cause pastern dermatitis; therefore successful treatment of this condition rests on determining the actual cause first, *before* treatment is initiated.

Moisture undoubtedly is a predisposing factor in the disease, therefore attempts at keeping the area dry and away from moisture are important. Obviously this may not be practical in the long term. However, stable rest on clean shavings may be an important step in breaking the cycle. In less established cases, and particularly in horses with feathers, cleansing with a surgical scrub and careful daily drying with a hand towel may be enough. Some owners report success following daily applications of liquid paraffin, or even pig oil to act as a barrier against the mud. What is certain, is that not all mud is alike! Slurry and mud mixed with faecal matter will predispose to a variety of skin conditions that will not respond without proper hygiene. I have seen hunters develop pastern dermatitis overnight following a hunt through a farmyard. In these cases, an allergenic component to the condition is probable.

Treatment: In severe cases, systemic treatment with antibiotics is advisable. Topical treatment with soothing creams combining corticosteroids and antibiotics, and bandaging are also very effective in

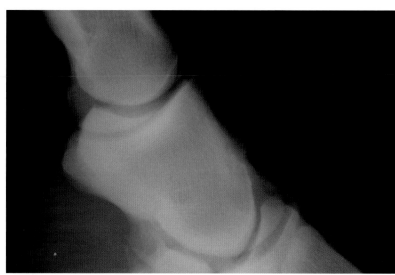

An old extensor process fracture on a twelve-year-old gelding. Notice the extensive remodelling of the joint which it caused

dissolving the scab formation and inducing healing. Severe crusting can be removed with 10% salicylic acid crème. Severely inflamed skin should always be treated with oral corticosteroids and/or topical burn ointments (Flammazine) to prevent reoccurring scab formation.

Although common literature cites oral ivermectin as a treatment for horses affected with *Chorioptes equi* mange, this is largely ineffective. Once mange has been established through the use of skin scrapings, the legs should be bathed in cattle ivermectin every other day for three consecutive treatments. This will always resolve the issue, although treatment is relatively costly.

Possible liver insult should be considered in all dermatitis cases.

Hoof abscess (subsolar abscess)

The inner structures of the hoof are a perfect breeding ground for anaerobic bacteria to multiply. These can gain access either via cracks within the hoof surface, or foreign body penetration, or even 'pricked' feet when the hoof nail comes too close to the sensitive structures of the foot. Horses that are already suffering with founder (chronic laminitis) or seedy toe are particularly at risk.

The lameness is acute and very painful, so much so that novices often diagnose a broken leg. The leg is non weight-bearing, and I have even experienced recumbent horses groaning in agony. If there is no obvious sign of a fracture, begin your examination with the foot. Remember, the intensity of the pulse in the palmar digital arteries of the foot will be increased. An exception to this occurs on occasion when a double sole has formed, which traps the infection. Therefore, a careful inspection with hoof testers is essential, as is careful palpation along the coronary band and heel in order to ascertain if the infection is ready to burst from these softer, less rigid areas.

Hoof testers are essential for locating pain within the hoof

An abscess has been found. Note the purulent grey pus oozing out

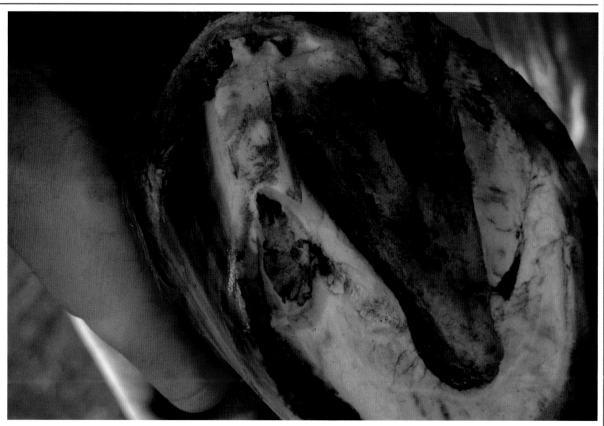
The infection has been cut out and the hoof carefully cleaned prior to bandaging

Treatment: Hoof testers should localize the area with the most pain. In many cases the shoe must be removed to expose the area underneath. Careful paring of the foot with a knife will demonstrate if a puncture wound is present. If not, the area should be searched with a hoof knife until the infection is released. Adequate drainage is essential. The horse should only be poulticed for a few days, but it may be necessary to bandage for longer, depending on the extent of the injury. It is often helpful to have the foot re-examined and trimmed after poulticing when the horse is more comfortable, and to monitor the drainage allowed.

Antibiotics will not affect infections within the hoof capsule as there is no blood supply there. Their use should be limited to occasions when the vital part of the foot is affected. NSAIDs may be helpful, though in my experience they are not particularly effective. Similarly, nerve blocks rarely block out the pain entirely and can often prove completely ineffective, therefore demonstrating the importance of a full clinical examination.

Radiographs can also prove useful when trying to find deep abscesses that are difficult to get to.

If a horse becomes suddenly lame again after initially releasing the infection, a problem with drainage may be present. However, it should be remembered that over-poulticing of feet, particularly thin-soled, flat feet, can also cause lameness, and these hooves only need drying out for the horse to become sound! Another problem can occur if the drainage hole is cut too deeply, allowing the sensitive corium underneath to protrude through. This is readily seen as a pink to deep red mushroom-like protrusion at the base of the drainage hole. It is sensitive to touch. This must be pushed back with the use of pressure! Fill the hole with gauze swabs, pushing the corium back behind the horn, and apply a pressure bandage. Caustic pencils or copper sulphate may also be useful.

All horses with hoof infections should be up to date with their tetanus vaccination.

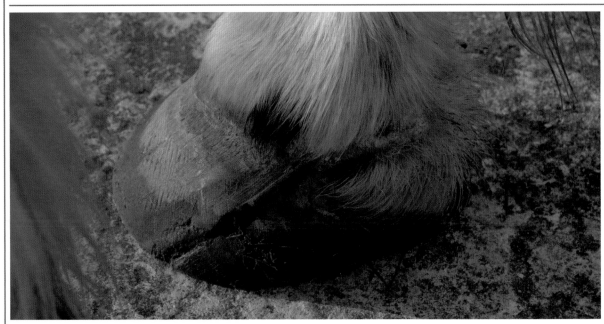

Without proper treatment, this hoof wall defect has no chance of resolving

112

Hoof wall cracks (sandcracks)

Hoof cracks can arise from a variety of causes. Although it may be as a result of dehydration, horses with damage to the laminae (laminitis, seedy toe, long toe conformation) are predisposed to this problem. Cracks will also arise if the coronary band has been damaged, in which case the crack will arise from the coronary band and extend distally; in the more usual scenario, the crack begins distally.

Treatment: Many cracks are superficial, and apart from the application of a hoof dressing to help with hydration, do not warrant any further treatment. Cracks that extend deeper into the sensitive structures of the foot, or continue to extend proximally towards the coronary band, do need to be treated.

The use of modern acrylics has greatly improved the treatment of cracks. However, corrective trimming and shoeing are still essential to success. If the crack occurs in the toe area, it is important to trim the toe back as far as possible. The entire crack should be resected out of the hoof wall, taking care to remove all the dead tissue and dirt until healthy tissue is found. In order to alleviate further pressure on the damaged area, I prefer to suspend this portion of the hoof wall. The hoof should be shod with a closed-bar shoe in order to alleviate excessive movement in the area. Primary defects of the horn arising from a damaged coronary band can only be treated symptomatically.

Keratoma

Although the name implies a cancerous tissue, keratomas are in fact masses of keratin-containing tissue growing between the hoof wall and the pedal bone. As pressure is exerted upon the sensitive laminae and/or

the pedal bone, they can cause the horse to go lame. They are also a continuous source of infection. Over time, keratomas can cause a pressure necrosis to the underlying bone.

A history of intermittent lameness is common, before a distortion at the coronet band and hoof wall becomes visible. An examination using hoof testers produces a painful response. On the solar surface, a distortion of the white line may be present. A ring block of P3 or an abaxial nerve block is necessary in order to improve the lameness.

Radiographically a discrete, well circumscribed lytic area may be visible; however, this is not always the case. The lesion can usually be differentiated from septic bone due to the smooth borders and lack of sclerosis.

Treatment involves the complete removal of the keratoma. Although this can be performed in the standing horse, for larger lesions and more fractious horses, general anaesthesia may be necessary. A tourniquet should be applied in order to minimize bleeding. Using an oscillating saw or motorized bur, two vertical cuts are made on either side of the lesion. The distal end of the hoof wall is then grasped and peeled upwards, taking care not to damage the coronet band. The mass is removed, and the underlying tissue and bone is debrided until healthy tissue is exposed.

A bar shoe with large clips on either side of the defect is nailed on to stabilize the weakened hoof. The defect is then carefully packed with soaked povidone iodine swabs, and bandaged. These swabs and bandages should be changed every three days until the area is cornified. After this, the area may be filled. The stabilizing bar shoe should be retained until the defect has grown out completely.

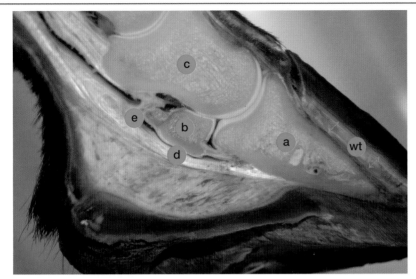

An anatomical overview of the foot: a) pedal bone; b) navicular bone; c) pastern; d) deep flexor tendon; e) navicular bursa; wt) distance between the pedal bone and hoof wall (wall thickness)

This cross-section of the foot shows the laminae responsible for securing the pedal bone

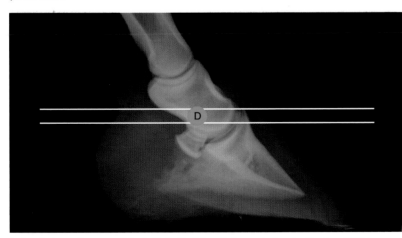

Lateral view of a normal foot. Note that the distance between the top of the coronet band and the top of the extension process (D) is narrow

Laminitis

I remember meeting Christopher Pollitt BVSc, PhD years ago at a veterinary conference. He has dedicated his whole life to academic research into the cause and nature of laminitis. I asked him if he would mind explaining to me the results of his latest research, as I wasn't sure if I understood them. His answer was, 'I don't understand laminitis either, even after all these years.' If he doesn't understand it, then it is perfectly understandable if you can't grasp the intricacies either!

The basics are simple enough. Literally, laminitis means an inflammation of the laminae, the connective tissue which attaches the pedal bone to the horn capsule and holds it in place. This inflammation causes a loosening of the bonds between the dermal and epidermal laminae, and the weight of the horse now works against it, forcing the bone down. At the same time, the pressure increase in the horn capsule pushes the tip of the pedal bone down, and the deep flexor tendon works as a fulcrum to facilitate this rotation. If unchecked, these forces will eventually cause the pedal bone to rupture through the horn capsule.

It is clear then, that two things can happen in laminitis: the bone can rotate, and it can sink. But how does laminitis occur in the first place? That is where the controversy lies, because laminitis can occur in several unrelated conditions:

- As a result of eating too much fresh grass or hard feed. Overweight ponies are particularly prone to this condition. Recent studies implicate an overabundance of fructose in rich grass as being a possible cause. Black walnuts have also been implicated.
- In cases of systemic disease which cause endotoxaemia, for instance placenta retention in mares, or acute septic peritonitis, or acute pleuropneumonia.
- In horses suffering from severe lameness which are forced to bear prolonged and extensive weight upon their other limbs, particularly the contra-lateral one. This in turn causes a stasis of blood flow to the

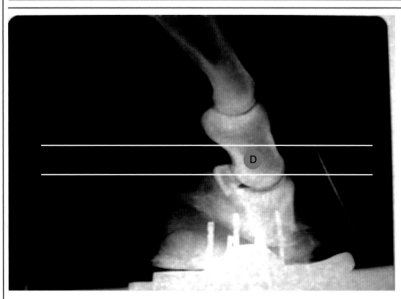

A chronically foundered horse. The distance is greatly enlarged, and the angle of the pedal bone is no longer aligned with the hoof wall. The extensive lysis in the toe is due to undue pressure on it, causing a pressure necrosis. The extensor tendon is contracted

weight-bearing limb, ending in the necrosis of the laminae tissue.

■ Concussion, as a result of exercising fat or unfit horses on hard ground.

■ It can be medically induced through the administration of corticosteroids.

■ As part of the Cushings syndrome. Endotoxins were first postulated as the cause of laminitis, arising either from feed or systemic disease. However, under experimental conditions, laminitis could not be induced with the use of endotoxins. Therefore, some other mechanisms must play a factor.

Studies have shown that under normal horn growth conditions, the attachments between the epidermal lamellae and the basal membrane of the pedal bone are constantly loosening and reattaching. This activity appears to be regulated by MMPs (metalloprotinases). The amount of MMPs appears to be increased in laminitic horses, but the substances which induce MMPs have not been identified yet. In other animals however, it has been proven that by-products of tissue degeneration, cytokines (tumour necrosis factor, interleukin-1 and transforming growth factor) do increase MMP production.

When considering treatment, it is helpful to define the condition as being either acute or chronic. The acute form lasts only approximately two days from the initial onset. The symptoms are diverse, depending on the severity of the pain induced. These include:

■ Mild lameness or a reluctance to move, particularly on a hard or uneven surface.

■ The inability to move, often resulting in the characteristic laminitic stance in which the hindlimbs are held directly under the body in order to carry a greater proportion of the weight, and the forelimbs are extended out in front of the horse in order to take as much weight as possible off them.

■ Recumbency, or lying down. It is important to remember that laminitis can occur in one, two, three or even all four hooves, which will necessarily change the symptoms exhibited.

During this acute phase, the bonds are loosening between the pedal bone and the hoof wall, but a separation will not yet have occurred. In mild cases, therefore, how can we be sure of our diagnosis?

■ The history must fit.

■ Because there is inflammation in the hoof or hooves, there will

always be an increase in the digital pulse in the affected limbs.

■ A sharp rap with a hard object on the dorsal wall will elicit a painful response. If the animal is moving about, making you unsure of its response, pick one leg up, lean over, and rap on the wall of the weight-bearing leg. The animal will either lean back dramatically or even jump if the rap causes pain. Simplifying matters somewhat: the growing pressure building up inside the hoof capsule must be very similar to that felt after striking one's fingernail with a hammer. Over time, as the pressure steadily increases, so does the pain. An increased pulse in the form of a throbbing finger also becomes noticeable. And of course, it takes only a slight increase in pressure or a light knock to make an already tender area really smart!

Treatment: must be prompt in order to curtail the amount of separation in the horn capsule.

■ The source of the condition should be found and eliminated from causing further damage. Ponies suffering from an overindulgence of grass will need stabling. A strict diet needs to be prescribed.

■ The hooves will need support. In mild cases or with small ponies, a deep bed of shavings will usually suffice, but straw is not sufficient! In more serious conditions, and particularly in heavier horses, the frogs should be supported as soon as possible. I have found old carpet to be an excellent and inexpensive material to use as a frog support, in the technique described on the next page.

■ Newer synthetics have proved invaluable in the treatment of acute and chronic laminitis, as it is now possible to glue, rather than nail on heart-bar shoes. The 'Imprint' shoe by Andrew Poynton is particularly recommended and is shown in detail on page 31.

■ An abaxial nerve block is recommended if the horse is unable to lift its leg for the placement of the shoe or frog support. Support bandages should also be considered.

- Medication should include NSAIDs, particularly flunixin meglumine due to its anti-toxin properties. A low dose of acepromazine has also been propagated as it is said to increase the blood perfusion to the foot. Glycerol trinitrate applied topically to the area just above the coronary band may also be beneficial to the blood flow in that area.

Regular monitoring and reassessment of the condition is important. A reduction in the pulse intensity in the limbs indicates improvement.

An 'old' remedy included taking blood to alleviate the pressure in the hooves. I can vividly remember as a young man watching a vet treat my laminitic pony. He asked me to get a bucket, and when I returned, he rammed the largest needle I have ever seen into the jugular vein of my pony and asked me to hold the bucket up to catch the free-flowing blood. I stood there wide eyed as the bucket began to fill, and when the entire bucket was filled, he mercifully removed the needle and asked me to pour the contents into the hedge. He then got back into his car and drove off.

The rationale behind this grotesque treatment was that this would alleviate the pressure in the hooves, thereby limiting the damage. This may be true in the short term, but a few hours later, after the horse or pony has had a good drink, the blood pressure will be right back up to normal again, albeit with a lot fewer red blood cells! So if you ever see this treatment being exercised, by all means ask the person with the needle to stick it somewhere else besides in the horse!

Some people propagated forced low-grade exercise in order to stimulate the blood flow in the hooves. This will, of course, increase the load on the already weakened laminae, and will result in more separation. Instead, horses should be allowed to lie down in order to take the strain off this area!

Another 'old' treatment was to force a horse to stand in a cool stream. While this approach does seem logical – after all, cold water is always good to reduce inflammation – not many of us have a fresh silted (not gravelled) stream running directly by our pastures. So if you do have one, by all means use it, but don't force your poor horse to walk miles in search of the 'miracle cure'.

If a tearing of the laminae does occur, resulting in a rotation and/or sinking of the pedal bone, the condition can be considered *chronic*. In general, everything that occurs now is a direct consequence of the acute damage, and the task of counteracting this damage can be difficult, time-consuming and expensive. Every owner should be aware of this from the outset!

In general, the aim of treatment is, over time, to correct the rotation in the hoof by continual trimming. In order to support the bone and take pressure off the tip of the pedal bone, it is necessary to equip the horse with shoes with built-in frog supports, called heart-bars.

Good quality radiographs using markers on the dorsal wall and tip of the frog are invaluable: only these will allow a full assessment for treatment.

Depending on the degree of rotation and sinking, a prognosis can be made concerning a return to athletic work, and in more severe cases, survival.

The toe must be rasped back along with the heels. Notice the bruising in the laminae

According to Robert Eustace of the Laminitis Clinic, a much poorer prognosis is given to horses where the pedal bone has sunk. The amount of rotation can be readily measured by taping a metal object, such as a flexible piece of lead, on the dorsal wall of the hoof, being careful to place it directly on the coronary band. Secondly, a drawing pin is placed at the very tip of the frog. After taking a lateral radiograph of the hoof, these markers on the hoof can now be seen to compare with the structures inside the leg. By drawing a horizontal line from the top of the coffin joint and another from the top of our marker over the coronary band, we can measure the distance between the two. Mr Eustace found that the greater the sinking distance of the pedal bone within the hoof wall, the less probability the horse had to a return to soundness, a founder distance of 15mm (½in) within the hoof capsule already reducing the horse's chances to approximately 37 per cent but still with a good

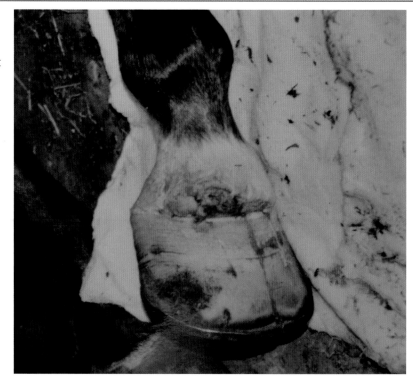

The final stages of laminitis – the laminae have loosened the bond completely and the horn wall is no longer attached with the rest of the foot. Note the extensive infection that has accumulated within the necrotic tissue

This is a correctly fitted heart-bar shoe, giving broad support to the heel and frog

This is not a proper heart-bar. What support can possibly be given by it? This ill-advised shoe cost the horse its life

prognosis for survival, while distances exceeding 21mm carried very poor prospects of survival.

If treatment is undertaken, it is of paramount importance to work together with an experienced remedial farrier. The radiographs should be examined and discussed by both the vet and farrier so that a common consensus is reached, and the amount of toe and heel that can be safely trimmed can be ascertained. In nearly all cases, heart-bar shoes, either metal or synthetic, must be employed. By using the marker at the tip of the frog, clear instructions for the farrier can be given as to how far forwards to place the bar of the shoe. A bar that is placed too far forwards will cause the horse to go lame, and will eventually lead to a pressure necrosis of the pedal bone!

In order to avoid any kind of miscommunication, I insist on meeting with the farrier personally to oversee the shoeing of the horse. Tragic events surround this decision. As a young assistant, I had been called to treat an Arab stallion that was suffering from laminitis. After

being assured that the yard farrier was a remedial farrier (after all, he had a very large sign proclaiming this on his truck), I phoned him to discuss the results of the x-rays. After giving him the measurements for some heart-bar shoes, I thought nothing more of the matter.

Two weeks later, the owner phoned me with the desperate news that the horse was even worse with the shoes on. I drove out immediately to find the horse recumbent, the pedal bone sticking out from the soles of the feet, and this abomination of a shoe nailed to its foot. I think of that horse and that 'remedial' farrier a lot. That shall not happen to me again.

The continual use of radiographs to monitor progress, and the necessity of constant communication between owner, vet and farrier, cannot be overemphasized. Affected horses often suffer from hoof abscesses caused by compression or dead laminae, and these must be found and removed. But given the right team effort, it is possible to treat many horses which previously would have been euthanased.

Navicular syndrome

My father often told me that bad words in the English language all had four letters; in the equine world, however, it has nine! The 'N' word is universally feared amongst horsey folk. Everyone knows of at least one horse with navicular syndrome that has had to be euthanased because of incurable lameness. On the other hand, everyone knows of at least one 'miraculous' recovery from a horse that hasn't had a day's lameness ever since. How can this be? The key to understanding this discrepancy is to realize that a 'syndrome' in medical terms means that a group of symptoms which may, or may not, be related have been lumped together because as of yet we are uncertain of their exact pathophysiology.

Horses suffering from navicular syndrome will often display a bilateral, intermittent forelimb lameness which can be exacerbated through work and/or a hard surface. Turning also makes the lameness more noticeable. The gait tends to be choppy, with the feet landing slightly toe first.

Test results tend to be unreliable, but the following results can be indicative of navicular syndrome:
- A lower limb flexion test is positive.
- Wedge tests to induce a coffin joint hyperextension are positive.
- An examination of the foot with hoof testers may elicit a painful response across the back of the heels or from the collateral sulcus to the opposite hoof wall.

Local anaesthesia of one limb with the aid of a palmar digital nerve block is positive, often causing a reversal in lameness. This indicates a bilateral problem in the area of the heels. But there is a huge problem in immediately assuming that we are dealing with navicular syndrome, because there are a lot of reasons for horses to go lame in the heels.

In order to find a diagnosis, a closer look at the anatomy of this complicated area is in order. Located deep within the heel is the navicular bone, a small flat bone. Around it a synovial structure is formed, the navicular bursa. This fluid-filled bursa usually communicates with the coffin joint. Curling around the palmar (plantar) aspect of the navicular bone is the deep digital flexor tendon (DDFT) and its tendon sheath, which inserts into the palmar aspect of the pedal bone. In short, we have two synovial structures, the navicular bursa and the tendon sheath of the DDFT, one tendon and the actual bone all packed into a tiny space.

Assume that all other simple lameness problems in the foot have been excluded (corns, sheared heels, bruising, and so on) by paying careful attention to any increase in the pulse intensity in the foot, and by methodical use of hoof testers. If there are any doubts, do not press on hurriedly into x-rays and further diagnostic tests. Rather, wait a few days, or even remove the shoe to have a good look at everything underneath. It is better to take a bit longer with your work-up to get the correct diagnosis, than to hurry and choose a wrong one. So provided we have done our homework, we are still confronted with the problem of knowing which structure or structures are the cause of our lameness. And here comes the real hitch: we can't – at least, not under normal clinical situations.

The advent of the MRI scanner has revolutionized diagnostics during the last five years, and continues to provide us with invaluable information about each individual structure at approximately 1mm intervals. Cost, however, is still a major obstacle limiting its use: only a few equine hospital facilities have the machine, and using it costs big money.

The guidelines for the diagnosis for navicular syndrome were hammered out before the advent of the MRI scanner, and recommended that the diagnosis for navicular syndrome could only be confirmed if the horse fulfilled the following criteria, namely that it blocked out to
- a palmar digital nerve block;
- a coffin joint block;
- a navicular bursa block.

Despite all the difficulties involved, in order to realistically diagnose navicular syndrome in a horse, it is wise to stick to those guidelines. But there is still one problem: we still don't know exactly which structures are involved!

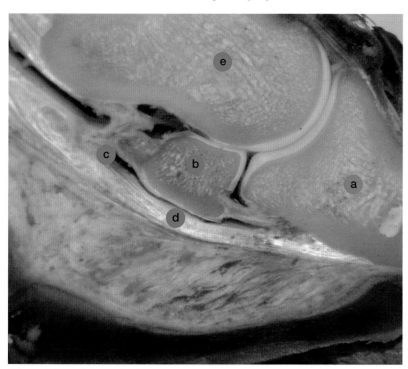

A lateral view of the navicular bone and bursa, and their relationship to the coffin joint: a) pedal bone; b) navicular bone; c) navicula bursa; d) deep digital flexor tendon; e) pastern

To complicate matters further, radiographs can only rule out other bony (osseous) causes of lameness.

Radiographs alone cannot be used to diagnose navicular syndrome in the horse.

This conclusion came as the result of bitter experience to the equine world. When I was a student, everyone was taking x-rays of the navicular bone and counting the number of enlarged fossae on it; depending on their size and shape, they were given different names ('lollipops', 'cones') and points. You then totalled up the points, and if you were over a certain number, the horse had navicular disease!

The problem with navicular disease, as it was called then, was that it didn't take into account any of the soft tissue structures mentioned previously! I can remember looking at radiographs of grand prix showjumpers, and based on the x-rays, fighting a nervous twitch to put them down. But they were sound! On the other hand, some horses with hardly an inclusion on the navicular bone were lame. Once this great discrepancy was realized, the disease name was changed to navicular syndrome, and everyone held up their hands in despair until the MRI came on to the scene.

This does not mean that radiographs should not be employed at all: what it does mean, is that they should be used in conjunction with clinical observations. In addition to the lateromedial and dorsopalmar views, a pedal bone view, 'Oxspring', and skyline view is necessary for a complete radiographic analysis. In order to alleviate radiographic scatter the shoes should be removed prior to radiographing, and the frog and hoof cleaned and trimmed. A contrast material such as Playdough should be packed into the frog on the Oxspring view.

The following changes can be found on the navicular bone:
1. A central lesion or cyst on the navicular bone, indicative of bone resorption and necrosis.

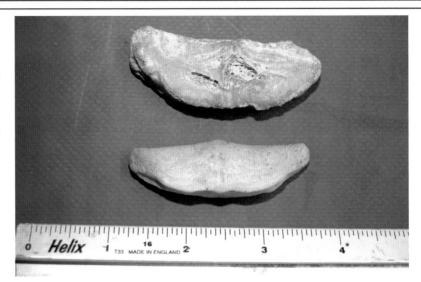

Two navicular bones. The lower one has normal pathology, the upper one has a central lesion

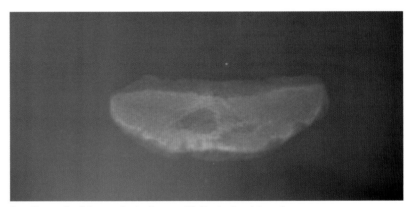

A radiograph of the navicular bone with the lesion (above)

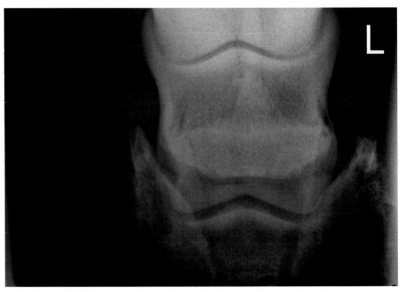

A radiograph of a horse suffering from navicular syndrome with only moderate x-ray findings

2. Enlarged fossae formation which, particularly when combined with sclerosis, may indicate concurrent coffin joint synovitis.
3. Calcifications or 'spurs' of the proximal suspensory ligaments, indicative of strain.
4. Remodelling of the proximal and distal borders, again indicative of ligament strain.
5. Flexor cortex changes, which are evidence of DDFT damage. Note that these changes can only be found on the skyline view.

Treatment: The focus should be on rebalancing and supporting the heels, and treatment of the inflammation. The hoof/pastern axis should be corrected if necessary, and when shoeing, two basic principles should be adhered to:

- Firstly, it is important to allow an easy breakover of the foot so that pressure is taken off the coffin joint; this can easily be achieved, for example, by using quarter-clipped shoes set under the foot.
- Secondly, heel support is essential; again, this is easily managed by using a closed-bar shoe such as an egg-bar. However, in my opinion, if egg-bar shoes are used over long periods of time, they can cause a collapsing and constricting of the heels, particularly in horses with an upright conformation. I prefer a short-tongued heart-bar shoe which applies pressure through the centre of the frog in an attempt to support the heels, while at the same time using the action of the frog to circulate blood through them.

It should be emphasized that there is no singular way to shoe a horse suffering from navicular disease. All sorts of orthopaedic shoes have been tried in the past, from wedges to natural balance shoes. Therefore, it pays to keep an open mind when it comes to shoeing, particularly when it is not always possible to know exactly what is going on within those heels. If one type of shoe doesn't appear to be helping or, worse, seems to be hindering things, then change it! An open discussion with your farrier is always helpful. I always have horses suffering from navicular syndrome reshod first before attempting any other treatment: that way, I can ascertain if there has been an improvement.

Horses suffering from navicular syndrome often suffer from a synovitis (inflammation) of the coffin joint. This can be judged while blocking the coffin joint. Given the fact that the coffin joint usually communicates with the navicular bursa, I will usually treat the coffin joint first with a combination of hyuloronic acid and methylprednisolone. If only limited improvement is experienced, then it is wise to resort to injecting long-acting corticosteroids directly into the navicular bursa.

The systemic use of NSAIDs can also be beneficial as can joint supplementation. Isoxsuprine to enhance blood circulation and warfarin to act as a thinning agent to the blood have also been used with varying success. It has recently been proposed that cartrophen has a synegistic chondroprotective effect when used with glucosamine.

If these treatment methods prove unsuccessful, then a referral for an MRI scan is sensible, as damaged soft tissue such as an insertional desmopathy of the DDFT must be suspected.

It has been reported that in some cases, a desmotomy of the navicular suspensory ligaments can also be effective.

As a last resort, the removal of the palmar digital nerves (neurectomy) can be contemplated. However, the ethics of such a procedure must be contemplated, as a neurectomy is not a treatment of the condition per se, rather a removal of the pain. The pathology is still present, and in some cases continues to grumble on. It should also be remembered that in the hands of an unscrupulous or ignorant client, the welfare of the horse will suffer. Without conscientious daily scrutiny of the feet, problems such as lacerations, infections, foreign bodies and suchlike, will go un noticed.

Navicular bone fracture

Fractures of the navicular bone (distal sesamoid bone) are rare. When they occur, they do so predominantly in the forelimbs. Fractures can be categorized as avulsion or chip fractures, simple and comminuted complete fractures. The majority of fractures occur secondary to bone demineralization in horses suffering from navicular syndrome. Rare cases may occur as a direct consequence of trauma or following a puncture wound to the navicular bursa resulting in an osteomyelitis.

Symptoms may be either acute or chronic. A palmar digital nerve block will improve, but seldom alleviate the lameness. Quality radiographs are needed to diagnose the condition. These require careful trimming of the frogs, and packing out the sulci (with Playdough for instance) in order to alleviate artefacts which may look like fracture lines. It should be remembered, however, that artefactual lines travel beyond the navicular bone.

Treatment: This condition requires similar treatment to that of navicular syndrome. However, a minimum of six months stable rest is necessary in order to achieve a union of the fragments. The use of wedged four pads cut at a three degree angle each under the shoes, removing one each month, is supposed to reduce the tension and compression forces on the navicular bone. Fixation of fragments using a single cortical bone screw is possible, although the value of such a procedure in severely diseased bone is questionable. The prognosis for a full return to work is poor. A neurectomy can be considered in unresponsive cases.

Pedal bone fractures

These fractures can occur either as a wing fracture or intra-articularly. Both usually present as an acute high-grade lameness shortly after athletic activity, such as racing, polo, and so on. I have also seen several wing fractures following a slip and fall on pavement.

Wing fractures are painful upon examination with hoof testers. Similarly, rapping the affected outside wing of the hoof with hoof testers will also elicit a painful response. Radiographs should be taken from all views, including oblique views. Undisplaced fractures are not always evident initially. Repeat radiographs taken approximately two weeks later will allow you better visualization due to the ensuing lysis around the fracture area.

Treatment: Prolonged stable rest and surgical shoeing with quarter-clipped egg-bar shoes to allay hoof movement. Casting is usually not necessary. Healing will usually be resolved in six months, though in some cases this may be longer. Follow-up radiographs should be taken to monitor progress.

Although intra-articular fractures may heal conservatively, because of the inconsistency of results, additional internal fixation using a lag-screw technique is recommended. However, this operative technique suffers from two disadvantages:
1. The screw does need to be removed following successful healing.
2. Given the difficulty with pre- and post-operative hygiene, osteomyeleitis of the pedal bone may ensue.

Pedalosteitis

As the name implies, pedalosteitis is an inflammation of the pedal bone resulting in a widening of the blood vessels, bone lysis and periosteal new bone formation, as well as rarefaction around the distal edge of the pedal bone, particularly the toe area. In most cases, this inflammation is a response to chronic bruising that is caused by

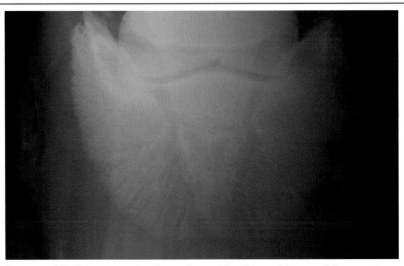

An unusual finding was made after radiographing this pedal bone. A bone cyst was discovered in the coffin joint

poor hoof conformation exacerbated by exercise on hard surfaces. It generally affects the forelimbs and is bilateral, although each limb may be affected to varying degrees.

Examination will reveal a mild to moderate pulse in the foot which can increase in intensity when examined immediately after walking. Hoof testers will elicit a painful response along the entire sole, with increased sensitivity in the heel and toe. When trotted, horses that are suffering from pedalosteitis will suffer from a shuffling, stuffy forelimb stride.

An abaxial or ring block to P3 will alleviate the lameness. Radiographs should be used in order to confirm the diagnosis.

Treatment: Rebalancing the feet and reshoeing the horse on seated-out shoes to take off the pressure from the sole is necessary. Bar shoes (egg-bar, straight-bar, short-tongued heart-bar) are advisable, at least in the short term. Pads are generally not beneficial as these tend to retain moisture and soften the sole. However, modern rubber adhesives that stick directly to the sole can be effective in reducing the amount of concussion to the foot. A course of NSAIDs is advisable. Stable rest need only be employed in severe cases.

Pyramidal disease

This term is applied to hooves that display a misshapen section of dorsal hoof wall, which appears as a bulge at the height of the coronary band and gradually extends downwards towards the sole. This malformation of horn should be seen as an indicator of underlying pathology which may or may not be a cause of lameness. The most common pathologies include large fractures of the extensor process of the pedal bone, or low ringbone formation. Lameness usually involves the coffin joint. Radiographs and a coffin joint block are essential to determine the extent of coffin joint degeneration.

Treatment: Intra-articular medication of the coffin joint should be included. If a chip of the extensor process has occured, this can be removed arthroscopically.

Quittor

A chronic infection of the lateral cartilage; this is usually preceded by an injury to the area. It is rare for the affected horse to be lame. As there is no blood supply to the cartilage, it is prone to infection. For this reason, quittor cannot usually be treated conservatively with the use of antibiotics.

Treatment: Surgical removal of the infected cartilage is indicated in cases of Quittor.

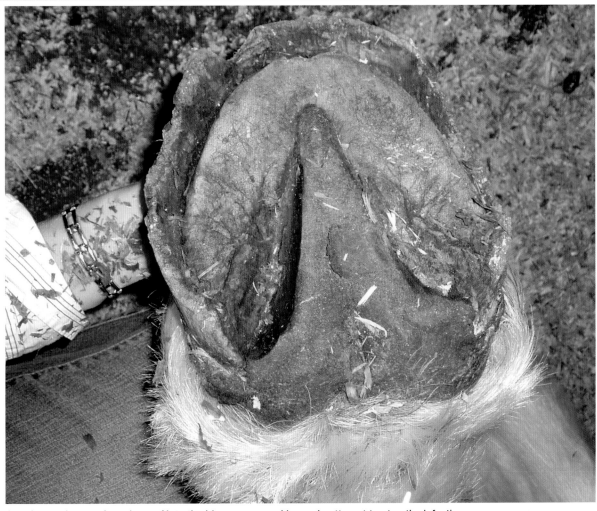

An advanced case of seedy toe. Note the blue spray, used in a vain attempt to stop the infection

Seedy toe

Occurs in areas where there is a separation between the laminae and the hoof wall. The hollow space fills with debris, which is a fertile breeding ground for bacteria, causing recurrent hoof abscesses. Post-laminitic horses are prone to this condition, but it can also occur in animals with excessively long toes. Examination of the sole of the hoof reveals a widening of the white line, and a light rapping on the dorsal wall of the hoof will emit a hollow sound.

Treatment: In these cases treatment can be difficult and prolonged. Radiographs should be taken to determine how much toe can be removed. In difficult cases, a partial hoof wall resection is indicated. The hoof wall is removed, along with all the underlying dead material, until healthy tissue is uncovered. It is advisable to bandage the exposed area for several days, taking care to keep the area clean. Topical antibacterial treatments with iodine or formalin are also beneficial. Then the area should be sealed completely, usually with a commercial synthetic glue (such as Vettec).

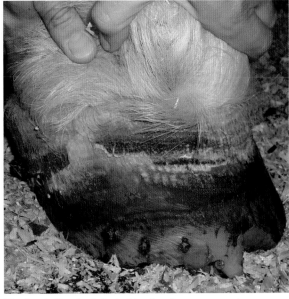

The hoof after the infected toe has been removed

Sidebone

Refers to a calcification of the lateral cartilage wings. Although this can be palpated, lateral and dorsopalmar radiographs are useful. Lameness is rare unless it involves a fracture. This is not to be confused with separate centres of ossification of the cartilage. Horses with chronically imbalanced feet often show extensive unilateral sidebone proliferation.

Treatment: Horses suffering with fractures should be shod with close-bar shoes and stable rested for up to six months. Imbalanced feet should be correctively shod.

Thrush

A bacterial infection of the sulci of the frog, which emits a characteristic foul odour. It usually arises from prolonged stabling in moist and unhygienic conditions, and careless management where the sulci of the frog are not cleaned daily. Horses with collapsed heels may be particularly prone. If untreated, the infection can spread to deeper and more sensitive areas of the hoof, resulting in lameness.

Treatment: Clean and dry stabling are prerequisites for successful treatment. Often this should be augmented with the use of daily bandaging and the use of topical disinfectants. Frequent trimming of necrotic horn is essential, as this harbours infection. Systemic antibiotics are rarely necessary unless the deeper structures of the foot become infected.

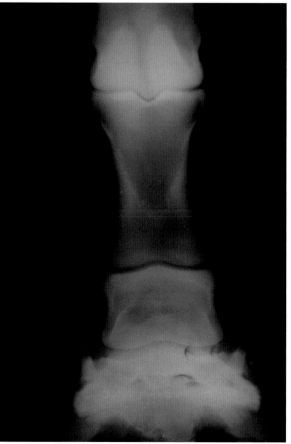

This horse has bilateral sidebone formation. This is an incidental finding and did not affect the soundness of the horse

A particularly effective way to treat infection in the heel is to pack a gauze swab into the heel and after trimming off the remaining end, pour a mixture of 5 per cent formalin and iodine into it. Change the swab twice daily. This will quickly kill off the bacteria, and more importantly, will dry the area out

Pastern problems

Fracture of the proximal phalanx

This is a common injury in athletic horses particularly, though fortunately most of these fractures remain non-comminuted. The lameness usually occurs suddenly after work, with a gradual worsening of symptoms over the following hour. Only then may swelling in the pastern area become noticeable. Palpation, particularly of the dorsal aspect of the pastern and fetlock, will be painful, as will distal limb flexion.

Pastern fractures are usually caused while the affected limb is weight-bearing and undergoes a rotation of the proximal phalanx. The convex sagittal ridge of the distal end of the third metacarpal (or metatarsal) bone then acts as a wedge to produce the fracture.

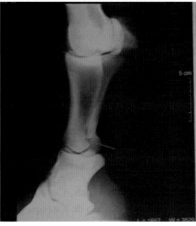

A Type 1 midsagittal fracture

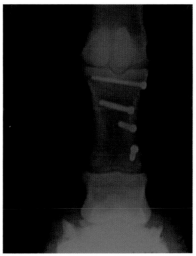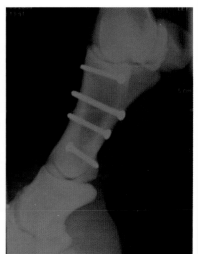

The same fracture following repair with the use of four lag screws

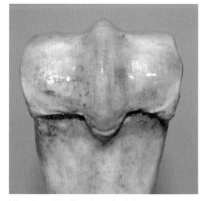

Viewing the distal end of the cannon bone, the wedge effect on the underlying bone becomes apparent

Horses suspected of having a fracture should be radiographed immediately from all angles, lateral, dorsopalmar, DPLMO and DPMLO. Particularly the dorso-palmar view is helpful. Nerve blocks should not be performed. Before transportation a dorsal splint bandage or cast should be applied.

Treatment: Non-comminuted proximal phalanx fractures have been classified into six different categories, and are treated accordingly:

Type 1: Midsagittal fractures, which are incomplete, non-articular fractures can be treated conservatively with Robert Jones bandaging and stable rest for six to ten weeks, followed by a gradual return to work. A periosteal callus usually forms over the dorsal aspect, but does not appear to affect the horse's athletic ability. Fractures any longer than 30mm (1¼in) should be operated on and fixed with two or three lag screws. Following surgery, the area should either be cast or supported with a Robert Jones bandage. Similarly, complete fractures should be internally fixated via lag screws, as this seems to produce less callus formation and joint degeneration than conservative treatment.
Type 2: Dorsal fractures.

Type 3: Distal joint fractures: these occur almost exclusively in hindlimbs, particularly in foals. Acute fractures are best treated by lag-screw fixation. In chronic cases, arthrodesis of the PIPJ is recommended.
Type 4: Palmar or plantar eminence fractures.
Type 5: Physeal fractures.
Type 6: Oblique or transvers diaphyseal fractures.

Comminuted fractures carry a much poorer prognosis for survival, particularly in those where there is no intact strut of bone present. Fixation techniques often suffer from secondary complications, notably infection. As a result, conservative treatments involving casting are recommended. If successful, these horses carry a high incidence rate of moderate to severe DJD.

123

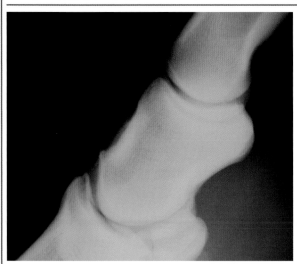
A large non-articular exostosis (low ringbone)

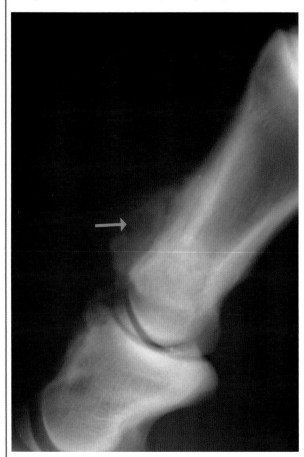
And another one higher up

Fractures of the second phalanx

The clinical history is similar to that described for fractures of the proximal phalanx. Unlike them, however, fractures of the middle phalanx occur predominantly in hindlimbs and are comminuted rather than simple fractures.

Treatment: Because accurate reduction of these fractures is difficult, arthrodesis of the proximal interphalangeal joint using three parallel cortical screws placed across the joint is recommended for all fractures involving the joint.

Ringbone (phalangeal exostosis)

A name commonly given to new bone growth in the pastern. This can be further differentiated as:

- Articular or non-articular, depending on whether the pastern or coffin joints are involved;
- High or low depending if the proximal and middle phalanx, or the middle and distal phalanx (pedal bone) are involved.

The distal area of the pastern should be palpated for signs of swelling, although the area is usually not painful to touch. Horses with non-articular ringbone may not be lame. However, if the ringbone is articular, the lameness symptoms will vary according to the extent of DJD.

An abaxial nerve block will improve the lameness, but a low four-point block is necessary to eliminate lameness. Additional intra-articular blocks and radiographs should be performed to ascertain joint involvement.

Treatment: Chronic cases are difficult to treat. Lameness involving the proximal interphalangeal joint can be improved through arthrodesis, particularly in hindlimbs. However, this cannot be recommended for distal interphalangeal joint problems. Here, intra-articular joint injections involving long-acting corticosteroids and/or hyuloronic acid in combination with systemic use of NSAIDs should be attempted. In all cases, remedial shoeing to correct balance and ease the breakover is important. Early stages of the condition can benefit from restriction of movement and shockwave therapy.

Fetlock problems

Chip fracture of the proximal phalanx

Chip fractures in the fetlock joint generally occur on the medial or lateral dorsal eminence of the proximal phalanx, and can be easily visualized on a latero-medial view of the fetlock joint. Oblique views should be used to determine which dorsal eminence is involved. The dorsal pouch of the joint may be distended. However, in many cases these chips may not produce lameness, and their finding may be incidental. It is therefore necessary to anaesthetize the fetlock joint to ascertain the significance of the chip.

Treatment: Fractures which cause lameness should be removed arthroscopically. If cartilage erosion is found during surgery, intra-articular medication is warranted.

Chronic proliferative synovitis

This refers to a thickening of the synovial pad just within the joint capsule on the dorsal aspect of the third metacarpal bone. The ensuing low-grade forelimb lameness is usually caused by repetitive trauma. This can often be accompanied by OCD lesions. The lameness is generally unilateral, with a noticeable swelling of the dorsal pouch of the fetlock joint. Distal limb flexion exacerbates the lameness. A four-point or intra-articular joint block alleviates the lameness.

Radiography of the fetlock joint should include the latero-medial, dorso-palmar and oblique views. A characteristic indentation of the third metacarpal bone can be readily seen on the latero-medial view. Ultrasonographic examination of the pad will reveal a thickening compared to the contra-lateral joint.

Treatment: Arthroscopic debridement of the pad and any osteochondral damage. The prognosis is good.

Osteoarthritis of the fetlock joint

This is a common injury in the athletic and geriatric horse. Initially only a joint distension may be palpated; however, flexion will exacerbate the lameness. A low four-/six-point block or intra-articular anaesthesia should eliminate the lameness. Radiographs should be taken using dorso-palmar, latero-medial and oblique views.

Treatment: Early stages of osteoarthritis may be treated using systemic NSAIDs and intra-articular medication with hyaluronate, and/or corticosteroids. Higher doses of intra-articular corticosteroids may be needed in more advanced stages of the disease.

Palmar annular ligament constriction

The annular ligament is a broad, inelastic band that wraps around the back of the fetlock, binding the digital flexor tendons and their digital synovial sheath within the sesamoid groove. When one of these structures swells or the annular ligament itself contracts, the ensuing constriction causes a notch which is easily seen, particularly on the palmar aspect of the limb. Studies have shown the most frequently affected structure to be the superficial flexor tendon.

Although a palmar nerve block will improve the lameness, it will not alleviate it entirely.

In determining a suitable treatment and prognosis, the actual cause for the palmar ligament constriction needs to be ascertained. An ultrasonographic examination of the superficial and deep flexor tendon, suspensory ligament, digital sheath and annular ligament will determine which structures are involved, and if there is adhesion formation within the digital sheath. Adhesions will reduce the effectiveness of surgical treatment.

Treatment: A surgical desmotomy of a constrictive annular ligament is indicated. Although this is a simple procedure, dangerous complications involving sepsis of the tendon sheath may occur. Due to the increased visibility and minimal trauma, arthroscopic surgery has proven more beneficial in horses with adhesion formation: these can be removed with an electric burr. However, recurrence is frequent, and post-operative exercise is essential to maintain flexibility.

Only short-term improvements may be achieved by conservative therapy involving the injection of 80–120mg of methylprednisolone into the flexor tendon sheaths.

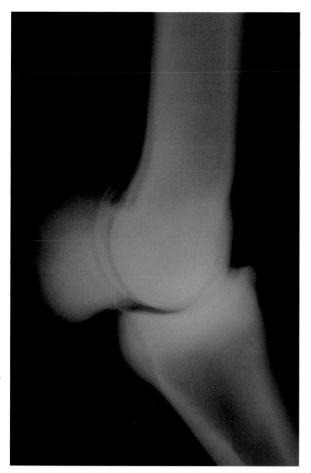

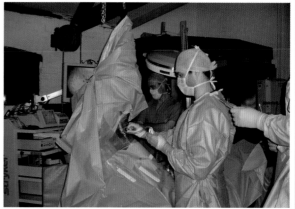

Arthroscopy is the safest and least invasive way to perform an annular ligament desmotomy

Osteoarthritis in a fetlock joint exacerbated by an OCD lesion 'chip fracture'

Proximal sesamoid fracture

Such fractures may occur either through direct trauma, or more frequently through hyperextension of the fetlock joint. The degree of lameness and swelling will depend on the size and location of the fragment, and the damage to the suspensory ligament. Fracture of both sesamoid bones will result in an over-extension of that joint, characterized by a dropped fetlock.

Radiography of the fetlock joint should include the latero-medial, dorso-palmar and oblique views, and if possible flexed lateral views. These will help determine whether the fracture is on the distal margins of the sesamoid bone or on the proximal palmar surface of the proximal phalanx. It is also useful to carry out an ultrasonographic examination of the suspensory ligament to aid diagnosis.

Treatment: Transported horses should be bandaged with a commercial monkey splint, or immobilized with a Robert Jones bandage or cast in order to minimize trauma to the suspensory apparatus. The treatment of proximal sesamoid fractures must be performed as soon as possible in order to achieve a favourable prognosis. Treatment will depend on the type of fracture involved: thus apical fractures involving less than one third of the sesamoid bone warrant surgical removal. The prognosis is good for these, provided there is no major damage to the suspensory ligament.

Basilar fractures, and fractures involving more than one third of the sesamoid bone, should be surgically stabilized with cortical bone screws or cerclage wire. Conservative attempts involving immobilization in a cast, and up to a year of stable rest, may have limited success.

Sesamoiditis

This is an inflammation of the proximal sesamoid bones and the overlying insertion of the suspensory apparatus. The clinical symptoms, including lameness, range from mild to acute. The area may be swollen, and painful to palpation and flexion. The lameness can be greatly improved with a four-/six-point block.

Radiographs taken of the fetlock joint should include the latero-medial, dorso-palmar and oblique views; these views will show increased vascularization and entheseophyte production along the sesamoid bones.

The condition often occurs simultaneously with suspensory desmitis, therefore careful palpation and ultrasonographic examination of the suspensory ligament is indicated.

The prognosis for a full recovery is poor to fair, as there is frequent recurrence of the condition.

Treatment: Prolonged stable rest, combined with oral NSAIDs (phenylbutazone and isoxsuprine) are the most common treatment methods. Shockwave therapy may also be indicated.

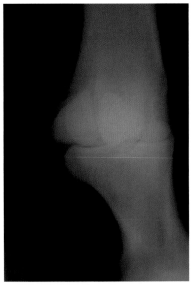

This horse received a kick which fractured its sesamoid bone. The fragments were removed, a fixation screw was not necessary

Metacarpal problems

In the course of its evolution the horse has adapted to the demand for speed combined with strength, by reducing the number of metacarpal bones needed to support its weight to one, the third metacarpal bone. Flanked on either side of it are the narrow, upside down, triangular-shaped second and fourth metacarpal bones, commonly known as splint bones. These serve only to support the carpus at their proximal end, distally forming only rudimentary bone protrusions which end at the distal third cannon.

The third metacarpal bone, flanked by the second and fourth metacarpal (splint) bones

Bucked shins (dorsal metacarpal disease)

This is a painful condition affecting the dorsal wall of the cannon bone in predominantly young racehorses. The continued stresses of high speed exercise cause periostitis and microfracturing within the yet immature cannon bones. The body adapts by producing new bone formation in this area, which can be readily seen as a swelling. The onset is usually acute following exercise, and improves after short periods of rest. The cannon bone is painful to palpation.

Nerve blocks are not usually indicated. In subacute dorsal metacarpal disease, latero-medial and dorso-palmar radiographs to the cannon bone may indicate an active periostitis, with new bone formation. Acute cases rarely show radiographic changes. Dorsal cortical fractures should be suspected in chronic cases that are unresponsive to therapy. These have a characteristic radiographic appearance, usually entering the cortex underneath distally, angling 30 to 45 degrees proximally. A periosteal callus has usually formed above the fracture line.

Treatment: Acute cases should be treated with rest, cold water hosing and bandaging in conjunction with topical and systemic NSAIDs. Most horses can be brought back into a reduced training regime after one to two weeks' rest and hand walking. High speed exercise should be halved, and only be increased as clinical signs continue to improve.

Dorsal cortical fractures may resolve after prolonged convalescent periods of up to six months. Radiographs should be taken every four to six weeks to assess healing. Unresolved cases are candidates for surgery, where a single cortical screw is placed in lag fashion; this can be difficult, due to the short depth of the cortex. Screw removal should be considered after two months, as failure to remove it will, rightly or wrongly, make it a scapegoat for future problems. The removal can be done standing. Recently, dorsal cortical drilling (osteostixis) has shown similar success rates (80 per cent) with a shorter convalescent period. In this procedure, five to seven holes are drilled through the cortex in a diamond pattern in an effort to induce healing. This can be performed in the standing horse.

Studies indicate that horses trained on turf have a lesser incidence rate of bucked shins than those trained on a wood-fibre track. Dirt tracks produced the highest rates of the condition.

Cannon bone fractures

Transverse fractures of the cannon bone are usually due to direct trauma, such as a kick. If the fracture is open, these carry a very poor prognosis and euthanasia is often the only justifiable course of action. Effective immobilization is of paramount importance, before transportation to a surgical facility. Only a small proportion of mid-metacarpal fractures will heal with

conservative therapy. In these cases, full limb casting for up to six months is necessary, as non-union and delayed union are frequent complications. The most effective form of treatment is internal fixation using a combination of compression plates and screws. However, the sheer forces of the horse's weight often lead to drastic rupture of the fracture line. Even given an assisted recovery, a particularly vulnerable time occurs during the wake-up period following general anaesthesia.

Condylar fractures occur more frequently after strenuous exercise. Fractures of the lateral condyle are more common. Palpation of the dorsal metacarpus reveals pain either over the lateral or medial surface.

Radiographically, most fractures can easily be seen using a dorso-palmar view. However, oblique radiographs may be necessary to demonstrate smaller fissure lines.

Treatment: Undisplaced condylar fractures can be treated conservatively with a knee-high cast. However, displaced fractures must undergo internal fixation using cortical bone screws before being cast or immobilized via a Robert Jones bandage. In most cases, removal of the cortical screws is not necessary unless lysis develops around the screw heads.

Inferior check ligament desmitis

The check ligament originates on the palmar surface of the distal carpal bones and extends distally, enveloping the deep digital flexor tendon until 'melting' within it around mid-cannon. If the check ligament is the only structure injured, this will cause only a mild forelimb lameness. A clinical examination will reveal swelling to the area, and palpation will elicit a painful response. The diagnosis should be confirmed with the use of an ultrasonographic examination.

Treatment: Whilst stable rest is generally only necessary for several weeks, followed by a controlled exercise programme, a full return to

exercise should not be allowed for at least six months.

Splint

The term 'splint' is often used to describe swellings on the second and fourth metacarpal bones. These can be due to localized trauma or imbalance. For instance, pigeon-toed horses often have splints on their medial splint bones, as these are placed under more strain. The localized inflammation of the bone (osteitis) and periosteum (periostitis) causes new bone growth. *Splints are often difficult to differentiate from splint fractures*. If there is any doubt, they should be radiographed before injection of corticosteroids into the area.

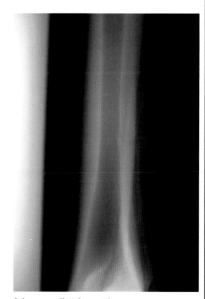

A large splint formation

Treatment: Splints should be treated promptly and aggressively to limit the amount of new bone growth. Cold hosing of the area, systemic use of NSAIDs, bandaging and topical applications of DMSO or even injections of 20–40mg of a long-acting corticosteroid such as methylprednisolone acetate subperiosteally will limit the formation of new bone growth. Not only are large splints unsightly, but their protrusion leaves them more exposed to further trauma, that is, continual flare-ups, resulting in yet further new bone formation. If

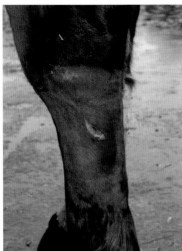

A typical kick wound...

...leading to a fractured splint bone

this begins to impinge upon the suspensory apparatus, the horse will go lame.

Surgical removal is the only treatment available for large splints that are unresponsive to treatment or impinge upon the suspensory ligament. The area is exposed, the periosteum carefully pealed back, and the splint is physically removed with the use of osteotomes. However, the chance of recurrence is high, and the same emphasis on aftercare applies here as for the treatment of splint bone fractures (below). Recent studies indicate that splint removal with the use of an oscillating saw may in fact be less traumatizing to the periosteum.

Splint bone fractures (second and fourth metacarpal bones)

Given their fragility, particularly distally, the fourth (lateral) and second (medial) splint bones are prone to fracturing. A fracture of the lateral splint bone is often due to a kick from another horse. Lower fractures are often accompanied by mild to moderate swelling of the cannon bone, but horses are usually able to walk without undue discomfort or difficulty. Palpation of the area is painful.

Owners can often mistakenly believe to have remedied the problem through cold hosing and bandaging, as the swelling subsides.

However, as soon as the horse begins to walk without a bandage, the area swells once again, due to the unstable fragments irritating the surrounding tissue. It is imperative to radiograph these cases.

Treatment: Although stable rest and bandaging alone will often suffice for the fragments to heal, this is often accompanied by extensive callus (new bone) formation. Not only is the swelling unsightly, but over time, it may impinge upon the suspensory apparatus, resulting

in chronic lameness. It is therefore recommended that all fractures involving the distal two-thirds of the joint be removed. In order to remove the fracture and damaged periosteum, it is preferable to perform surgery on the operating table. If this is not possible, however, simple fractures can be removed in the standing horse.

Proximal splint bone fractures should be stabilized with small bone plates and/or cortical screws.

In order to achieve good cosmetic results, it is important to minimize the swelling to the area. Approximately eight weeks of stable rest, combined with bandaging and NSAIDs, are usually necessary before the horse can commence work. Carelessness during the convalescence time, or a return to work early, will stimulate unwanted callus formation.

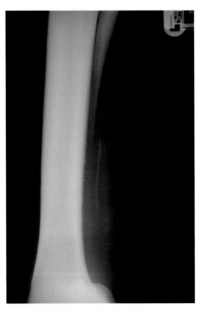

A distal fracture of the fourth metacarpal bone

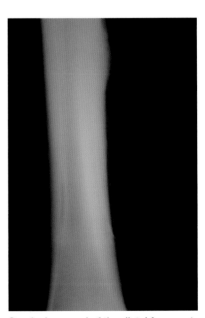

Surgical removal of the distal fragment will ensure an uncomplicated healing process

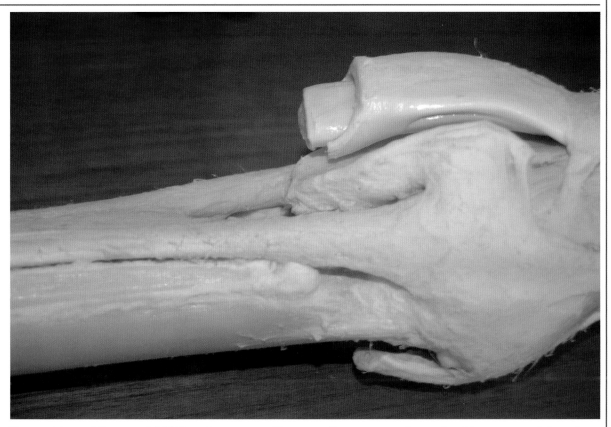

The overlying soft tissue and DDFT have been removed to expose the suspensory ligament as it branches medially and laterally just above the fetlock

Suspensory ligament desmitis

The suspensory ligament lies sheltered between the second and fourth metacarpal/tarsal bones at the palmar/plantar aspect of the cannon. It should be pictured as a slightly oval, thick fibrous band which extends distally from its origin at the proximal cannon bone until it divides just above the fetlock joint into medial and lateral branches which attach to the abaxial surface of the sesamoid bones. Damage to the suspensory ligament can occur to the insertion, body or branches.

Lameness can often be subtle. With the horse standing, the leg should be carefully palpated for signs of heat or swelling. Then holding the leg with one hand, carefully palpate the surface of the suspensory ligament down its entire length. Do not apply undue pressure as this will always produce a painful reaction, even in a healthy suspensory ligament. Always compare your findings with the opposite leg, as this will help you gauge if you are dealing with an overly sensitive horse, or if you have indeed found a sore area.

Provided the lesion is not in the lower branches of the suspensory ligament, *the lameness can often be exacerbated by an abaxial nerve block:* the nerve block causes a slight relaxation and subsequent lowering of the fetlock area, which forces the suspensory ligament to stretch a bit more, so that when the horse is trotted up, the damaged, over-stretched ligament is more painful.

A subcarpal or a subtarsal nerve block will alleviate the lameness.

An ultrasound scan is invaluable for visualizing the pathology within the suspensory ligament. However, it should be remembered that many artefacts can be seen on an ultrasound scan which may not necessarily be the cause of lameness. (Important pointers regarding ultrasound anatomy are given on pages 130–131, and the correct use of the ultrasound scanner on page 72.) Let it suffice here to give the following advice when a suspensory ligament lesion is suspected:

1. Always nerve block the limb in order to ascertain the area of the lameness.
2. Radiographs of the limb are helpful, as fractures of the medial splint bone often accompany suspensory ligament injuries. They can also reveal damage to the sesamoid bones where the suspensory ligament branches insert. Radiographs can be particularly helpful when insertional desmopathies are suspected. These often show sclerosis of the cannon bone, enthesiophyte production or even avulsion fractures in the area of the suspensory insertion.
3. Ultrasonographic findings in one limb should always be compared to the opposite limb. Furthermore, it should be remembered that there is always an area of hypoechogenicity in the insertion of the suspensory ligament.

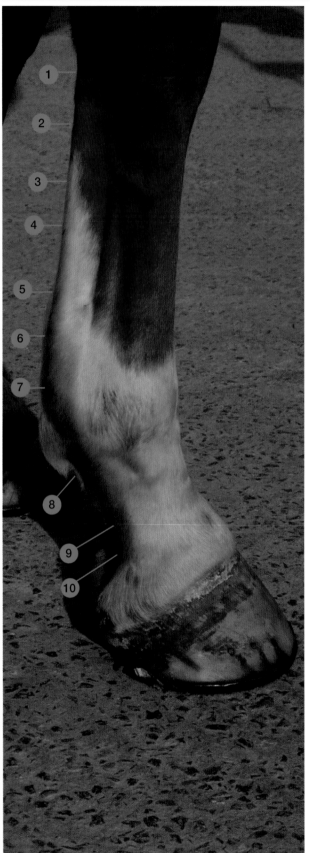

Treatment: Rest is the most important treatment for suspensory injuries. Depending on the severity of the lesion, horses should be confined to stable rest or limited turnout in a small, level paddock. The acute phase of the injury should be treated with the judicious use of systemic and local anti-inflammatories, and with bandaging and cold hosing. Shockwave therapy has also proved helpful in the treatment

KEY

CL Check ligament

SDFT Superficial digital flexor tendon

DDFT Deep digital flexor tendon

SUS Suspensory ligament

CAN Canon bone

V Vein

CC Carpal canal

DS Digital sheath

SB Sesamoid bone

IL Intersesamoidean ligament

OBSL Oblique Intersesamoidean ligament

P1 Phalanx 1

P2 Phalanx 2

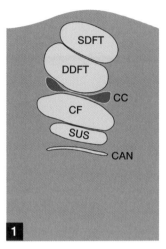

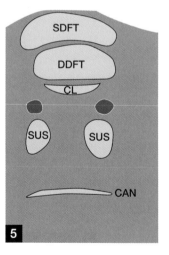

Ultrasound scans of the suspensory apparatus at the numbered points indicated (left) reveal the internal structures shown in the diagrams (right)

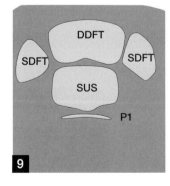

of suspensory ligament damage. Controlled exercise during the following six to twelve months is essential. Follow-up scans will determine the extent of healing. Turnout or exercise in deep mud should be avoided at all costs, as this will further damage the already weakened suspensory ligament.

A complete rupture of the suspensory apparatus can occur, particularly during racing or speed training, when the affected horse is severely lame. If forced to bear weight, the palmar aspect of the fetlock sinks towards the ground. These horses will not return to athletic pursuits. If treatment is opted for, this should be immediate and should consist of a cast to support the fetlock and prevent further soft tissue damage. Radiographs should be performed, as the sesamoid bones may be fractured.

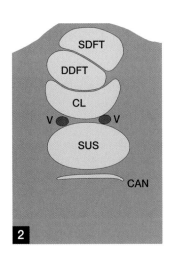

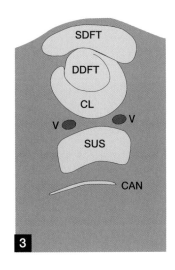

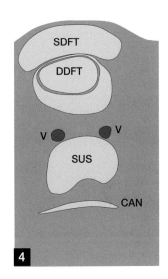

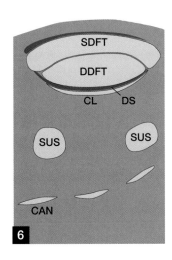

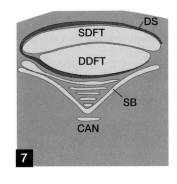

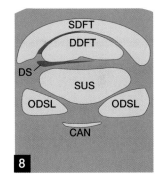

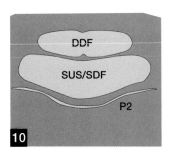

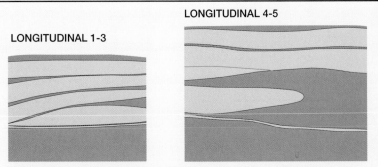

Holding the scanner head perpendicular to the tendons will produce a transverse scan of these structures

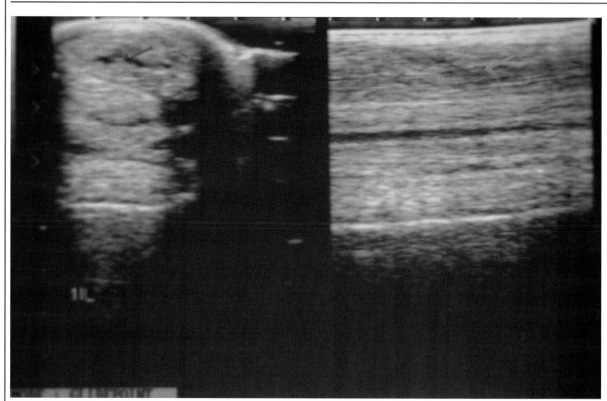

A large lesion in the superficial digital flexor tendon

Tendonitis

Lying directly over the suspensory ligament, first the deep and then the superficial digital flexor tendons complete the palmar/plantar aspect of the metacarpal/metatarsal area. As their name implies, they are responsible for the flexion of the distal limb. Tendonitis occurs only rarely in the hindlimb. In the forelimb, the overwhelming majority of tendon injuries occur in the superficial digital flexor tendon (SDFT). As the cross-section of the tendon is smallest and therefore weakest mid-cannon, it is not surprising that most SDFT injuries occur here. The characteristic swelling in this area gives rise to the term 'bowed' tendon.

Note that it is only horses with moderate to severe tendon damage that show lameness! Minor tendon injuries only show a small amount of heat and swelling.

Care and attention should be paid to these symptoms in order to avoid subsequential disastrous tendon damage.

As with the suspensory ligament, picking up the leg and palpating the length of the deep and superficial flexor tendons for a painful response is the most important method of diagnosing acute tendon injuries. Always compare your findings to that of the opposite leg!

Chronic tendon injuries are easily recognizable, as the scar tissue formed increases the thickness of the tendon. However, the scar tissue is composed of type III collagen, which is always of inferior strength to normal type I collagen. In addition, the normal longitudinal formation of the individual tendon fibres is also disrupted, causing a reduction in the overall elasticity of the tendon.

Treatment: Horses that are suffering from acute tendonitis should always be cold-hosed and bandaged, and should then be stable rested. Extensively damaged tendons should be supported on the spot where the damage has occurred so as to avoid any further injury to the tendon structure. If necessary, a cast or Robert Jones bandage should be applied. Systemic anti-inflammatories should also be prescribed.

Water therapy plays a vital role in the reduction of swelling, and the affected limbs should be cold-hosed twice daily. In the later stages of rehabilitation, water treadmill therapy may also be considered.

'Core lesions' in the SDFT are well defined areas within the tendon in which the tendon fibres have been broken. Over the years, a number of therapeutic agents have been used to inject into these lesions in the attempt to increase the quality of healing. These include hyaluronate, said to reduce the number of adhesions, and beta-aminoproprionitrile (BAPN), a medication that is said to increase collagen cross-linking. The most promising results have been achieved recently with the use of stem cells, available generically (A-cell) or cultivated from cells removed from the individual animal's bone marrow.

A superior check ligament desmotomy has been advocated as part of the treatment in SDFT lesions.

The main difficulty in the treatment of tendon injuries is the poor blood circulation found in these tissues, and the lack of understanding of the pathophysiology within these structures. Hence a wide variety of often spurious and primitive methods has been employed to help increase the blood flow within the tendon tissue. 'Blistering' as well as 'firing' are both designed to produce a localized irritation to the area in the hopes that the increased blood flow will assist with the healing process. Much can be said against these methods, but particularly within racing circles they are still frequently employed, and until we fully understand the tendon's function, they shall continue to be so.

No matter what treatment method is employed, a simple rule of thumb is six months off for SDFT injuries, and twelve months off for DDFT lesions.

← ↑ Tendon injuries often afflict athletic horses

133

Conditions of the Upper Forearm

Carpal problems

Hygroma of the carpus

This refers to a large subcutaneous swelling of the dorsal aspect of the carpus, usually immediately following trauma to the area. Neither palpation nor flexion elicits a painful response. Radiographs should be made to ensure that there is no carpal bone involvement. A contrast media should be injected into the hygroma to ensure that there is no synovial hernia or fistula. These conditions require surgical intervention.

Treatment: In the acute stages, drainage of the fluid and injection with corticosteroids and pressure bandaging can be attempted, to reduce the size of the hygroma. In chronic cases, a penrose drain will need to be sutured in place for a week, with a sterile pressure bandage being reapplied daily.

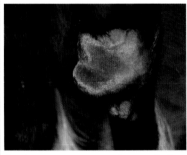

The knee is a frequent place to find foreign bodies. Here an abscess is removed

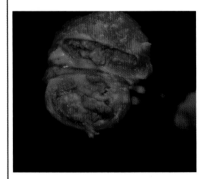

Fracture of the radius

This is almost always the result of a kick, the fracture usually occurring mid-shaft. The prognosis is very poor, and the only available treatment – internal fixation using two bone plates placed laterally and cranially – is very expensive. Compound fractures in which the skin is pierced further worsen the prognosis.

Treatment: Most animals that have sustained this type of injury are euthanased. If surgery is opted for, the immediate immobilization of the forearm is crucial, using a large Robert Jones bandage strengthened dorsally and laterally with timber.

More distal fractures of the radius can sometimes be treated using external immobilization alone.

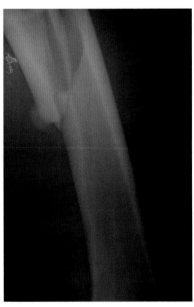

This horse suffered a radial fracture following a kick. The prognosis for a full recovery after such an injury is poor

Fracture of the ulna

Fractures of the ulna carry a much better prognosis than that for the radius. Following direct trauma to the area (probably a kick or a fall), the leg becomes non-weight-bearing and the animal is unable to extend the elbow. In addition to swelling, crepitus may be felt. Latero-medial radiographs should be taken.

Treatment: Non-displaced distal fractures can be treated conservatively. However, more proximal fractures should be treated surgically using a dynamic compression plate placed along the caudal border of the olecranon and the ulna. This will prevent the pull of the triceps muscle from displacing the fractures.

If the fracture involves the elbow joint, subsequent degenerative joint disease may cause a chronic low-grade lameness in this area.

Hygroma of the elbow (capped elbow)

This is a subcutaneous swelling in the area of the elbow. Unless the skin is damaged and becomes infected, it is not painful and is mainly a cosmetic blemish. It is caused either by not enough depth of bedding, or from the shoe rubbing as the horse is lying down.

Treatment: Similar to the treatment of other hygroma, acute conditions can be treated by injecting cortico-steroids locally. In more persistent cases of the condition surgical drainage and skin resection can be used to help avoid the chance of recurrence. Most importantly, deep bedding should be employed.

Shoulder problems

Although a favourite diagnosis of inexperienced horsemen, true shoulder lameness is uncommon in horses and ponies.

Bicipital bursitis

Viewing the horse from the side, the downward slope of the shoulder ends in a point, and it is here that the tendon of the biceps brachii runs through the intertubercular groove of the humerus. To help cushion and protect the tendon, the bicipital bursa is also located here. This exposed position makes it vulnerable to external trauma. A clinical examination reveals pain, heat and swelling to the area. The animal is markedly lame, but able to bear weight on the affected leg. Flexion and abduction of the leg are also painful. Radiography of the area is difficult as the necessary stretching of the limb may not be well tolerated. Ultrasound will reveal an increase of fluid in the bursa.

Treatment: Most cases respond to rest and systemic anti-inflammatories. Open wounds in this area almost always involve an infection of the bicipital bursa. Fluid samples should be collected in order to confirm the suspicion. In the meantime, broad-spectrum antibiotic therapy is indicated.

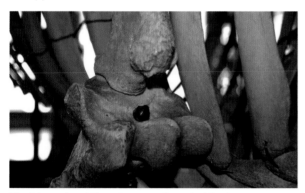

The biceps brachii tendon runs through this, the intertubercular groove of the humerus. A kick here can cause acute lameness without bone damage

Humeral fractures

Given the muscle mass surrounding the humerus, any fracture of this bone may be difficult to diagnose and/or radiograph. However, the prognosis for a humeral fracture is slightly better than for other long-bone fractures. Extensive manipulation is not indicated due to the proximity of the radial nerve.

Treatment: Recent studies indicate that conservative therapy carried a greater chance of success than surgical intervention. Healing is slow, however, the only sensible measures being limited support of the limb via a Robert Jones bandage. I prefer to keep horses cross-tied for several weeks with their back ends placed in a corner to help support them.

Scapular fracture

Many scapular fractures will heal with conservative therapy. However, given the location of the fracture, these carry a varying prognosis: thus fractures of the scapular spine carry a good prognosis, whereas fractures of the supraglenoid tubercle or comminuted neck fractures carry a poor prognosis.

Treatment: Simple neck fractures may need internal fixation using bone plates.

Suprascapular nerve damage (Sweeney)

This damage usually occurs as the result of trauma, and results in the atrophy of the infraspinatus and supraspinatus muscles, making the scapular spine more prominent. Due to the lack of stabilization on the shoulder joint, when weight is placed on the affected limb, the shoulder joint rotates outwards.

Treatment: Stable rest and systemic anti-inflammatory therapy may be prescribed. If no improvement in nerve function is noted after twelve months, surgery to free the suprascapular nerve is indicated. Following removal of the scar tissue surrounding it, a small groove of bone is removed from the scapula to help protect the nerve. Although the prognosis is good for horses undergoing surgery, the return to full nerval function is slow.

Successful conservative treatment of humeral fractures relies on the character of the horse. This patient was confined to box rest and immobilization of the limb for six months

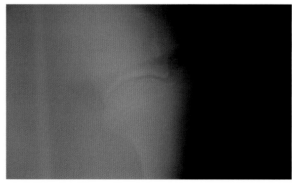

X-ray of the healing shoulder injury

Conditions of the Hindlimb

Problems in the hock

Bog spavin

This is the name given to a distension of the tibiotarsal (tarsocrural) joint with synovial fluid. The swelling is not painful to palpation. However, radiographs should always be taken to ascertain if there are any OCD (chips) present within the joint. These must be removed arthroscopically.

Treatment: If no lesions are present, drainage of the joint and an intra-articular injection with 200mg of medroxyprogesterone acetate may be attempted in order to achieve a better cosmetic result.

Bone spavin

Bone spavin refers to osteoarthritis of the tarsometatarsal and distal intertarsal joints. It is the most common cause of chronic hindlimb lameness in the horse, particularly in older animals.

The hock joint is a complex joint consisting of the high motion, low pressure tibio-tarsal joint, and the low motion but high pressure tarso-metatarsal, proximal and distal intertarsal joints. Due to the high pressures and torque movement exerted upon them, focal necrosis of the joint cartilage occurs more readily. The resulting cell degeneration leads to a progressively aggressive and deteriorating joint environment, which in turn causes further joint cartilage destruction. The joint surface and underlying bone continue to erode, whilst at the same time the body compensates by producing new bone. This ongoing process continues along the entire joint margin. Gradually the distance between the joints (joint margin) narrows, and local fusing occurs (sclerosis). The end stage is the complete destruction and fusion (ankylosis) of the joint.

Once a complete fusion has occurred, these destructive processes cease and so does the pain. Because the joints involved are

low-motion joints which do not affect the mechanics and movement of the tibio-tarsal joint, the horse becomes sound, losing only that minor bit of flexibility that a healthy multi-joint construction would have afforded it.

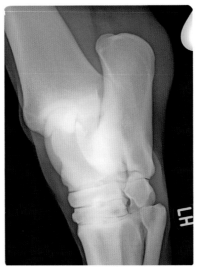

A horse suffering from bone spavin will often have an excess of bone growth in this area

This hock shows a slight narrowing of the tarso-metatarsal joint. This is a common finding in older horses and may or may not be the cause of lameness

Horses with chronic bone spavin – that is, are still in the stage of joint destruction and bone production without fusion – will show a reluctance to 'step under' with their hindlimbs. The condition is usually bilateral. No real power is gained from the hindquarters as proper engagement is impossible. Chronically affected horses may show gluteal muscle wastage. The lameness can be exacerbated on a 15m circle, particularly in the transition from trot to canter. Affected horses often 'bunny hop' hectically or kick out, and their owners often misinterpret these actions as playfulness or even naughtiness.

Palpation of the hock joints will usually not reveal anything of significance, except in cases of chronic spavin where the 'seat of spavin' on the medial aspect of the distal intertarsal and tarso-metatarsal joint reveals a marked bony exostosis.

Flexion of the hock joint is usually positive.

Confirmation of the diagnosis should be made via intra-articular anaesthesia of the tarso-metatarsal and distal intertarsal joints. Following a positive result, radiographs should be taken from both the lateral-medial, dorso-plantar and oblique views. It is imperative that the legs are straight, and that the x-ray machine is focused directly on to the hock joints, otherwise radiographs will not be diagnostic. For instance, if the x-ray beam does not travel directly into the joint margin before hitting the plate, but travels at an angle from either above or below the joint, the joint margins will overlap each other, and will falsely cause the impression of a joint narrowing. As new bone production (entheseophyte) can be most readily seen on the oblique views, it is vital that the correct angles are used. Because of these difficulties, and also the need for accuracy, it is often wiser to have affected horses radiographed where there are proper developing or digital facilities.

Treatment of the condition centres around alleviating pain and helping to encourage the breakdown of the joints until complete fusion is achieved. In some cases, NSAIDs and daily exercise may be sufficient. In addition to this, however, most horses benefit from intra-articular medication using a long-acting corticosteroid. It may be necessary to repeat these injections from time to time.

Unfortunately, it is not possible to predict how effective intra-articular corticosteroid therapy is, how long the effects will last, and how many injections will be necessary in order to complete fusion: some horses need only be injected once or twice, whilst in other patients the injection appears to wear off after only a few short weeks.

It should be remembered that, over time, all horses will begin to show wear and tear in their joints, particularly in the hocks, and it is up to the individual rider to understand this, and tailor the exercise programme accordingly. Horses with a history of spavin, and older horses in general, will need a longer warming-up period before engaging in athletic exercise; they cannot be asked to collect and engage right away, but will need thirty minutes or more of easy, straight-line exercise before more should be asked of them. Proper husbandry is also essential – thus it is counter-productive to stable rest a horse with spavin: it needs daily turnout and exercise to keep it from 'stiffening up' in its arthritic joints.

In some cases, wedged heel shoes may be beneficial, as they change the angle of pressure within the hock joints. In my opinion, it is better to have the wedges built on to the shoe rather than relying on plastic inserts. With wedges it is important to exercise on hard ground or road surfaces, as otherwise the effect of the wedge is lost.

Most horses are able to cope with the previously outlined measures. However, there are instances in which either the corticosteroid injections have proved ineffective, or have needed to be repeated too often in order to be practical. In my experience, hocks which display a lysis – meaning there is a continual degeneration of surrounding bone – are less responsive to these conservative measures. In these cases, arthrodesis can be achieved either chemically or through surgery.

Over the years, a number of chemicals have been injected into the hock joints of horses in order to break down the cartilage chemically and achieve complete arthrodesis. The procedure is simple and inexpensive, and on the face of it appears to be the logical alternative. However, the most commonly employed agent is sodium monoiodoacetate, which has one very important side effect: it is extremely painful for the horse, so much so, in fact, that many practitioners refuse to use it. Most recently, hock joint arthrodesis using alcohol as the chemical agent has provided good initial results. As it does not appear to be nearly as painful, it may become the drug of choice for this procedure.

Surgical arthrodesis has been well documented. The horse is put under general anaesthesia, and three 3.2mm holes are drilled through the length of the hock joint. After this procedure, arthrodesis can take up to a year.

Capped hock

A capped hock refers to a swelling at the point of the hock due to trauma. This results in an inflammation of the underlying bursa (bursitis). Fluid may accumulate there or in the subcutaneous tissue surrounding it (hygroma).

Treatment: In the initial acute phase, the area should be cold-hosed and bandaged. Medication should include local and systemic anti-inflammatories. Although the fluid could be drained and injected with corticosteroids, this mainly cosmetic procedure needs to be weighed against the risk of creating a sepsis in this area. Surgery should not be attempted.

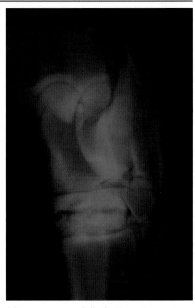

After numerous failed attempts to achieve an arthrodesis with corticosteroids, a surgical arthrodesis was attempted. This has only partially succeeded

A capped hock is best left alone

Curb

A curb refers to a plantar swelling approximately 10cm (4in) distal to the point of the hock. The aetiology is unknown, although sickle hock conformation may play a factor. Usually the swelling is due to a desmitis of the plantar ligament which has its origin on the plantar aspect of the calcaneus, running distally to its insertion on the fourth metatarsal bone. However, an ultrasonographic examination is beneficial in order to ascertain if there is additional damage to the SDFT. These patients carry a poorer prognosis to make a full recovery. In cases where trauma is suspected, radiographs may reveal a periostitis along the plantar border of the calcaneus.

Treatment in the acute phase should include systemic and local use of NSAIDs, cold hosing and bandaging. Local injection of the area with corticosteroids is also an option. Most horses make a full recovery within six weeks' time.

A curb caused by a previous injury to the area

Peroneus tertius rupture

The peroneus tertius originates on the distal part of the femur, and inserts on the dorsal aspect of the proximal third metatarsal bone. The affected animal is able to bear weight, however when it moves forwards, the hindlimb is unable to flex at the hock. An examination of the limb reveals that when the limb is lifted, it is possible to extend the hock while the stifle is flexed.

Treatment: Strict stable rest for several months is the only known treatment.

Stringhalt

Stringhalt is a term used to describe horses that suffer from the sudden involuntary flexion of one or both hindlimbs. A 'goose-stepping' gait, which subsides with exercise, is characteristic. The exact aetiology is unknown, although plant toxicity has been indicated in cases of bilateral stringhalt. Unilateral stringhalt can occur following direct trauma to the extensor tendons on the dorsal aspect of the tarsus.

Stringhalt causes a sudden flexion in the hindlimbs

Treatment: As the exact pathogenesis of the disease is unknown, the treatments are varied. Many cases will resolve spontaneously over a period of months or years. Horses suspected of suffering from plant toxicity should be relocated to different pastures. Oral phenytoin (15mg/kg bid) has been used to improve the signs of stringhalt. Baclofen, a GABA inhibitor given orally at 1mg/kg tid, has also shown some success.

Talus fracture

The talus is usually fractured by direct trauma in the form of a kick. The tarsocrural joint is effused. The degree of lameness will depend on the severity of the fragment: these can range from small fragments off the distal lateral trochlear ridge or proximal medial trochlear ridge, to complete sagittal fractures.

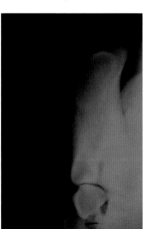

Treatment: Smaller fragments should be removed arthroscopically. In acute cases, internal fixation of the fragments is preferred to removal via arthrotomy.

A pressure necrosis to the talus is removed surgically. The dead bone material has subsequently infected the calcaneal bursa and the tarsal tendon sheath

Tarsocrural joint OCD

The tarsocrural joint is the joint most commonly affected by osteochondrosis. Often, the only symptoms are an effusion of the tarsocrural joint.

Treatment: Fragments should be arthroscopically removed if possible. If surgery is not possible, intra-articular medication will help hinder, but will not prevent further damage to the articular surface. OCD is particularly likely to occur in large horses that have grown rapidly, often due to their being overfed; Warmbloods seem particularly prone to this condition. It is advisable in high risk horses to have overview radiographs taken of their joints before they are broken in to ensure that no chip fragments are present.

Thoroughpin

A thoroughpin refers to a tenosynovitis of the tarsal sheath. Clinically, a swelling both laterally and medially above the point of the hock can be seen and palpated; it is not usually painful. This swelling must be differentiated from a false thoroughpin, which is a haematoma in the same area. Lateral-medial, dorso-plantar, oblique and skyline radiographs should be used if trauma to the area is suspected, as the sustentaculum tali may reveal exostosis. Ultrasonography of the area is also of benefit to ascertain if there are any adhesions present.

Treatment: Acute cases should be treated with cold hosing, bandaging, and the systemic use of NSAIDs. Chronic cases should be drained and injected with long-acting corticosteroids, unless lesions of the sustentaculum tali are present. It is beneficial to remove these arthroscopically, although the prognosis for a full return to work is more guarded.

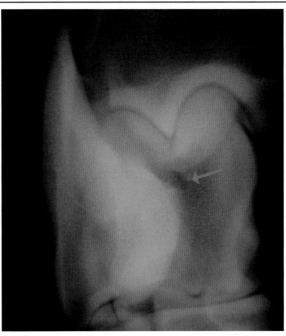

A chip fracture in the tibiotarsal joint

A large thoroughpin

Tibial fractures

Fractures of the tibia can be divided into the following three main categories:

1. Tibial stress fractures: These occur commonly in young racehorses, particularly along the lateral aspect of the proximal tibia. Fracture lines may not be visible, though later radiographs may reveal callus formation.

Treatment: At least six months of box rest is required before a return to work can be contemplated.

2. Tibial tuberosity fractures: These occur frequently through direct kicks to the stifle area. Due to its prominence, the tibial tuberosity is particularly vulnerable to fracturing, although this does not always become immediately apparent. Horses suffering from such fractures display a high-grade lameness, with swelling over the cranial aspect of the stifle. Palpation of the area is very painful.

Treatment: These fractures must be repaired surgically, usually with a dynamic compression plate. The prognosis is relatively good.

3. Diaphyseal and physeal fractures in adult horses are nearly always comminuted and open.

Treatment: Only euthanasia is appropriate in these cases. In younger horses, spiral fractures are more common and may warrant internal fixation.

Problems in the stifle

Fibrotic myopathy

This is a condition in which the semi-membranosus or semi-tendinosus muscles become damaged. Although this usually occurs through trauma, intramuscular injections and even damage of the sciatic nerve due to pelvic injury have been implicated. The condition causes a characteristic shortening of the stride, with a stamping movement of the hoof shortly before it touches the ground. Palpation of the muscles, though not painful for the horse, reveals a thickened area of tissue.

Treatment: Surgical transaction of the tendon of the semi-tendinosus muscle near its insertion on the proximal tibia will usually resolve the horse's lameness.

Gonitis

This simply means an inflammation of the joint, which may be due to soft-tissue damage or bony lesions. Intra-articular anaesthesia will help localize the lameness to the joint. It must be remembered that radiographs only reveal approximately 50 per cent of possible damage within the stifle; however, these remain invaluable for the assessment of fractures, OCD lesions and arthritic or septic conditions. Ultrasonography will help ascertain the viability of the patellar ligaments, collateral ligaments and abaxial parts of the menisci. However, the best visualization of the joint structures can only be obtained through arthroscopic examination.

Treatment: Can be achieved by eliminating the cause of the inflammation. Supportive therapy includes rest and systemic use of anti-inflammatories. Highly distended stifle joints may benefit from drainage and intra-articular medication.

Locking stifle (upward fixation of the patella)

An upward fixation of the patella occurs when the patella lodges on the proximal end of the medial trochlear ridge. Horses with straight leg conformation are prone to this condition, as well as Shetland and mini Shetland ponies. Another frequent cause can often be seen in horses that are currently not in work: the resulting loss of muscle tone in the horse's quadriceps muscle removes the tension upon the stifle, and so it becomes even more prone to locking.

Horses can be affected on one or both limbs, though usually only one at a time: the entire limb locks in extension and cannot be flexed in order to move forwards, the resulting straight leg forcing the toe to drag on the ground. Often, simply making the horse back up will remove the fixation; more stubborn cases can be manually dislodged.

Treatment: Systemic use of NSAIDs is indicated in order to help reduce the swelling in the area. If the patella locks continually, it is helpful to tape an approximately 3cm wedge of carpet underneath both heels in order to alter the angle of the stifle. If this proves helpful, then wedged shoes can be nailed or glued on by a competent farrier.

Most cases will respond well to controlled exercise, in particular walking up hills, in order to build up the quadriceps muscles. In time, the medication and wedged shoes can be withdrawn.

Chiropractic care to ensure that the pelvis is balanced and not under unequal muscular tension may also be beneficial.

Surgical intervention should only be attempted if all else fails. In the standing, sedated horse, a 2.5cm stab incision is made just proximal to the tibial crest between the middle and medial patellar ligaments. A blunt instrument such as a pair of closed scissors is pushed between the ligaments, and a blunt-nosed bistoury is then used to sever the medial patellar ligament completely. The subcutaneous tissue is left open, and only the overlying skin is sutured. Four weeks of convalescence is necessary before a return to work.

There have been cases of OCD fragmentation to the apex of the patella following surgery.

A locking stifle has a dramatic effect, particularly when it occurs bilaterally. It causes the limb to be unnaturally straight and forces the animal to drag the limb severely when attempting to move forwards

Luckily, most cases can be treated conservatively through correct trimming of the hoof, raised heel wedges, NSAIDs and exercise

Luxation of the patella

A luxation of the patella – that is, a dislocation of the patella from its normal position – can occur either through trauma or through a congenital hypoplasia (incomplete development) of the lateral trochlear ridge of the femur. The congenital form occurs predominantly in miniature horses and causes a shallowing of the trochlear groove, making it easier for the patella to slip laterally over the flat lateral trochlear ridge.

Treatment: Radiographs are important to determine the extent of the hypoplasia and assess secondary damage to the joint. Surgical correction is necessary by performing a lateral release on the tissues which support the outside of the joint and by placing tightening sutures medially (medial imbrication). In cases where there is severe flattening of the lateral trochlear ridge, the groove may be deepened surgically (trochleoplasty).

Meniscal tears
Provided they are not substantial, meniscal tears carry a reasonable prognosis for the horse's return to athletic competition.

Treatment: Arthroscopic surgery is necessary to visualize the entire extent of the damage. Furthermore, the burring away of the torn meniscal fronds helps to re-establish healthy joint healing.

Osteochondrosis dissecans of the stifle joint (OCD)
This condition occurs frequently within the horse, the predeliction site being the lateral trochlear ridge of the femur.

Treatment: OCD fragments can be removed, and damaged articular cartilage curetted. Most lesions carry a good prognosis, although the ensuing convalescent period can take up to six months.

Patellar fractures
Treatment: Patellar fractures can generally be removed arthroscopically and carry a good prognosis. Small base fractures can be treated conservatively.

Subchondral bone cysts
As their name implies, subchondral bone cysts are lesions within the articular surface of the joint cartilage, which reach into the bone matrix. Due to cartilage flaps and fronding blocking their entrance, bone cysts do not always respond to intra-articular anaesthesia.

Although the lameness usually presents unilaterally, cysts often occur bilaterally; therefore radiographs should always be taken from both stifles. It is important that latero-medial, caudo-cranial and flexed latero-medial views are taken. Care should be taken to ensure that these are not underexposed, as this may cause the cysts to be overlooked. Although cysts can present anywhere within the joint, the predilection site is the medial femoral condyle. The size of the cyst is not related to the degree of lameness exhibited.

Treatment: Conservative treatment involves paddock rest for up to a year, however the prognosis is poor. Arthroscopic surgery usually involving the curettage of the cystic cavity is indicated. Intra-lesional injection with long-acting corticosteroids, combined with micro-picking of the surface area, may also be of benefit.

Paradoxically, stifle joints that have not displayed cystic lesions and are examined arthroscopically, often suffer from subchondral bone cysts following surgery. The reason for this is unclear.

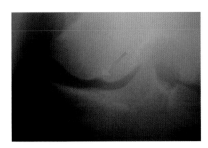

Subchondral bone cysts occur most commonly in the stifle joint. A photograph of the actual cyst is included on page 92

Tibial crest fractures
Treatment: These can be removed arthroscopically, and carry a fair prognosis, provided the cranial cruciate ligament is undamaged.

Tumoral calcinosis
This refers to large, calcified swellings in the subcutaneous tissue. These occur frequently just distally to the stifle joint. Although they appear unsightly, they do not usually cause lameness.

Treatment: Surgical removal is the only treatment option. However, as many of these lesions have a tendency to attach to the stifle joint capsule, making the exposure of the joint necessary for their removal, it is usually not warranted.

Hip and pelvic problems

Femoral fractures
Femoral fractures are fairly common in the horse. In the adult horse, they are usually comminuted with a hopeless prognosis.

Hip joint dislocation
The round and accessory ligaments connect the femoral head to the pelvic pan. Trauma to this area can lead to rupture. This lack of stabilization can in turn lead to the dislocation of the hip joint. The affected horse is unable to advance the hindlimb, and shows an outward rotation of the entire leg.

Treatment: Surgical relocation is difficult. Open reduction or femoral head resection is only an option for salvaging ponies.

Tibial crest fractures can cause severe lameness, often some time after the injury (usually a kick). The prognosis for a full return to work is usually fair following surgical removal of the fragment

Neonatal Diseases

Osteochondritis dissecans

Rachitic disease

This disease is believed to be the result of calcium, phosphorus and vitamin deficiencies, and usually develops in horses between 6 and 12 months of age. Clinically it resembles DJD of the PIPJ, but there are no corresponding bone or cartilage changes.

Congenital angular limb deformities

These are common conditions and refer to a deviation of the limb either laterally (valgus) or medially (varus) at birth. The causes are multifactoral, including intra-uterine malpositioning, overfeeding of the mare, incomplete ossification of the cuboidal bones and, most importantly, joint laxity.

Many congenital angular limb deformities are due to joint laxity, and through gentle regular exercise, the condition will resolve itself. Conditions that are unresponsive will reveal an instability in the lateral-medial direction without crepitus.

Treatment: A large Robert Jones bandage or cast should be applied from the proximal radius to the distal metacarpus, thus leaving the distal limb exposed for the foal to walk on. Swimming may also be useful.

Bandages should be changed every three days in order to avoid pressure sores. Corrective trimming of the hooves is also essential.

It is important to correct the angular limb deformity before closure of the growth plates and to prevent changes in areas distal to it.

Fetlock deviation (metacarpophalangeal and metatarsophalangeal joints)

Treatment: Ideally, treatment should be initiated within the first 30 days post natum. After 60 to 80 days, only surgery will correct the deformity. As it is not possible to reduce the angle manually, angular deformities in excess of 5 degrees need early surgical management.

Surgical hemicircumferential transection and elevation of the periosteum (HCTP) or periosteal stripping (PS) aims to accelerate growth on the concave aspect of the limb, thus laterally for valgus and medially for varus deformities. Under general anaesthesia, the position of the physis can be identified.

For a carpus valgus deformity, a 4–6cm (1½–2in) longitudinal incision is made between the common and lateral digital extensor tendons, starting just proximal to the physis. The incision is extended through to the periosteum, using a curved scalpel blade parallel to the physis, at the distal end of the initial incision (parallel to the skin incision) forming an inverted T. The periosteal flaps are elevated with the aid of a periosteal elevator and then allowed to return to the normal position. It is important to transect the remnant of the ulna, or if the ulna is ossified, it should be removed with the aid of rongeurs. In foals with hindlimb tarsus valgus the veterinarian should bear in mind that a fibular remnant may be present.

The success rate for hemicircumferential periosteal transaction and elevation is good, although the original success rate figure of 80 per cent is now deemed too high. The procedure may be performed again if needed, as overcorrection has not been noted.

Transphyseal bridging is performed on the convex side of the angular limb deformity to decelerate bone growth on that side. This can be achieved by using cortical screws with cerclage wire wrapped in a figure of eight, with a dynamic compression plate, or with orthopaedic staples. Follow-up radiographs are necessary so that the correction can be monitored and the implants removed in a timely fashion in order to prevent over-correction.

It is possible to use these techniques concurrently.

Once there is physical closure, only step ostectomy (sagittal plane), step osteotomy (frontal plane) or wedge ostectomy may be used as salvage procedures.

Incomplete ossification of the cuboidal bones

The cuboidal bones are present in both the carpus and tarsus in cartilaginous form before ossification occurs, usually within 30 days post natum. Ossification difficulties are particularly prevalent among premature and dysmature foals. Often there is a congenital angular limb deformity, particularly a valgus present, which worsens rather than improves during the first two weeks of life. The condition is frequently bilateral.

Radiographs reveal one or more abnormal cuboidal bones, especially the fourth, ulnar and third carpal bones in the forelimb, and the third or central tarsal bones.

Treatment: The limb should be manually realigned, and stabilized with the use of a Robert Jones bandage from the proximal radius to the distal metatarsus, again to allow the foal to walk. A commercial Farley-brace/Redden-brace is available for the forelimb. This allows movement of the joints while maintaining joint stability.

Once complete ossification has taken place, a prognosis can be made, depending on the changes within the cuboidal bones and the presence of OCD lesions. Unfortunately, DJD often develops as a later complication of this condition.

Congenital flexural deformities...

These are often referred to as 'contracted' tendons. However, this is incorrect, as the tendon is simply shortened in relation to the bones, rather than contracted. The affected joints include the coffin joint, fetlock joint, carpal and tarsal joints. There has been much speculation concerning the aetiology of the condition, which can include one or more joints. These include intra-uterine malpositioning, toxic insults in the embryonal stage, genetic factors, and influenza virus infection of the mare, amongst other things. None of these is particularly satisfactory.

A careful clinical examination of all the joints and ligaments in the limbs should be conducted in order to ascertain if there are other pathologies present. Radiographs are also extremely useful in determining joint abnormalities.

...of the distal interphalangeal joint

This condition is relatively uncommon and affects either one or both joints. The affected limb will bear weight on the toe only, causing excessive wear there. These foals are commonly called 'ballerina foals'.

Treatment: In the treatment of this condition, regular exercise on a hard, flat surface is essential. Backing the animal up, making it hop on one leg while holding the other, and walking up steep slopes are also helpful. The use of NSAIDs to help alleviate pain and encourage movement is indicated. Corrective trimming should include mild heel rasping and a small acrylic toe extension to protect the toe from wear.

An infusion of 3g of oxytetracycline in a 250–500ml saline bag given in the first several days post natum is said to cause a relaxation by chelating free calcium ions which would otherwise have attached into muscle fibres. This dosage may be repeated.

Casting rather than splinting seems to be effective, and should incorporate the foot up to the carpus or tarsus. The cast should be regularly monitored and changed every seven to fourteen days, as pressure sores are very common. Two weeks should usually suffice to correct the deformity.

...of the metacarpo-metatarso-phalangeal joint

This is the most common congenital flexural deformity and is most likely to affect the hindlimb. It often occurs in conjunction with distal interphalangeal joint deformities. The animal tends to knuckle over on the dorsal surface of the fetlock, and in extreme cases will be walking on it.

Treatment: A similar regime as described above should be employed, with mild cases responding to manipulation, exercise and bandaging. Although commercial splints are available, applying a padded PVC tube to the palmar/plantar aspect over a Robert Jones bandage is effective as it forces the extension of the affected limb. Pressure sores are common, making the monitoring and frequent changing of bandages a necessity.

...of the carpal joint

Flexural deformities of the carpal joint are usually bilateral, causing the foal to knuckle forwards at the carpus or, in severe cases, to be unable to stand.

Treatment: The splint bandages or lower limb casts should be used, being careful to avoid the fetlock and distal phalangeal joints. Foals with bilateral difficulties may be unable to get up and it will therefore be necessary to assist them in this so they can suckle. Unilateral cases frequently cause overuse of the opposite limb including carpal varus. Surgical intervention includes tenotomy of the insertions of the ulnaris lateris and flexor carpi ulnaris muscles.

...of newborn foals

The cause of this condition is unknown, although it is more commonly seen in premature and/or systemically ill foals. Both hindlimbs and occasionally all four limbs are usually affected. The digital hyperextension severity varies, but may cause the fetlock to make contact with the ground; this causes the foal to walk on the heel of the hoof with the toe extended into the air, which gives rise to a rounded 'rocker heel' over time. Chronic cases will develop a subluxation of the DIP joint, eventually leading to DJD.

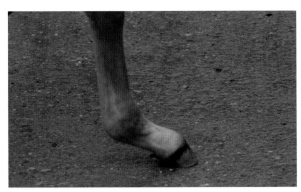

This foal is suffering from a congenital flexural deformity. Prompt treatment is required

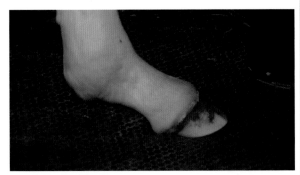

This foal is suffering from weak tendons. This problem will usually resolve itself provided that exercise is restricted and the foal is kept on firm ground

Treatment: Many cases will resolve spontaneously. Treatment should include light supportive bandaging, removal of the rocker heel, and plastic heel extensions. Surgery is not usually necessary.

Rupture of the common digital extensor tendon

This is a relatively uncommon condition which usually affects both forelimbs. It may have a hereditary component. In many cases, however, it occurs secondarily to other severe flexural deformities. Frequently, hypoplastic carpal bones are present.

A characteristic swelling is noted on the dorsolateral surface of the carpus. Palpation of the tendon sheath reveals the ruptured tendon. The foal frequently has a tendency to stumble.

Treatment: The foal should be given prolonged box rest until it is able to resume exercise without stumbling. Splint bandages will help to align the normal limb angle, and speed the ossification of hypoplastic carpal bones. The bandages should be changed every three days, and may be necessary for up to eight weeks. Surgical treatment of the ruptured extensor tendon is not necessary.

144

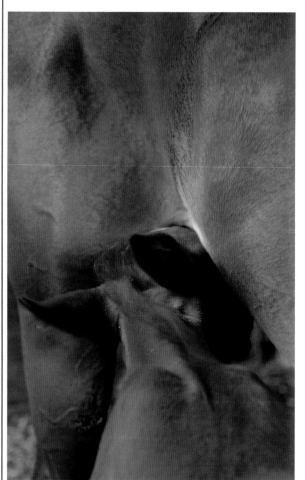

Sufficient colostrum intake in the first twenty-four hours is vital for the foal's health and vitality

Joint ill

'Joint ill', or 'septicaemia', accounts for approximately 30 per cent of mortality in young foals. It is induced by a massive intake of bacteria, either directly from a systemic disease in the mare, through the lining of the stomach while it is permeable during the first 24 hours ante natum, or through an infected remnant of the umbilical cord. Frequent histories include the foal not suckling for the first few hours and/or the mare discharging colostrum before giving birth. Certainly, an immune deficiency will predispose for infection.

Affected foals deteriorate rapidly. Gram-negative bacteria such as *E. coli* and *Klebsiella* are often involved: these release endotoxins, which stimulate the body's inflammation mediators such as cytokines and phospholipase A2, causing fever, vasodilation, hypertension, hypoglycaemia, and eventually DIC, septic shock and death. And, if a foal manages to survive this acute state, bacteria can settle into various joints, particularly the fetlock and hock joints, causing an acute septic arthritis.

Treatment: Recognition and treatment must be rapid; the follow-on treatment is prolonged and expensive. An affected foal should be transported with the mare to a dedicated 24-hour nursing site following on-site treatment for shock. This should include intravenous isotonic fluids and 5 per cent dextrose solutions, systemic antibiotics, colostrum supplementation and hyperimmune antiendotoxin serum. Treatment for septic arthritis should meet with a similarly rapid response in order to curtail irreparable damage to the cartilage. More information as to the treatment of septic arthritis can be found under that separate heading, see page 94.

Physitis

Physitis is a bone disease which causes the enlargement of growth plates in certain long bones in young horses. The disease can be multifactoral. However, it frequently involves heavily muscled and overweight foals that have been overfed. This excessive weight, coupled with excessive exercise, places undue strain on the immature bones, leading to 'physeal compression'. This causes a thickening of the physis, characterized by swellings on the distal aspects of the radius, tibia, and cannon bones. Although the swelling is usually painful to deep palpation, lameness symptoms range from no more than a slight stiffness to overt lameness.

The most common radiographic findings include a widening of the physis, with paraphyseal bone production, often called 'physeal lipping'. Angular limb deformities and osteochondrosis lesions may also be present concurrently.

Treatment: A reduction in turnout is required and the foal's feed should be carefully evaluated. This should

A recumbent foal should always be viewed critically since this may be the first sign of ill health

be reduced in quantity, particularly the grain intake. In some instances, an analysis of the diet may reveal an inadequate calcium intake or a low Ca-P ratio. Therefore, besides a reduction in grain intake, calcium carbonate supplementation may be necessary.

The use of NSAIDs is indicated. In some horses, a course of anabolic steroids has been recommended, as this may quicken the closure of the physes.

White muscle disease

White muscle disease is a degeneration of the red muscles in foals due to deficiency of selenium and possibly vitamin E. This usually already occurs during

the developmental stage. Therefore, an important method in preventing disease development lies in the supplementation of selenium and vitamin E to mares during pregnancy, particularly those on selenium deficient soil. Foals with myocardial degeneration may be born dead or die suddenly post natum. Skeletal myodegeneration occurs more slowly. Affected foals may be weak or recumbent or initially exhibit a stiff gait.

Treatment: Prompt treatment of the condition is vital through parenteral administration of selenium (0.5-0.7 mg/kg) and vitamin E (100 IU/kg/day). Stable rest, the avoidance of stress exposure and adequate nursing are essential until the condition is reversed.

Conclusion

A glimpse through dated veterinary and medical books shows with what speed medicine has evolved over the last century. And with the passing of each decade, its pace quickens. Man's reliance in the Technology God has reaped untold rewards and saved millions of lives. But this blind faith in the wonders of technology is already now beginning to show cracks that are more than surface deep. The world of the tiny micro-organism is beginning to become resistant to our efforts to contain it – the rise in resistance of bacteria, virus and even parasite will continue to challenge our efforts and mute our victory.

But perhaps even more challenging and certainly more terrifying are the ethical questions which modern medicine demands we answer. Genetics allows us now to build 'Dolly the Sheep'. Cell technology has already incorporated the use of embryonic stem cells in its research. The use of these cells to grow new cartilage in joints or even grow new organs to replace failing ones, is certainly the most promising development in medicine to date. It is exciting when you consider that this new age technology seeks to mend, rather than contain an otherwise incurable condition. But the moral and ethical decisions which the use of this technology provokes are not truly being considered, debated and acted on by our society. I will never forget sitting in a lecture room in 1996. The professor stood at the blackboard and stared up at us. He said, 'And all of you would like to debate the ethics of medicine with me. I tell you now, that train is long gone. It is out of the station and we are staring at the back of it, trying to make sense of what we have seen. But it will continue onward, without us!' The thought of technology unleashing a monster that we can no longer control but which will have a deep, lasting and profound impact upon mankind is not new. But the professor's words had a terrifyingly true ring to them. If our society does not assume responsibility for this new technology, somebody else will. It is better therefore, to influence and direct the implementation of this new technology than to sit helplessly while less scrupulous elements continue to work in secret.

But for a successful future, medicine also needs to look to the past for guidance. I have been told that Chinese doctors get paid while their patients are healthy, not ill. Whether or not this is still true I have no way of knowing, but the idea is profound. Preventative medicine, i.e. taking a more proactive approach in our outlook towards ourselves and our animals is something which is so simple and yet so often ignored. It does however, place the responsibility upon you the horse owner to keep your animal well. You must feed it properly, neither too much nor too little. You must have it shod regularly and well. You must exercise it properly. You must ride it properly. You must stable it properly. You must allow it to graze under safe conditions. You must know what is normal for your horse so that you will quickly detect what is abnormal. If you assume responsibility for implementing these measures, then you will have a much healthier and more athletic horse and a much smaller veterinary bill. I sincerely hope that this book assists you in your continuing efforts to ride a *sound* horse!

Milton Abbas, 2007

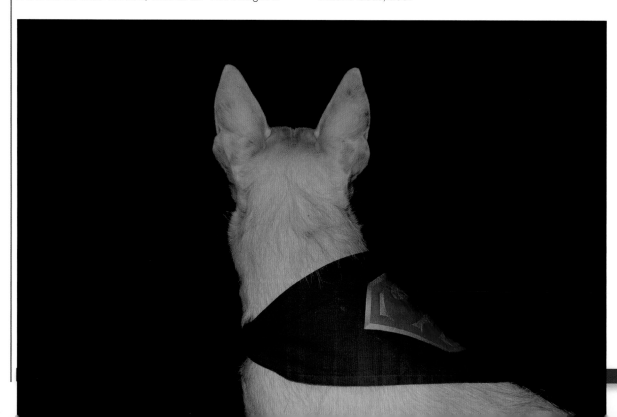

Glossary

Abaxial Away from the central axis of the limb

Aetiology The reason or cause of a disease

Apical Belonging to the tip

Arthrodesis Operative procedure to remove joint movement in a dysfunctional joint

Arthroscopic(ally) With the use of minimal invasive keyhole surgery, a technique designed to diagnose and treat joint and synovial cavity pathologies

Avulsion fracture A rupture of the bone at the insertion of a ligament

Axial to In line with the central axis of the limb

Buccal Cheek of the mouth

Caudal(ly) Directional term meaning towards the tail

Caudocranial Directional term moving from the head to the tail end

Caudomedial Directional term meaning towards the tail and the central axis of the torso

Cerclage wire Surgical wire used for bone fragment stabilization

Condylar Pertaining to the widened end of a long bone

Contra-lateral Belonging to the opposite side

Cortical Belonging to the cortex of the bone

Cranial Directional term meaning towards the head

Curettage The debriding and scraping of tissues using a curette, a medical instrument shaped much like a small ice cream scoop

DDFT Acronym for deep digital flexor tendon

DJD Acronym for degenerative joint disease

DMSO Dimethyl sulphoxide, a chemical compound with free radical scavenging properties. It can seep through the skin so is often used with a corticosteroid to treat localized inflammation

DPLMO Acronym for dorsopalmar (or plantar) lateromedial oblique, a directional term used for a standard radiographic view

Debridement Surgical removal of necrotic tissue and bacteria in order to clean a wound

Desmitis Inflammation of a ligament

Desmopathy A disease or pathology of a ligament

Desmopathy (insertional) A disease or pathology of a ligament at its point of insertion

Distad Distal to

Desmotomy The surgical transaction of a ligament

Diasthema The toothless area in the mouth between the canine and wolf tooth

Distal Directional term relating one object below another

Dorsal Directional term pertaining to the back

Dorsolateral Directional position on the head side and outside of the body

Dorsopalmar Directional term to describe the movement from the dorsum to the sole

EDTA An anti-coagulant

Echogenicity Term used to describe the density of an object based on the amount of ultrasound wave reflection

Entheseophyte New bone formation at the insertion of a ligament

Exostosis A bony outgrowth

Fetotome wire A cutting wire used to cut surgically

Fibrin A substance necessary for blood clotting.

Hypergranulation An excess of granulation tissue which often forms in the healing process

Hypertonicity Decscibes bone and other dense material which reflects back ultrasound waves

Hypoechogenicity Describes fluid and other non dense material which does not reflect back ultrasound waves

147

Interphalangeal Directional term meaning between the digits

Lateral Directional term pertaining to the perimeter of an object

Lateromedial Directional term describing a movement from the perimeter to the middle or inside of an object

Lingual Directional term used to describe the tongue side of the mouth

Luxation A complete dislocation of a joint

Lysis The destruction of a cell by an antibody

Lytic Degredation or destruction of a substance by another agent

MMPs Acronym for metalloproteinases which regulate the attachment between epidermal lamellae and basement membrane

Medial Directional term pertaining to the middle of an object

Midsagittal Directional term referring to the central longitudinal axis

NSAIDs Acronym for non-steroidal, anti-inflammatory drugs, widely used to control arthritic, post-operative and other painful processes

Ostectomy An excision of bone or part of a bone

Osteochondral The bone–cartilage junction

Osteotomes A surgical instrument for chiselling out bone material

Osteotomy A surgical separation of bone

Palmar Directional term referring to the sole of a forelimb

Perineural Directly next to a nerve

Periosteal Pertaining to the periosteum, a thin membrane surrounding a bones surface

Periostitis an inflammation of the bone surface which affects the periosteum

Plantar Directional term referring to the sole of a hindlimb

Portal A surgical opening from which to gain access

Proteoglycans Proteins that are combined with a carbohydrate

Proximal Directional term relating one object above another

Sclerosis A hardening of tissues

Scoliosis A lateral curvature of the spine

SDFT Acronym for superficial digital flexor tendon

Subcarpal Directional term for below the knee or carpus

Subperiosteally Beneath the periosteum

Subluxation A partial dislocation of a joint

Tenosynovitis Inflammation of a tendon sheath

Tenotomy The surgical severing of a tendon

T-square A metal object, shaped like the letter T, used for determining hoof balance in farriery

Vascularization The synthesis of blood vessels

Ventral Directional term referring to those surfaces of the body in the same orientation as the belly

Bibliography

Bennett, Deb, PhD *Principles of Conformation Analysis Vol. I* Fleet Street Publishing, Gaithersburg MD, 1988, pp.67-79.

Boden, Edward *Blacks Veterinary Dictionary*, 19th edition, A & C Black Ltd., London 1998.

Brown, Christopher, Bertone Joseph J. *The 5-Minute Veterinary Consult* – Equine, Lippincott Williams & Wilkins, Baltimore, MD, 2002.

Budras, Klaus-Dieter, Rlck, Sabine *Atlas der Anotomie des Pferdes*, Schlütersche, Hannover, 1991.

Butler, Janet A., Colles, Christopher M., Dyson, Sue J., Kold, Svend E., Poulos, Paul W. *Clinical Radiology of the Horse*, 2nd edition, Blackwell Science Ltd., Oxford, 2000.

Christenson, Dawn E. *Veterinary Medical Terminology*, W. B. Saunders Company, Philadelphia, 1997.

Clayton, Hilary M., Flood, Peter F., Rosenstein, Diana S. *Clinical Anatomy of the Horse*, Mosby Elsevier, Edinburgh, 2005.

Colahan, Patrick T., Mahew, I. G., et al *Manual of Equine Medicine and Surgery*, Mosby, London, 1999.

Curtis, Simon *Corrective Farriery – A textbook of remedial horse shoeing*, Vol. 1, R&W Publications Ltd., Newmarket, pp. 106-130.

Frankeny, Rebecca L. *Miniature Horses: A Veterinary Guide for Owners and Breeders*, J. A. Allen, London, 2003

Hayes, Capt M. Horace *Points of the Horse*, Stanley Paul & Co Ltd., London, 1968, pp. 85-118,140-248.

Hinchcliff, Kenneth W., Kaneps, Andris J., Geor, Raymond J. *Equine Sports Medicine and Surgery*, Elsevier Ltd., Edinburgh, 2004, pp. 210-259.
Langdon, William G. Jr. *Bits and Bitting Manual*, Langdon Enterprises, Colbert, 1989.

Lavin, Lisa M. *Radiography in Veterinary Technology*, 2nd edition, W. B. Saunders Company 1999.

McBane, Susan *The Essential Book of Horse Tack & Equipment*, David & Charles, 2000.

McIlwraith, Wayne C., Trotter, Gayle W. *Joint Disease in the Horse*, W. B. Saunders Company, Philadelphia, 1996.
Mills, Daniel & McDonnell *The Domestic Horse – The Evolution, Development and Management of its Behaviour*, Cambridge University Press, Cambridge, 2005, pp. 5-31.

Poe, Rhonda Hart 'What is a Gaited Horse?', *The Gaited Horse*, Fall 2006, pp. 16-19.

Pollitt, Christopher C. *Color Atlas of the Horse's Foot*, Mosby-Wolfe, London 1995.

Popesko, Peter, *Atlas der Topographischen Anatomie der Haustiere, Band III:* Becken und Gliedmassen, 3., Durgesehene Auflage, Ferdinand Enke Verlag, Stuttgart, 1989.

Ramey, David W. *Concise Guide to Arthritis in the Horse*, Ringpress Books Ltd, 1998, pp. 15-36.

Richardson, Robbie C. *The Horse's Foot and Related Problems*, 11-23

Rose, Reuben J., Hodgson, David R. *Manual of Equine Practice*, 2nd edition, W.B. Saunders Company, Philadelphia, 2000

Ross, Mike W., Dyson, Sue J. *Diagnosis and Management of Lameness in the Horse*, Saunders, Philadelphia, 2003.

Stashak, Ted S., Adams *Lameness In Horses*, 5th edition, Lippincott Williams & Wilkins, Philadelphia, 2002.

Stührenberg, Kaja *Faszination Tölt* website, www.kajastuehrenberg.de

Speirs, Victor C., Wrigley, Robert H., *Clinical Examination of the Horse*, W.B. Saunders Company, Philadelphia 1997.

Taylor, F.G.R., Hillyer, M.H. *Diagnostic Techniques in Equine Medicine*, W.B. Saunders Company Ltd., London, 1997, 232-269.

Varcoe-Cocks, K., Sagar, K. N., Jeffcott, L. B., McGowan, C.M. *Pressure algometry to quantify muscle pain in racehorses with suspected sacroiliac dysfunction*, Equine Veterinary Journal (2006) 38 (6) 558-562.

Ziegler, Lee *Easy-Gaited Horses*, Storey Publishing, MA, 2005, pp. 1-41.

Acknowledgements

The author's name on the front of a book simply does not reflect the scores of people who each in their own way have contributed to its making. It is appropriate therefore, that at least some mention is made of their efforts, without which this book would have never left the planning stages.

First and foremost I would like to thank Jane Trollope, Commissioning Editor for David & Charles for placing her confidence in me, and Anne Plume, Jodie Lystor, Jennifer Fox-Proverbs, Emily Rae and Prudence Rogers for putting the time, effort and enthusiasm into something which after all, is simply another day's work for them.

Circumstances never quite allow you to thank fellow colleagues, supervisors and friends and I should like to take time out to name four in particular:

Dr Dörte Böhm for the precision and professionality of her work. I am forever thankful to have worked with her during my first employment.

Peter Scott Dunn, L.V.O., MRCVS, a truly gifted veterinary surgeon with an astute eye for lameness and a practical approach for solving problems – a truly quintessentially English horseman who has influenced all that have worked with him.

John Walmsley for his inspiring leadership in establishing Liphook Equine Hospital as one of Britain's finest bespoke hospitals. John truly showed how things could be done. And yet, he ably maintained his hobbies and home life, a talent which very few of us really have.

Craig Simon for his dedicated, but light-hearted approach to work, but most of all for his friendship. It was a privilege to have worked together. I wish him all the best back in Australia.

My wife Katy has my undying gratitude for the patience and understanding she has always shown towards my work and the long hours it involves.

My work colleagues Charlotte Shepherd, Kirstin Slorach and Caroline Matthews have been particularly patient, not only for putting up with the occasional time off for me to disappear and work on this book, but also for the perpetual photo taking that they have had to endure. Kirstin Slorach kindly assisted me in the writing of the western saddle. Charlotte, Kirstin, Caroline and I together make up Whistlejacket Equine Surgery, Fishmore Hill Farm, Milton Abbas, Dorchester, DT11 0DL.

Mr. Bruce Bladon, BVM&S, Cert EP, DESTS, Dipl ECVS, MRCVS kindly provided the photographs for scintigraphy and MRI. Bruce is a partner in the Donnington Grove Veterinary Surgery, Oxford Road, Newbury, Berkshire RG14 2JB, which has some of the finest equine veterinary facilities in the country. Exceptionally qualified, Bruce is always available to lend a professional hand or give a grounded opinion. It does not go unnoticed.

My dear uncle Dr Kai Christian Otte, fellow veterinarian and expert on Paso horses greatly aided me in understanding the movement of gaited horses. It is a privilege to include him in this book. Kai breeds horses on his farm,

Oberadelhof, in 92287 Schmidmuehlen, Germany.

My great friend Mr George Bingham provided me with many laughs and some of the sketches to the book. George is a very talented bronze sculptor and builder. His artwork can be admired on his website, www.georgebingham.com.

Mr. Dietrich Graf von Schweinitz, BSc DVM MRCVS Cert Vet Ac, provided the example thermography photographs. Dietrich successfully uses this diagnostic method at his practice, Southern Hills Equine Veterinary Clinic, Greyfriars Farm, Puttenham, Guildford GU3 1AG, United Kingdom.

Mr Peter Coutanche, a keen and talented farrier, readily endured all my photo sessions and good natured banter with him. Pete works out of his forge in Weymouth, Dorset, United Kingdom.

The brilliant example of a hospital plate was kindly forged during late hours by talented farrier, Mr Phillip Thomas, 'Taff' of County Forge, 5 Haywards Farm Close, Verwood, Dorset BH31 6XW. His help in time of need was greatly appreciated.

Mr Andrew Poynton, farrier and inventor of Imprint shoes, kindly donated pictures of his plastic shoes. Andrew runs his business from Town Forge, 60 High Street, Malmesbury, Wiltshire, SN16 9AT, United Kingdom.

My special thanks go to the Royal Veterinary College in North Mymms, United Kingdom and the Ludwig-Maximillian University in Munich, Germany for kindly allowing me to photograph their anatomical specimens.

Many thanks go to Simon Jackson, College Librarian, and Elspeth Keith, Assistant Librarian of the Royal Veterinary College in North Mymms, Hatfield, Hertfordshire for kindly allowing me the use of their research facilities and specimens for photography. Kate Warner of the Camden Campus on Royal College Street in London was also very generous with her assistance.

My sincere appreciation extends to the many clients and horses who have kindly allowed me to take their photograph whilst working. It must be remembered that some of the horses pictured in this book have not survived. May these photos help reduce the suffering of other horses out there.

Last, but not least, I would like to remember my faithful dog Monty who stood by me so many years. Monty sadly passed away this year from a sudden heart failure after watching the Grand National. He was a true vet's dog until the end! He shall not be forgotten.

Index

152